The Compleat Home Winemaker & Brewer

The Compleat Home Winemaker & Brewer

BEN TURNER

William Luscombe

First published in Great Britain in 1976 by
William Luscombe Publisher Limited
The Mitchell Beazley Group
Artists House, 14 Manette Street
London W1V 5LB
Reprinted 1979

© 1976 by Ben Turner

ISBN 0 86002 067 3 (cased) ISBN 0 86002 162 9 (limp)

Set in Monotype Photina by
Tradespools Limited, Frome, England
Printed in Scotland by
Morrison & Gibb Ltd, Edinburgh

Editor Alan Folly
Production Bob Towell
Design & art direction Anthony Nelthorpe MSIA
Arka Graphics, London
Colour illustrations Joyce Tuhill
Line illustrations Arka Graphics
Cover photograph Harry Scotting

To
William Luscombe my Publisher
and above all my Friend

whose support both in sickness & in health
has meant so much to me

Contents

Contents

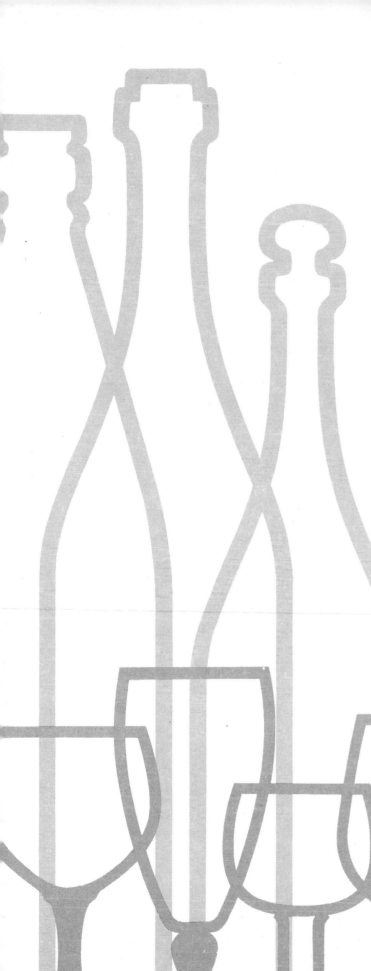

You know, my Friends, with what a brave Carouse
I made a Second Marriage in my house;
Divorced old barren Reason from my Bed,
and took the daughter of the Vine to Spouse.

Rubaiyat of OMAR KHAYYAM
Stanza 55 (Fifth Edition)

Preface

For the blossoming adolescent a little knowledge of wine is the beginning of education for a civilised way of living.

For the newly-married burdened with a mortgage, a baby, bills and the taxman, wine brings hope for better days and contentment with the present.

For the middle-aged, flagging in the rat race, wine diminishes tension, aids digestion, restores ego and makes life worthwhile.

For the elderly, wine engenders warmth and comfort. It brings back happy memories and becomes a rosy filter in the spectacles of disillusion.

Your own wine adds to all these gifts the satisfaction of creation and brings you a little nearer to the mystery of life.

Make your own wine, then, for your own sake.

Ben Turner

 Why Wine

FROM long before the birth of Christ the medicinal qualities of wine have been appreciated. The Ancient Greeks used wine as a medium for the essences of herbs or spices known, or thought, to contain ingredients that relieved pain or sickness. The bitterness or unpleasant flavour of the medicine was masked by the wine and thus became more acceptable to the patient. This practice continued throughout the centuries. Indeed in most countries one can still buy wines containing health promoting additives. Usually described as tonic wines, they are frequently taken by the chronic invalid or the convalescent, as well as by the hypochondriac.

Antiseptic

The antiseptic quality of wine has long been known. It was common practice to wash wounds in wine before binding them, and it was accepted that this helped the healing process. It was not known of course that the acid and alcohol killed bacteria, because bacteria were not recognised as the cause of infection until the middle of the 19th century.

Anaesthetic

The anaesthetic qualities of wine and spirits were also known. Before an operation the patient would be made quite drunk so that the pain of amputating a limb, for example, could be endured. The blood pressure was lowered, too, although this advantage may not have been appreciated.

Healing

The beneficial qualities of various flower, vegetable and other wines may not yet be fully understood. It was once believed that celery wine was helpful to people suffering from rheumatism. Fig wine was thought to be good for people afflicted with chronic constipation. Elderberry wine is still considered helpful for those suffering from a cold or cough. Dandelion wine was supposed to be helpful to those suffering from a disorder of the bladder — and so on. Scientists may yet find that these old tales are not complete nonsense.

Tonic & Relaxing

Today, wine is widely regarded as a tonic, in the form of an aperitif, for the jaded appetite. It is also considered to be an aid to digestion. It is known that wine can relieve tensions and relax taut nerves. It reduces inhibitions and ensures sociability. Whilst beer and spirits are frequently forbidden to the obese or the sick, wine is only excluded during a fever. It is often prescribed during convalescence. Even the diabetic, for whom sweet food and drink can be a positive danger, is not forbidden a glass of dry wine.

Because wine stimulates sociability, it is not usually associated with alcoholism, a disease of the lonely or troubled who more often turn to spirits for relief.

Liquid refreshment — almost certainly home-brewed — flows freely in Peter Breugel's painting of the Peasant Wedding

How Much

Recent American research has reported that moderate consumption of alcohol — around half a bottle a day — leads to a longer, healthier life than that enjoyed both by those who drink none and by those who drink much more. Like many other matters, this is something that mankind has really been aware of for generations without being able to prove it in statistical terms!

Reveal the Mystery

There is no harm in giving a sip of wine even to babies, and there is much to be said for allowing young children a small glass of wine diluted with water. Because no prohibitions are made there are no secrets for the child to discover by surreptitious drinking. A glass or so at a meal for the young adolescent does no harm, improves the sense of

belonging to the world of adults and is a step on the path of sophistication. The important advice to young people is the same as it is for ourselves — moderation. Amateur winemakers, usually with a substantial stock of wine available to them, tend to be moderate social drinkers. Whilst at parties they may drink their fill, it is extremely rare to see one 'under the weather'.

Aphrodisiac
Some wines are said to have aphrodisiac qualities. Around the year AD 200 it was recorded by Atheneus 'that wine from Heraea (a town in Greece) drives men out of their senses and makes women inclined to pregnancy.' Mead too has long been thought to be something of a sexual stimulant. The probability is more likely that the moderate and regular drinking of wine or mead helps to keep one

well, dynamic and full of vitality. When the wine or mead is shared with an appropriate partner, tension is relaxed and inhibitions depart. There is no evidence that wine or mead directly stimulates the sexual senses.

Comfort
Elderly people benefit from a glass of wine taken regularly. It not only comforts them but has a warming effect at a time in life when they begin to feel the cold more than ever before.

There can be no doubt that in moderation wine is beneficial and health promoting to people of all ages, from the cradle to the grave. Those of us who have wine in abundance should be thankful for such a blessing when so many are under-nourished. Thanks be to God. Amen.

This ancient stone carving from Carthage in North Africa shows the god Baal holding a goat in one hand and a bunch of grapes in the other

A short History of Winemaking

The birthplace of wine

NOBODY knows when man first made wine for himself and his family, but it must have been at least 10,000 years ago. For Western Civilisation it probably started in the land between the Tigris and Euphrates, those two great rivers that flow from the mountains in Eastern Turkey to the Persian Gulf. Almost certainly the wine was made from grapes. Perhaps someone out collecting them fell and squashed a quantity, the juice ran free and soon began to ferment of its own accord. However harsh and rough the taste, it was no doubt of interest to the picker who probably repeated the exercise!

Some 2,000 years later it would seem that the grape vine was being cultivated for making wine. Indeed, there is reason to believe that the vine was the very first plant to be cultivated. Archaeologists have discovered mounds of grape pips among the foundations of early settlements, and with their scientific equipment have dated the pips to around 6000 BC.

The ancient Persian civilisation may well have been sufficiently sophisticated for the leaders at least, to have drunk wine with their food. The situation may well have been similar in China, for wine has certainly been made there for thousands of years. At this time Britain was just becoming an island detached from Europe!

Wine was well known to the first Egyptian civilisation since drawings and carvings exist from this period depicting the vine, the grape and the making of wine. At the time of the building of the Great Pyramids 2,500 years BC, it was recorded that the leaders of the people drank wine and the slave workers a kind of beer.

Other wines were known too, including palm wine, which may have been made from the milky sap of the tree rather than from the fruits.

From Egypt the craft of making wine spread to the early Greek civilisation. Our word 'wine', comes not from the Latin *vinum* but from the Greek *oinos* which in turn came from the ancient Arabic language. Our words 'oenologist' – one who studies wine – and 'oenophile' – one who loves wine – come from the same source.

Perhaps because it was man's first cultivated plant, perhaps because of the euphoria that the drinking of wine induces, there has always been an association between wine and religion. The Greeks

Part of the decoration on a household wine amphora. Wine drinking has always been an enjoyable social activity

no doubt took over the Persian practice of pouring a libation to the gods when the harvest was gathered.

The Greeks called their god of agriculture Dionysius and those who lived by working on the land, worshipped him and offered sacrifices for a good harvest. The harvest was an occasion for drinking, feasting and merrymaking then just as it was in the Middle Ages in England and still is today in agricultural countries.

From the Aegean the vine was taken to Italy where it flourished. The Romans worshipped Bacchus as their god of wine. That they did so to good effect is evidenced by the word 'bacchanalian' which we still use to describe a drinking party that has become something of an orgy.

Long before the birth of Christ, wine, together with oil and wheat were the principal commodities of trade although there was also some trade in silks

Top left: *The top strip of an Ancient Egyptian frieze showing the storage jars or amphorae. Note the pointed ends stuck in the sand*

Top right: *Bottom of the same frieze, clearly showing the cultivation of the vine and the treading of the grapes*

with animal fat and stored in the sand to keep cool. There were many wine shops whose distinguishing feature was a marble slab containing holes in which the amphorae could be stood and supported. These can be clearly seen in the ruins at Pompeii. The amphorae were glazed and pointed at the end that stood in the sand. Today the best storage jars for home winemakers are still stoneware jars. Although heavy, they keep the wine insulated from sudden changes of temperatures.

Throughout the Middle East and the countries bordering the Mediterranean, wine was well-established as the staple drink to accompany food. Because wine was as common as bread the fervently religious Jews had long been accustomed to offer their thanks to God with bread and wine on the eve of their Sabbath. This custom was later adopted by Christian religion and given a new and special significance.

From Italy the vine was taken to Spain and France where the climate and the soil, in places, was particularly suitable. Attempts were made by the Romans to bring the vine to England but with no great success. At one time, however, when there was a shortage of corn for bread, our vines were dug up and wheat was planted instead. Some years later, when the crisis was over, vines were planted again. Indeed, the variety Wrotham Pinot is thought to be one of those brought to England by the Romans. England never became even self-sufficient for wines, however, and it was recorded about us in AD 200 that 'The rich drink wine from Italy or from around Marseilles. The poorer classes drink beer made from wheat and prepared with honey.'

When the religious orders formed and started to build monasteries, abbeys and priories, the monks planted and cultivated the vine, not only for their own use, but also to sell or exchange for other items that they needed. The system of viticulture was studied and new varieties of the vine were developed. Methods of preparing, fermenting and storing the wine were improved, especially in matters of hygiene and in the use of casks.

Wines of a sort were made from other fruits, notably by the Greeks, but the only agent for sweetening the must was honey, so the results were melomels rather than wine. This situation applied in England in the Middle Ages. The staple drink was ale of different kinds, with mead and cider for

and spices, jewels and ornaments, rugs and marbles. Fermented drinks are mentioned in the Old Testament and our word cider is thought to have come from the word *seider* which in turn came from the early Hebrew word *sekera*.

The Romans, like the Greeks, were never completely satisfied with wine from the grape. The Greeks added fruits and honey and even tried to prevent it from going sour and turning to vinegar by steeping pine cones in it. The Romans mixed wine with water, even sea water. Civilised Roman society always diluted the wine with three parts of water and only the young rakes and rebels drank it neat. No doubt it was often cloudy, frequently sour and beyond the palates of the ladies.

As they did with so many matters, the Romans brought order to vine growing. They stored their wine in baked clay amphorae which they sealed

special occasions. The better-off drank imported wine. Because of the marriage of Henry II to Eleanor of Aquitaine in the 12th century, there was ready access to the wine-producing country around Bordeaux. Trade was encouraged and more wine, per head of the population, was then imported from Bordeaux alone, than is now imported from the whole world. The wine was shipped in a large cask holding about 1,000 litres called a tun. So many ships were involved in the wine trade that it became common practice to define the size of the ship by the the number of casks that it could carry; hence a ship of 60 tuns – a phrase that still remains with us.

Sugar, although known about since 500 BC was not imported into England until 1264. It was very expensive. Even when the first sugar refinery was started in the 15th century, sugar remained very expensive and honey continued to be the main sweetening agent for all purposes until the latter part of the 17th century.

The first printed book on wine came from William Turner, a physician to Queen Elizabeth I. It was published in 1568 and entitled *A New Book of Wines*. An excellent copy still exists in the Wine and Food Society's Library. The common ailment of that time was the stone which developed in the kidneys and passed painfully into the bladder. William Turner thought that this might be due to the red wine from Bordeaux. He associated the colour red with fire and thought that the red wine heated the blood and formed the gravel. He advocated the drinking of light white wines from the Rhineland which he thought would cool the blood and eliminate the sediments in the body. An interesting theory that throws light on the state of

medical knowledge at that time.

By 1675 advice was being given in books on the best time to rack wine from its sediment, how to feed fermenting wines and how to clear cloudy wines. Drunkenness was as common as dishonesty. Many books gave advice on how to adulterate wine, the best being to blend fruit wines made in England with grape wine imported from France and to sell it as the best French wine! This practice in reverse, *ie* mixing grape juice concentrate with our fruit musts, enables us to produce much better wines than before, now comparable in quality with commercial wine. The making of wines from fruits was well established in England by the end of the 17th century. Whether from climatic, economic or political reasons, growing grapes for wine never became a commercial proposition. Cider apples flourished and cider comparable in quantity with the

Top left and right: two stages in mediaeval winemaking, from contemporary sources

Above: *Detail from the famous Bayeux tapestry. The Normans were famous trenchermen who appreciated good food and wine*

white wines of the day was made in Hereford and sold in London (*John Worlidge 1676*).

The Spanish emigrants had taken the vine to America, from where it spread both north into California and south into Chile and the Argentine although a different species already grew there. Later it was taken to South Africa and Australia where it also flourished in certain places.

The 18th century was a period of great domestic development in England. Cooking of all kinds, baking, jams, pickles, preserves, wine, beer, cheese all were made in the country homes and countless recipes were published. Alas, the Industrial Revolution was looming and with it the drift from the land to the factory. Long hours of work without access to the free fruits of the hedgerow, saw the decline in country winemaking and the craft as part of the normal domestic scene, dwindled

slowly away throughout the 19th century. Tea had supplanted wine as a drink and cheap gin created a little euphoria. Indeed in the early 18th century Hogarth had already depicted many tragic scenes caused by drunkenness resulting from gin.

The Great War (1914–1918) gave the final kick to winemaking at home and it virtually disappeared until immediately after the Second World War. No wine had been imported for some time and thus it was very expensive. Yet returning soldiers had developed a palate for wine and many of them determined to make their own. The Author made his first wine in September 1945 and has continued to do so ever since.

Shorter working hours and cheap foreign holidays, gave impetus to the interest, but for some years the activity was derided and the source of many jokes. By 1965, however, some of the more aware companies saw the opportunity for big business. Equipment and ingredients specifically for winemakers and home brewers were manufactured and marketed. As inflation increased the winemaker had an opportunity to laugh and thousands upon thousands of people turned to the ancient craft. Winemaking in the home is now an established hobby which has spread throughout the English-speaking world. Standards are improving rapidly with the development and use of specialised equipment, ingredients and knowledge. Making wines, beers, meads, ciders, liqueurs and fruit vinegars of great variety is now an activity undertaken, for the enjoyment it brings, by several million people in the United Kingdom. This book is designed to help them increase that enjoyment by improving the quality of their products wherever they live.

15

Glossary of Terms

Acid
The sharp taste in a fruit or wine. The common acids found in fruit are citric, malic and tartaric. Citric acid is most pronounced in lemons, malic in apples, and tartaric in grapes. The one acid to avoid is acetic acid which tastes of vinegar. Acid is an essential ingredient. Without it yeast cannot ferment the sugar.

Aerobic and Anaerobic
The presence or absence of oxygen. Also a description applied to micro-organisms such as yeast, which can live with or without air.

Air-lock
Any device used during fermentation which enables carbon dioxide to escape but prevents air getting in.

Alcohol
Many kinds of alcohol can be formed during fermentation. The most common is ethyl alcohol, an intoxicating spirit which gives the characteristic flavour and satisfaction to wine.

Aldehydes
A group of chemical compounds formed by the partial oxidation of an alcohol. The most important in wine is acetaldehyde which is formed during the yeast fermentation and is a major contributor to the bouquet and flavour of wine.

Aperitif
A wine served before a meal to stimulate the appetite.

Body
The fullness of a wine. The opposite of thin and watery.

Bottles
Punted wine bottles as used in Bordeaux, Burgundy or Champagne. Green for red wines, colourless for white. Standard size is 75 cl, equal to $26\frac{2}{3}$ fl. oz. 6 bottles are equal to 1 Imperial gallon or 4.5 litres.

Bottoms
Another word for lees or sediment. The dead yeast cells, fruit pulp and precipitates formed during fermentation, settle on the bottom of a jar during maturation and storage, and are left behind with a small amount of wine after racking.

Bouquet
The vinous smell caused by esters and volatile acids, given off by a wine when mature and poured into a glass.

Campden Tablet
A chemical called potassium metabisulphite which releases a gas called sulphur dioxide when dissolved. 1 tablet forms 50 parts per million of gas in 1 gallon.

Carbon Dioxide
The gas formed during fermentation. It rises in tiny bubbles to the surface of the wine and bursts with a slight hissing sound. It is also formed during the bottle fermentation of sparkling wines. When it rises in the glass it is called 'the bead'.

Casks
Small oak barrels in which wine may be stored. The minimum size is 6 gallons. In smaller casks the ratio of surface to volume is too high and causes deterioration.

Decant
The action of carefully pouring wine from a bottle containing sediment into a carafe or decanter in such a manner as to separate the clear wine from the sediment.

Diastase
A complex of enzymes which convert starch to sugar. Sometimes described as 'Fungal Amylase'.

Demijohn
The standard glass fermenting and storage jar. It has a capacity of $8\frac{1}{2}$ pints (4.8 litres) and fills 6 wine bottles.

Dry
The term used to describe a wine in which there is no taste of sweetness. The opposite of a sweet wine.

Enzyme
A protein which acts as a catalyst causing a complex molecule to change into a simpler molecule. Essential in digestion and fermentation.

Ester
A volatile compound formed by the combination of an alcohol with an acid. The most common in wine is ethyl acetate, an important part of the bouquet.

Fermentation
The process by which sugar is converted into alcohol.

Filtration
The removal of minute solid particles suspended in a wine by passing it through some substance which will extract the solids in that wine.

Fining	The process of clearing a cloudy wine with a substance that coagulates the suspended matter and deposits it on the bottom of the jar.
Flor	A wrinkled greyish skin that forms on the top of a wine from which the air is not perfectly excluded.
Fortification	The addition of vodka or grape spirit to a wine to increase its alcohol content. Sometimes used when imitating port, sherry or madeira-type wines.
Gallon	8 pints each of 20 fl. oz. (160 fl. oz.) make 1 Imperial gallon. A so-called 'gallon jar' usually contains $8\frac{1}{2}$ pints. The U.S.A. gallon consists of 8 pints each of 16 fl. oz. (128 fl. oz.). The metric equivalent of an Imperial gallon is 4.5 litres.
Invert Sugar	A simple mixture of the two mono saccharides fructose and glucose, sometimes called levulose and dextrose. Invert sugar is immediately fermentable and is widely used in brewing beer.
Invertase	An enzyme secreted by yeast and which by its presence causes sucrose to separate into fructose and glucose.
Lees	*See Bottoms.*
Malo-Lactic Fermentation	Malic acid is converted into lactic acid and carbon dioxide by bacteria of the *gracile* family. It usually occurs during storage and sometimes causes a blown cork. Lactic acid is less sharp tasting than malic acid and so the flavour of the wine is often improved.
Maturation	The ageing of a wine to the stage in its development where it is most pleasant to drink.
Must	The name given to a liquid prior to fermentation into wine. It may or may not contain solid matter such as fruit pulp.
Nutrient	The name given to yeast food. It consists mainly of ammonium phosphate, vitamin B1 and traces of minerals, salts and amino acids.
Pectin	A gelatinous substance found in many fruits. Useful when making jam but undesirable in wine since it causes haze. Readily removed by pectin-destroying enzyme, of which there are many proprietary brands available.
Proof	The measure of alcohol in wine, liqueur or spirit. 100% Proof is equal to 57.06% alcohol by volume. Wines or liqueurs that are 30, 40, 50, etc degrees proof are that percentage of 57.06%. It follows that a wine that is 21° Proof contains 12% alcohol by volume.
Racking	Removing clear wine from a jar containing sediment into a clean jar after fermentation or during maturation.
Saccharomyces Cerevisiae: Variety Elipsoideus	The true wine yeast developed for used by home winemakers.
Sparkling Wine	One in which a secondary fermentation has created a pressure of carbon dioxide which is released when that wine is poured.
Sulphite	The short name for both sodium and potassium metabisulphite. The sulphite kills weak bacteria, moulds, fungi, wild yeasts etc., and inhibits the growth of others. Is more effective when used in conjunction with citric acid. It prevents oxidation. It is used for sterilising equipment as well as for must and wine. *See also Campden tablet.*
Yeast	A botanical cell, invisible to the naked eye, which secretes enzymes which act as catalysts in reducing sugar to alcohol and carbon dioxide. There are many different varieties of yeast of which only a few are beneficial to the winemaker and brewer.
Wort	The name given to a liquid prior to fermentation into beer.
Zymase	A complex of enzymes secreted by yeast and which by their presence cause fructose and glucose to be reduced to alcohol and carbon dioxide.

17

The Ingredients used in Winemaking

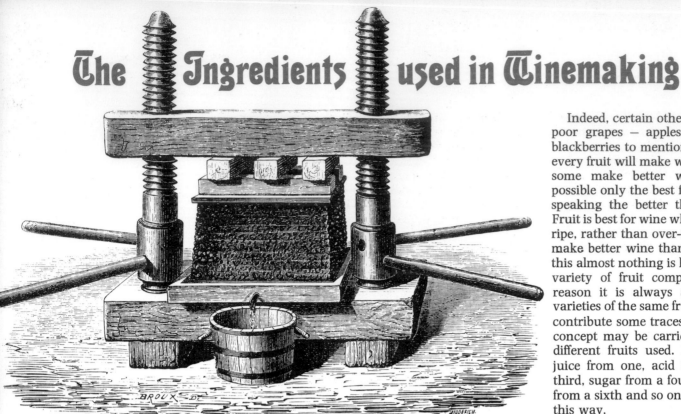

The type of wooden wine press that was used for generations in the French countryside. This one, from the Hérault District, could be moved from vineyard to vineyard on a horse-drawn cart

EVERYONE will probably agree that there is no ingredient more suitable for making wine than the grape. Wherever the vine will grow mankind makes wine from its fruit. Almost everywhere man has settled he has taken the vine with him to plant and make his wine. So 'what's in a grape?' The analysts report the average contents as follows:

Water	between 70	and 85%	of the weight
Glucose	8	13%	
Fructose	7	12%	
Tartaric acid	0.2	1.0%	
Malic	0.1	0.8%	
Citric	0.01	0.05%	
Tannins	0.01	0.10%	

But there are also important trace elements often lacking in other ingredients. Twenty-one different kinds of amino acids, nitrogenous compounds and vitamins including many of the B group, thiamine, riboflavin, pyrodoxine, pantothenic acid, biotin, nicotine acid and many more. Minerals including calcium, magnesium, potassium and sodium. Black grapes have anthocyanin in their skin to give that beloved robe, and white grapes have anthoxanthins and flavours. Bouquet comes from the volatile aroma constituents including ethyl and methyl alcohol, ethyl and methyl acetate, acetaldehyde and B-phenyl and ethyl alcohol. But this list is by no means exhaustive and some varieties of grape have individual differences of content. That is why almost all vignerons grow several varieties of grapes and blend them together to make their wine. Not all grape varieties are ideal for making wine, however. Some are best eaten, others are best dried. Some make a wine that it is best to distil into brandy. Some make great wine, some alas, make poor wine.

Indeed, certain other fruits make better wine than poor grapes — apples, gooseberries, bilberries and blackberries to mention but four examples. Virtually every fruit will make wine, although, as with grapes, some make better wine than others. Wherever possible only the best fruit should be used. Generally speaking the better the fruit the better the wine. Fruit is best for wine when it is just ripe, or just under-ripe, rather than over-ripe. Cooking varieties usually make better wine than dessert varieties. Apart from this almost nothing is known about the merits of one variety of fruit compared with another. For this reason it is always advantageous to use several varieties of the same fruit if possible. Each variety will contribute some traces of different constituents. This concept may be carried yet further and a blend of different fruits used. In this way one can obtain juice from one, acid from another, tannin from a third, sugar from a fourth, body from a fifth, flavour from a sixth and so on. Superb wines can be made in this way.

Frozen fruit, when thawed, make wine just as well as fresh fruit, with the added advantage that they are easier to mash. Canned and bottled fruits may also be used. They are usually packed in a sugar syrup that should be used in the must because it also contains a good deal of fruit flavour. It is always necessary to check the specific gravity of such a must before adding extra sugar.

Fruit juices and purées are equally suitable provided they contain neither saccharin nor preservative. Dried fruits have been a great stand-by to the amateur winemaker for many years. All of them make good wine but the quantity to use depends on their flavour and the comparison between their dried weight and their fresh weight. Apricots and figs, for example, are highly flavoured and this becomes very concentrated upon dehydration. Citrus peel is not suitable because it contains pith that makes the wine bitter.

Jams, conserves and pie fillings are eligible ingredients for winemaking. Jams contain a good deal of sugar and therefore much less needs to be added. They also contain much pectin and so a double quantity of pectolytic enzyme should be added and left in the must for 24–48 hours. Marmalade is not usually suitable since it frequently contains the whole of the orange skin including the pith.

Some vegetables are suitable for making wine. They should be fresh and fully grown, not old and withered. Full bodied wines are usually made from root vegetables and they tend to be best when strong and sweet. The surface vegetables tend to make lighter wines. All need acid, tannin and grape to give them some vinosity.

Grains may also be used, although they tend not to make very palatable wines on their own. All need the grape to give them a little vinosity. Some diastase should be added instead of pectolase. This reduces the starch to fermentable sugars. Flaked grains are better for winemaking than whole grains.

A number of flowers and herbs may be used either fresh or dried. Many flowers are poisonous, however, and details of these are provided. Some leaves, such as those from the vine, walnut and oak trees and sap from the birch and sycamore trees, may also be used.

There remain yet other ingredients which can be used for flavouring wine, notably ginger, coffee, tea and vanilla pods. Aniseed, caraway, clove and coriander have also been used.

Water

It is essential that all water used in making wine be pure and wholesome. It doesn't seem to matter if the water is hard or soft; at least, no significant difference has ever been noted. There is a body of opinion in favour of using boiled water. It not only precipitates some calcium carbonate but also sterilises the water beyond doubt and dissipates any dissolved gases, such as chlorine, used in purification. Spring water is highly regarded, but well water is often thought to be suspect, and boiling is recommended. Rain water should never be used without first filtering it through a sterile chamois cloth and boiling it thoroughly. It often contains sulphur impurities. Distilled water is not recommended since it lacks trace elements of mineral salts so often beneficial to the yeast.

When adding water to a fruit must, it should be remembered that fruit consists mainly of water. If the fruit is well crushed and pressed, up to 80% of its weight can be extracted with equipment suitable for use in the home.

Water is added not only to dilute acids but also to leach out flavour, sugar and body, as well as all the nourishment. Some ingredients such as vegetables need to be boiled for this purpose.

Flavour

Flavour is a combination of taste, odour and texture. There are four main tastes — salt, sweet, sour, bitter — and three ancillary ones — metallic, fatty and alkaline. Odours have been categorised into five groups — ethereal, camphory, floral, musky and minty. Texture in this context, refers primarily to the degree of 'thickness'.

Flavour naturally differs with every ingredient and from one year to another, or one place to another with the same ingredient. In some fruits, flowers and vegetables it is very strong and to avoid an overwhelming flavour care must be taken not to use too much of the same ingredient. By reducing the quantity of fruit to obtain a satisfactory flavour the total body, acid and nourishment are also reduced and these must then be added to make a balanced must.

In some soft fruits there is a flavour change during fermentation due partly to the withdrawal of sweet-ness from the flavour. Wines made from these ingredients taste better sweet than dry.

Concentration sometimes has the same effect and this is noticeable in rosehip syrup. Dried herbs and dried flowers are also extremely concentrated in flavour and a very small packet goes a long way.

Opinions differ on the merit of using boiling water to assist in the extraction of flavour. Whilst there are many who use this method with excellent results there are others who prefer to use cold water, arguing that this does not dissipate any of the flavour or volatile acids of the ingredients. By fermenting a must on the pulp, the alcohol helps to extract the flavour and 4 or 5 days is usually sufficient. Furthermore, the off-coming carbon dioxide helps to prevent the invasion of spoilage micro-organisms.

Sugar

Most winemakers use ordinary white granulated sugar, since this is still the least expensive, the most convenient and the best. Soft brown sugar may be used in the making of madeira-type wines to produce a caramel taste akin to the madeira flavour. Cube sugar, caster sugar and icing sugar are all more expensive but nevertheless suitable. Golden syrup or a light treacle may be used in red wines or strong dessert white wines, but the colour and flavour of this sugar affects the colour and flavour of light white wines. Fructose or glucose may also be used, preferably some of each, though they can be used singly. Invert sugar is simply a mixture of fructose and glucose which ferments very rapidly. It can be made by boiling a solution of ordinary white granulated sugar with a teaspoonful of citric acid for 20 minutes. Although invert sugar is used extensively in the brewing industry its advantages in winemaking are less apparent. Commercial invert sugar contains 25% water, so 4 measures of this is equal to 3 measures of granulated sugar.

Honey may be substituted for sugar in the ratio of 4 parts honey to 3 parts sugar. It will affect the flavour slightly and it is recommended that not more than one quarter to one third of the sugar be so replaced, unless a honey flavour is required in the wine. Similarly, malt extract may be used and the same proportions apply. Black treacle and molasses should always be avoided since they impart a most unpleasant taste to a wine.

Cereal as a source of carbo-hydrate has limited merits. Although the starch in the cereal can be converted to sugar by the enzyme diastase, the grain imparts a flavour which can hardly be described as vinous. They are most effective when used as an additive to provide some body to a wine, rather than as a main source of sugar.

Most winemakers add sugar to a must in its dry, granulated crystals form, and stir till it is dissolved. Others prefer to use a sugar syrup to effect a quicker dissolution of the sugar without so much stirring, with its consequent admission of air and, therefore, oxygen to the must. The usual formulae is 2 lb sugar dissolved in 1 pint of boiling water to produce 2 pints of syrup (1 kg dissolved in 62 cls produces 1 litre). The solution is covered and left to cool before use. If a syrup is used, less water is required.

Lactose or milk sugar is sometimes used for sweetening a dry wine. It cannot be fermented by ordinary wine yeast. The quantity to use depends on the amount of sweetness desired; about 20 grams ($\frac{3}{4}$ oz) per bottle is enough for the average palate. Saccharin – which is more than 500 times as sweet as sugar – may also be used to sweeten a fermented wine. It has no carbohydrate content and cannot be used for fermentation.

Acid

Acidity in a must has been described as the cornerstone upon which flavours are built. Without sufficient acid a wine tastes medicinal, will not ferment well, is prone to infection, will not keep and lacks balance.

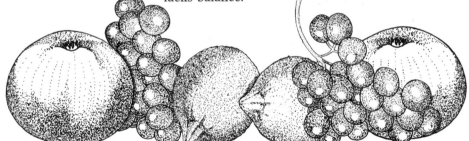

These fruits contain the acids essential to good wine: lemons (citric acid); apples (malic acid); and grapes (tartaric acid)

The common acids found in fruit, other than grapes, are citric or malic. Most winemakers add citric acid to their musts, partly because of its general availability and partly because it stimulates a quick fermentation. Tartaric acid, the major acid in grapes, is used by some winemakers, however, because any excess is precipitated during maturation as potassium tartrate – little glass-like crystals. Malic acid also has advantages in that it is frequently subject to a malo-lactic fermentation by members of the lacto-bacillus group. The sharp-tasting malic acid is then converted to the mild-tasting lactic acid. A combination of the three acids has all the advantages, but is less widely used than it deserves.

As a general rule a dry wine needs an acidity of between 3.5 and 4.5 parts per 1,000. A sweet wine needs a little more, between 4.5 and 5.5 parts per 1,000 to balance the sugar. Strong wines which it is hoped to mature for 10 years or so, need more still, and 6 or 7 parts per 1,000 would not be too much.

As a general guide a mixture of 2 parts tartaric acid to 1 part malic acid should be added to fruits containing citric acid, and a mixture of equal parts citric and tartaric acids to fruits containing malic acid. To vegetable, flower, cereal and herb musts a mixture of the three acids in the proportion 2 parts citric, 2 parts tartaric and 1 part malic acid, make a

suitable blend.

For must containing no acids at least 20 grams ($\frac{3}{4}$ oz.) and preferably 28 grams (1 oz.) of acid should be added per demijohn of must, *ie* for 6 bottles of wine. This quantity may be increased up to 40 grams ($1\frac{1}{2}$ oz.) for a strong dessert wine, that is to be matured for a number of years.

Acid, in the form of crystals, keeps for years in an airtight jar stored in a cool dry place. It is best to buy the crystals in bulk so that you always have plenty when needed.

Tannin

This is the substance which gives wine 'zest' or 'bite' and contributes substantially to a wine's character. Wines lacking tannin have an insipid taste, do not keep well and seem rather 'spineless'. Grapes, of course, have an abundance of tannin, to be found in skin, stalk and pips. Many fruits have some, including apples, apricots, bananas, blackcurrants, bilberries, damsons, elderberries, peaches, pears and sloes. Most fruits have insufficient, however, especially after dilution. Flowers, vegetables, cereals and herbs have no tannin. It is readily available to the home winemaker in the form of grape tannin powder and about half a level 5 ml spoonful should be added to all musts. Some winemakers add a quantity of strongly brewed cold tea left in the pot, varying from 1 tablespoonful to $\frac{1}{2}$ cup. The process of fermenting a must on the pulp, extracts the maximum amount of tannin from fruit.

Nutrients

It is essential that the must should contain sufficient nourishment for the yeast cells, if a satisfactory fermentation is to be effected. This can be added in the form of a mixture of different salts of ammonium phosphate and sulphate and vitamin B. Experience has shown, however, that some fruit mucilage is also needed to produce a good wine. Some grape juice concentrate, fresh grapes or dried grapes should therefore be added to every must and especially to flower, herb, grain and vegetable musts.

Pectic Enzyme

Fruit juice is contained in a cell surrounded by a wall composed of cellulose and a mixture of substances called pectin. Pectin acts as a protective colloid or haze-forming particles and unless it is destroyed prevents a wine from clearing and becoming star-bright. It does not respond to fining agents or to filtering and has to be treated with an enzyme called pectinase. This enzyme is present in many fruits, especially the grape, and will clear many musts during fermentation. Pectinase is inactivated by heat, however, and the pouring of boiling water over fruit damages it.

Artificial pectinase is available mostly as a white powder, but it can also be obtained in liquid form, when it has a brownish colour. It is marketed under various brand names and may be bought as Pectolase, Pectozyme, Pectinol or simply 'pectin destroying enzyme'. The powder should be stored dry in an air-tight jar in a cool place, and will then keep for up to one year. The liquid form is damaged by light and its shelf life, however protected, is much shorter than the powder form.

Most winemakers automatically add some pectin destroying enzyme to every fruit must. The actual quantity, depending on the brand being used, can vary from one 5 ml spoonful per demijohn to 1 tablespoonful. It should be added when the must is cool and before the addition of sugar, which retards its action. Twenty-four hours is usually long enough for it to destroy the pectin in the must.

All fruits and vegetables contain pectin to some extent but the following have more than others, and a pectin-destroying enzyme should always be added to musts containing these ingredients: apricot, damson, peach, plum and sloe, parsnip and potato.

Yeast

It is little more than 100 years ago that Louis Pasteur proved that yeast cells cause fermentation.

Bread leaven was known long before the birth of Christ, and ale yeast too. Throughout the centuries it was used without knowing how it worked or even what it was. Around 1800 it was generally thought that fermentation was a purely chemical process. Some, however, thought that it was due to spontaneous generation.

It wasn't until 1835 that a Frenchman, de la Tour, and a German, Schwann, discovered separately that beer and wine yeasts were living spherical organisms able to reproduce themselves and that their presence was essential for fermentation. De la Tour, studying drops of beer under a microscope, saw the yeast cells forming buds that grew, parted from the parent buds and soon formed buds themselves. Schwann discovered that the cells needed nitrogenous matter as well as a sugar solution in which to thrive. He called them 'zuckerpilz' which simply means sugar fungi. Shortly afterwards Von Meyer, another scientist studying yeast cells, suggested the name 'saccharomyces' as a generic name for sugar fungi and this remains today.

A catalyst

To isolate the cause of fermentation was not the same as understanding how it worked. It was only known that yeast cells were always present during fermentation and that they flourished and multiplied. The Swedish chemist, Jons Berzelius, had recognised that some substances, simply by their presence, caused other substances to react, without themselves being changed in anyway. He described such a substance as a catalyst, a name he derived from the Greek word 'Katalysis', meaning 'dissolution'. In 1839

Berzelius suggested that yeast was a catalyst since by its very presence in a sugar solution it caused a reduction of the large sugar molecules into ethyl alcohol and carbon dioxide in almost equal proportions.

In 1857 after a series of experiments based on his own thinking, Pasteur published an article on lactic fermentation. Further experiments proved that if a yeast which had been cultured in a germ-free medium was introduced into a beer wort that had been sterilised fermentation was quickly started. He was soon able to proved beyond doubt that the yeast cell alone caused alcoholic fermentation.

Yeast Enzymes

Other scientists, notably Jorgensen and Hansen in Denmark, developed these researches and later it was discovered that the yeast cell secreted a number of enzymes which were the actual catalysts that caused fermentation. Invertase split the sucrose molecule into glucose and fructose and then a whole

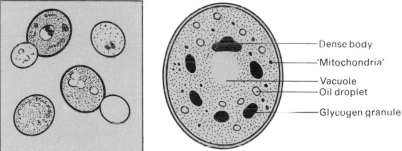

— Dense body
— 'Mitochondria'
— Vacuole
— Oil droplet
— Glycogen granule

series of different enzymes, called the apo-zymase complex for simplicity, carried on the complicated process of reduction, first to one chemical, then to another and so on throughout at least 15 changes, until ethyl alcohol and carbon dioxide were formed. (*See Table Number 8*)

Once the yeast cell was known, scientists soon discovered many different varieties and sub-varieties of yeasts amounting in all to nearly 2,000. Only a very few are of interest to the winemaker and brewer. These are:

The yeasts we use

SACCHAROMYCES CEREVISIAE: the circular yeast cell used for fermenting bread doughs and beer worts. The word *cerevisiae* probably came from the noun *cerevisia*, a Gaulish word meaning beer. A Spanish word, *cerveza*, also means beer. The word was in use at least 200 years before the birth of Christ and well before the Romans came into contact with the Gauls from whom they probably took the word we use today.

SACCHAROMYCES CARLSBERGENSIS: a bottom fermenting yeast that works best at a low temperature and is used in the making of lager beer. It was named after the founder of the famous Carlsberg brewery in Denmark.

The simplified diagram of a yeast cell gives an idea of what can be seen under a high powered microscope. The enzymes are secreted inside the cell and the molecules of sugar pass through the cell wall, are changed into alcohol and carbon dioxide which then pass back into the must. The carbon dioxide rises to the surface in the form of a bubble and bursts with a hissing noise. The alcohol remains in the young wine

SACCHAROMYCES ELIPSOIDEUS: an eliptical shaped yeast that is most commonly found on the grape. It is fairly tolerant to sulphur and to alcohol. It imparts a good bouquet and flavour to wine and usually falls firmly to the bottom after fermentation. For these reasons it is the most suitable yeast to use when making wine.

Yeast forms

Nowadays wine yeast is widely available in many forms and sub-varieties. Most commonly it is available in tablet form, as dried granules, and in liquid form. It is also available as a culture on an agar slant in a sealed test tube. In good conditions, yeast in liquid form will keep for up to two years and in dried and tablet form even longer. They should be kept cool, dry and dark.

How many millions

Inevitably there are bound to be some dead or weak cells in a sachet, tablet or phial, as well as millions of

The older the yeast, the less efficient it becomes, as this diagram demonstrates. After three months, less than half the cells are viable

cells in dried granules and tablet form naturally need a little time in which to hydrate before beginning to reproduce themselves, and therefore should always be prepared in a starter bottle.

Subtle differences

Whilst there has certainly been some controversy on the subject, there is now an increasing amount of evidence to support the long-held belief of certain winemakers that different sub-varieties of yeast, given the right conditions, can and do subtly affect the bouquet and flavour of the finished wine.

The Sauternes yeast for example, ferments glucose somewhat reluctantly and produces glycerine. As a result its wine tends to have a relatively high residue of glucose and glycerine which imparts a body and sweetness that is characteristic of this wine.

Bordeaux yeast is characterised by increasing the organic acid level of a wine, leading, with adequate maturation, to an enhancing of the bouquet. Burgundy yeast, like Bordeaux, has an alcohol

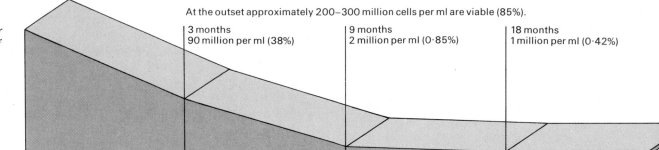

At the outset approximately 200–300 million cells per ml are viable (85%).

3 months
90 million per ml (38%)

9 months
2 million per ml (0·85%)

18 months
1 million per ml (0·42%)

living cells. At the outset the proportion is about 85% viable to 15% non-viable. The older the yeast preparation becomes, the smaller will be the proportion of viable cells. When preparing yeasts for distribution the count of living cells is extremely high – some 200 to 300 million cells per ml of culture. After three months the viable cells might be around 90 million per ml. After a further six months the number is likely to be down to 2 million per ml. After another nine months, when the preparation is some eighteen months old, the count is likely to be down to around 1 million cells per ml. Even at this substantial age a 5 ml spoonful of liquid yeast will contain about 5 million living and active yeast cells. Dried yeast granules naturally contain a much greater number of cells, around 20,000 million per gram. Their shelf life is at least three years if they are kept dry and cool. Moisture and warmth cause rapid deterioration.

Activate them first

Before adding yeast to a must, it is highly desirable to activate the cells in a starter solution containing a variety of nutrients and vitamins, some acid, some sugar and, of course, water. This ensures that the living cells can recover their vitality and reproduce themselves to form a large enough colony to start a fermentation of a must without delay. The yeast

tolerance of only up to 15%. So, too, has Hock yeast.

There are varying degrees of alcohol tolerance between the sub-varieties as well as varying precipitation characteristics. Port yeast, for example has a tendency to clump together more than others, but surprisingly it has an alcohol tolerance of no more than 15%. Indeed, when making a port-type wine it is a good idea to start the wine off with a port yeast and when about 8% alcohol has been formed, to introduce a really active and vigorous madeira yeast. With sufficient nutrient this will carry the fermentation along to around 18% alcohol, virtually the maximum attainable. Tokay yeast, too, has an extremely high alcohol tolerance and in the right circumstances can ferment a must up to 18% alcohol.

Sherry yeast is often a combination of at least two strains, *saccharomyces fermentati* with an alcohol tolerance of about 16%, and *saccharomyces beticus* which sometimes forms a 'flor' or skin on the surface of a fermented must. Sometimes a sherry yeast will contain other strains as well, to contribute towards the distinctive bouquet and flavour of a sherry-type wine.

The Sherry Flor yeast is derived from *saccharomyces ovaformis* and microscopically forms tetreds and triads. It also produces rather more acetaldehyde than one would normally expect, again enhancing the bouquet.

Champagne yeast has the remarkable capacity to withstand a high pressure of carbon dioxide, up to 90 lb per square inch. It does not impart off-flavours to the wine in the way that other yeasts do when left in contact with the wine after fermentation. It has a relatively low alcohol tolerance of only up to 14%.

Cereal yeast is capable of fermenting dextrins and starches within limits and should be used with musts containing a higher proportion of these carbohydrates. This yeast is not intended for use with purely cereal or starch ingredients since it is extremely difficult to produce a quality wine with these ingredients alone. It will ferment up to 16% alcohol in the right circumstances.

The experienced winemaker can discern subtle differences in bouquet and flavour in at least the major sub-varieties when used in conjunction with a sympathetically balanced must. This is due to the slight differences in the bio-chemical action of the yeast types.

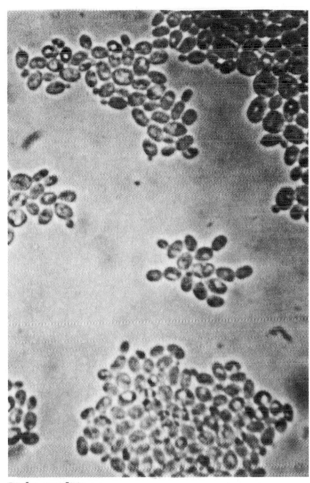

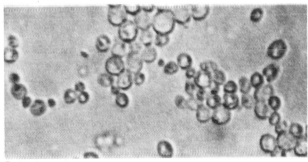

Extreme left: *Sherry Flor yeast cells*

Left: *Burgundy yeast cells*

Super yeast

There is a growing belief that a mixture of different yeast strains will improve the rate of fermentation, the degree of fermentation, the precipitation after fermentation and the cleanliness (ie freedom from off-flavours). One well-known proprietary brand — C. W. E. Formula 67 yeast — claims just this. So does another — Unican Super Yeast. Both are available in granule form and certainly work wonders. They ferment extremely vigorously and need plenty of head room at first. Fermentation begins within a few hours and is often over within seven to ten days. By adding extra sugar at intervals, up to 16% alcohol can be formed without difficulty. After fermentation the sediment falls cleanly to the bottom. The performance is quite dramatic.

The full nature of the contribution of yeast to bouquet and flavour is not yet properly understood. We do know, however, that this contribution is important and significant, provided the right chemical and physical environment is maintained. During fermentation, small but important quantities of glutannic, malic, lactic and succinic acids are formed, the last named contributing particularly to the winey smell. Adequate sulphite in the wine stimulates the production of acetaldehyde, perhaps the most important constituent of a good bouquet.

Right conditions

An inadequate nitrogen supply, due to insufficient ammonium phosphate and/or ammonium sulphate, encourages the production of fusel oils, one of which, amyl alcohol, combines with acetic acid to form amyl acetate, the unpleasant 'pear-drop' smell. Lack of pantothenic acid, one of the vitamins in the wide B group, leads to the formation of hydrogen sulphide, the bad egg smell.

For the best results, a balanced nutrient should be used which includes a full range of minerals, vitamins and salts necessary for a flourishing yeast colony. Such formulations are sometimes called yeast energisers or boosters. The grape naturally includes all these elements and the inclusion of grape in one form or another in every must, helps enormously in providing the right environment for the yeast to function effectively.

Fermentations need to be conducted at an even temperature of between 20° and 24°C (68° to 75°F) for the best results.

Thus far we know, but research continues in this relatively new science of fermentology and we can look forward with confidence to improved yeast strains, better balanced nutrients and new methods of controlling the quality of wine made in the home during the years to come.

Fermentation & Maturation

Converting the Must into Wine

THE world, as we know it, is continued by a process of creation and decay. Without decay the accumulation of dead organic matter of all kinds, would so clutter the earth that life itself would be stifled. This decay is caused by micro-organisms that break down the debris to elements that will sustain further life as it is created. One stage of decay — a stage that is only one of a cycle in the overall process — is fermentation which causes effervescence, heat and a change of properties.

The creation of wines and beers is caused by fermentation. It is the action of yeast which decays, or breaks down, the sugars in vegetable matter. This fermentation of sugar is but one stage in converting vegetable matter which contains sugar (eg fruit) from its complete form to chemicals and compost. After the yeast has reduced the sugar to alcohol and carbon dioxide, other yeasts and bacteria cause further fermentation that ultimately reduces the wine to carbon dioxide and water. This full process

Equation A

Sucrose plus water in the presence becomes glucose plus fructose
of invertase

$$C_{12}H_{22}O_{11} + H_2O \rightarrow C_6H_{12}O_6 + C_6H_{12}O_6$$

Equation B

Glucose in the presence becomes carbon plus ethyl plus large calories
or fructose of zymase dioxide alcohol of energy

$$C_6H_{12}O_6 \text{ complex} \rightarrow 2CO_2 + 2C_2H_5OH + 15.4 \text{ kg cals.}$$

Equation C

Maltose plus water in the presence glucose plus glucose
of maltase becomes

$$C_{12}H_{22}O_{11} + H_2O \rightarrow C_6H_{12}O_6 + C_6H_{12}O_6$$

has only been understood in recent years, and better control of the production of wine and the prevention of spoilage during and after its production has resulted.

The sucrose which is present in a must, either from the raw materials, or from the addition of sugar, is hydrolysed into simple sugars by the enzyme called invertase, secreted by the saccharomyces yeast. (See Equation A).

The yeast also secretes a complex of enzymes, called zymase, which causes the glucose and fructose to change into carbon dioxide and ethyl alcohol whilst releasing energy. (See Equation B).

The escaping carbon dioxide gas produces the

effervescence which is called the visible signs of fermentation. The ethyl alcohol is the basic part of wine, and the large calories of energy are utilised by the yeast.

Maltose, used in the brewing of beers, is hydrolysed and fermented in a similar manner. The difference is an enzyme called maltase which hydrolyses the maltose to glucose only. The glucose is then fermented by the enzyme complex as described above. (See Equation C).

It was generally believed at one time that to exist all forms of life required oxygen as an energy source. It was believed that in a covered must the yeast obtained oxygen from sugar as a result of fermentation. It is now certain, that wine yeasts do not require oxygen as an energy source. The energy they require is that released by the fermentation and they take no oxygen.

Otto Myerhoff conclusively proved in 1948 that yeast only required oxygen for reproduction; it can live without oxygen but will not reproduce itself. This oxygen is obtained from the air or from the oxygen dissolved in a solution. Thus the sole purpose of fermentation, as far as the yeast is concerned, is to provide itself with energy not oxygen.

The optimum conditions for maximum fermentation and the production of the best wines are accordingly as follows:
1 the use of a pre-activated wine yeast;
2 a constant temperature between 20°–24°C;
3 the correct balance of acids, nutrients and sugars;
4 the exclusion of air by means of an air-lock.

The duration of fermentation of wine under optimum conditions is approximately three weeks, but for no apparent reason may continue for many weeks longer. Unfavourable conditions in one form or another can protract fermentation to six or nine months, or even longer.

If the conditions are unfavourable various micro-organisms can attack the wine, either during fermentation or maturation. They continue the process of decay, either by oxidation or fermentation. Spoilage actions cause the wine to have off-flavours, develop hazes, become vinegar, or, finally, to be reduced to carbon dioxide and water. The one exception is the malo-lactic fermentation which is permitted to occur in wines of high malic acidity in order that it may be reduced; even so, the wines can be spoilt by a 'mousey' taste. Prevention of spoilage fermentations is achieved simply by the exclusion of air and the use of sulphite.

Fermentation of sugars in a solution often produces frothing and bubbling. In the beginning and at the higher temperatures, the bubbling can be so vigorous that the must appears to boil. Hence the derivation of the word fermentation from the Latin fervere — to boil.

Some wines develop visible signs of fermentation in the Spring after their production. This has given rise to the idea that a wine may act in sympathy with its parent plant, e.g. gooseberry wine starts fermenting again with the blossoming of the gooseberry bush. However, in fact it is not that they act in sympathy, but that both activities are the result of the same factor – the rise in temperature. Wines kept in a constant temperature do not develop the 'sympathetic' fermentation. These Spring fermentations are more frequently produced by enzymes and micro-organisms, such as lacto-bacilli, than by yeast fermentation of sugar.

When the last bubble of carbon dioxide has passed through the air-lock on a jar of fermenting wine, the period of maturation begins.

To make sure that fermentation has actually finished and not just stuck, however, it is advisable to check the specific gravity. If it is not what it is expected to be from the kind of fermentation conducted, then the fermentation may be inhibited and incomplete. A fermentation can stick for any of the following reasons:

1 The wine has become too warm and the yeast has become lazy.
   Remedy: move the jar to a somewhat cooler place with an air temperature of around 20°C (68°F).

2 The wine has become too cold and the yeast has become lazy.
   Remedy: move the jar to a somewhat warmer place with an air temperature of around 24°C (75°F).

3 There was insufficient nutrient in the wine and it has all been used.
   Remedy: add some yeast booster consisting of a broad range of nutrients and vitamins.

4 There was insufficient or no acid in the must and the yeast is inhibited.
   Remedy: dissolve a teaspoonful of citric acid in a bottle of the wine and stir it into the bulk.

5 If too much sulphite was used in the preparation of the must, or the yeast was added too soon, or not first activated, then the yeast colony may have been too weak and thus may nearly have died off.
   Remedy: aerate the wine by pouring it into another jar in such a manner as to expose the wine to as much air as possible. In this way any sulphur dioxide will be dissipated and oxygen will be absorbed. The yeast colony should then be able to reproduce and enlarge. If fermentation doesn't soon start, a new yeast culture will be necessary.

6 If the specific gravity of the must was not checked it may be that the total content of sugar, from that added and that already in the fruit, is too much for the yeast to ferment.
   Remedy: If the specific gravity is in excess of 1.100 the must should be diluted with cold boiled water.

7 If all the remedies have been tried and the fermentation remains stuck, then prepare a new yeast starter from a yeast with a high alcoholic tolerance such as Tokay or Madeira. When it is thorough-

ly active add it to half a bottle only of wine and stand the bottle in a warm place with a plug of cotton wool loosely in the neck. When this is fermenting well, add it to a full bottle of wine and wait again for a day or so for this to ferment well. Then add another bottle of wine and so on until the entire quantity is fermenting once more.

If the specific gravity is as low as expected, then fermentation is complete.

The wine should be moved to a cool place; around 10°C (50°F) seems ideal but cannot always be achieved. During a week or two at this temperature, all the solid particles of yeast and debris should settle firmly on the bottom of the jar and the wine should begin to clear from the neck downwards.

As soon as there is a firm deposit, siphon the clearing wine from the lees into a clean, sulphite-rinsed jar. With care all but the actual paste can be removed but there is likely to be a small air space at the top of the newly-filled jar. Except for sherry-type wines, air should be excluded by topping the jar up with some of the same wine, a very similar wine or a little cold boiled water – or even some sterilised glass marbles.

Some sulphite should now be added to prevent infection and oxidation. Fifty parts per million is adequate for a dry wine and 100 p.p.m. for a sweet wine. Insert a clean cork or rubber bung into the jar, soaking the one and rinsing the other in a sulphite solution. Shake off any loose solution but do not dry the cork or bung. Push either well home in the neck of the jar, label the jar with details of the wine and store it in a cool dark place, free from vibrations.

Now comes the hard part of winemaking – waiting for the wine to mature. This period of impatience varies with every wine and no firm guidance can be given. In general terms light wines mature more quickly than heavy wines, whites quicker than reds, wines low in acid, tannin and alcohol quicker than wines containing larger quantities of these three ingredients.

A few will mature in three or four months but wines made at home tend to be somewhat high in alcohol and often a year is needed before a wine has developed its bouquet and flavour to the full. Dessert wines of the Sherry, Port, Madeira and Tokay type may take from two to five years to reach maturity. Each wine differs and only experience of tasting different wines can give guidance about any particular wine.

After some months in bulk store, a wine may be bottled for further storage. It is quite remarkable that nearly every wine benefits from a period of storage in bottle. Every effort should be made to give a good wine a minimum of three months and preferably six to nine months or even longer in bottle. By the time the wine is ready for bottling it should have been racked twice and, of course, be absolutely star-bright. Hazy wines do not mature in bottle.

Basic Processes

CERTAIN activities are the same in the making of every kind of wine. They include such matters as hygiene, the keeping of records, checking the acid and sugar contents, racking, fining and filtering.

Hygiene

The greatest care should be taken to ensure that all the equipment and ingredients used are clean and free from spoilage organisms of whatever kind. Much of the equipment used, such as casks, jars, bins, buckets, funnels, wooden spoons, corks, bungs, and so on, afford hiding places for fungi or bacteria. Indeed, put away damp in a dark place and there is soon a visible mould growth upon them. Unless sterilised, such equipment could rapidly spoil a new wine.

It is most important then, that all winemaking equipment be put away clean and dry after each using, and that it be freshly sterilised before each subsequent use. This applies especially to bottles, pressing cloths or bags and corks.

The most common spoilage organism is *mycoderma aceti*, sometimes called 'aceto-bacter'. This is the vinegar bug which causes wine to smell and taste of acetic acid — the main constituent of vinegar. The bacteria is frequently carried by the little fruit fly — *drosophila melanogaster*. It alights on ingredients and equipment, leaving behind enough bacteria to begin a colony. But there are many similar organisms, including wild and unwanted yeasts and the large family of lactic acid bacteria, all of which cause an unpleasant smell in the bouquet and a bad flavour in the wine. *These organisms like access to oxygen and dislike sulphur.*

Sulphur has long been known for its purifying qualities. Before simpler ways were known, a sulphur candle was burned inside a cask to purify it. It took many years of research before sulphur could be prepared in such a way as to be safe for use in the human body but eventually the answer was found in sulphonamide. Amateur winemakers have a safe access to the anti-toxic qualities of sulphur in the crystals of sodium or potassium metabisulphite, both of which are equally suitable. Winemakers refer to them simply as sulphite. They are available as loose white crystals or in tablet form marketed under the name of Campden tablets. One tablet dissolved in a gallon of water releases 50 parts per million of the gas sulphur dioxide which is the anti-toxic element. If crystals are bought loose, 450 grams (1 lb) dissolved in 4.5 litres (1 gallon) produces a solution of which two 5 ml spoonsful are equivalent to 1 tablet. This is, of course, the cheapest way of buying and using sulphite. For most people 100 grams of sulphite dissolved in 1 litre of water is an ample quantity. If kept well-stoppered and stored in a cool place it will keep for several months. The effect of sulphite is enhanced in an acid solution. Always add, therefore, 10 grams of citric acid cystals per 100 grams sulphite crystals.

Cleanliness is essential

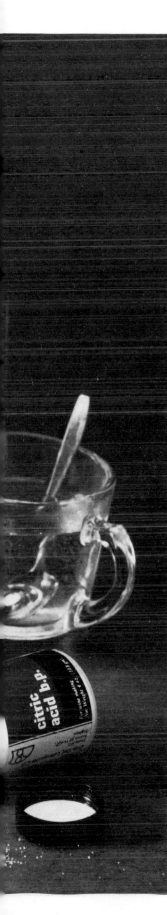

Normally 50 parts per million is sufficient sulphur dioxide to purify clean equipment or a clean must. Dirtier equipment or some damaged fruit need double this quantity, *ie* two tablets or four 5 ml spoonsful of standard solution. Before using any equipment it should be rinsed in this solution. Corks should be soaked for half an hour in it, larger equipment should be washed over in it. Bottles when washed and ready for use should be sterilised by pouring a sulphite solution from one bottle to another and leaving them to drain. Do not subsequently wet them again.

Sulphite has a further advantage for the wine-maker in that it is an anti oxidant, *ie* it prevents oxidation. When preparing fruit, the appropriate quantity of water together with sufficient sulphite to produce a 50 parts per million solution for first class fruit and 100 parts per million for second class fruit, together with a few grams of citric acid, should first be placed in a mashing bin. As the fruit is crushed or cut to remove stones, it should be dropped into the bin. In this way, browning (which is oxidation) will be prevented. The quality of the resulting wine will then be enhanced and there will be no taint of oxidation.

Because the sulphur dioxide gas given off by the sulphite in a must is toxic to all micro-organisms, wine yeast should not be added until 24 hours after the sulphite. In this way the sulphite has time to kill all the micro-organisms and prepare a clean must in which the active yeast can begin fermentation without competition, so to speak. The small amount of sulphur dioxide left in the must after 24 hours does not inhibit the true wine yeast.

If a sulphite solution is used regularly in the winery for sterilising all equipment and ingredients, for wiping over surfaces and floors, problems of infection by spoilage organisms can be eliminated. But all equipment means ALL equipment and small items such as a funnel, an hydrometer, a thermometer, a siphon, a filter or a spoon should not be over-looked. Similarly with ingredients. Dried fruit should always be washed in a sulphite solution of 100 parts per million and then you can be sure that you are starting your must off in a clean and hygienic condition. Sulphite is the winemaker's best friend. It is not as well appreciated as it deserves.

For both the beginner and the experienced wine-maker the keeping of records is most important. It is so easy to forget whether this ingredient or that was included and, if so, how much; to remember specific gravity readings and dates; to remember even, the basic ingredients. When mature, all white wines look similar and do not necessarily taste of their main ingredient; and the same applies to red.

A simple card such as that illustrated is quite adequate and can subsequently be filed when fermentation is complete. At that stage a tie-on label can be used giving brief details of name, date and reference. Stick-on labels are generally less satis-

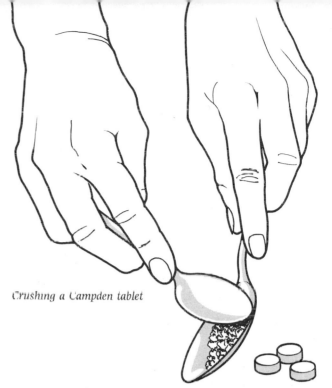

Crushing a Campden tablet

factory. They sometimes come unstuck and get lost, or else remain so firmly stuck that they cannot be removed. Experience shows that for every wine you need to look up your records at some time, whether on the preparation, fermentation, maturation or consumation stages.

Records may be brief and simple, or as elaborate as you like but records of some sort are imperative.

A Record Card

Name of wine	Quantity made
Date started	Yeast used

Ingredients	Quantity	Description
Grape juice concentrate/ Sultana/Raisins		

Sugar	Water
Acids	Tannin

Pectic Enzyme	Sulphite	Nutrients

S.G. of must before sugar added

S.G. of must before yeast added

S.G. of wine at end of fermentation

Date of first racking	Date of fining
Date of second racking	Date of filtering

Date of bottling

Method used

Acidity

Since acid is an essential ingredient in the making of wine, it is wise to check how much natural acid is already present in the must. This is not difficult to determine at home and it is especially important to do so in the preparation of quality wines.

There are two simple methods. The first is by titration. A precise quantity of the must, usually about 2 ml, is diluted in twice the quantity of distilled water. Six drops of *Phenolphthalein* are then added as a colour indicator and the whole is gently shaken so that all three are well mixed. A measured quantity of an acid-testing reagent – usually sodium hydroxide – is then added, drop by drop, until the whole solution turns pink. This is easy to spot with white wines but harder with the very dark reds. If the must is very dark, more distilled water may be added.

When the pink point is reached the quantity of reagent used is noted. The test is then done a second time and if the quantity of reagent used is not precisely the same the average is taken. The number of ml of reagent is then multiplied by $2\frac{1}{2}$ and the answer is the quantity of acid in the must, measured in parts per 1,000 (p.p.t.) of sulphuric acid. Sulphuric acid is used as a constant with which all other acids are compared. The comparisons between sulphuric acid, citric, tartaric and malic are given in table 14 section A. If more acid is required, stir in sufficient to increase the p.p.t. as necessary according to section B.

For example, if titration reveals a sulphuric acid equivalent content of 2.5 p.p.t. and you propose to add citric acid to bring the acidity of your must up to 5 p.p.t. citric acid, you will need to add just under 7 grams ($\frac{1}{4}$ oz) of citric acid per demijohn. It will be seen from table 14 section A that the equivalent p.p.t. of sulphuric acid for citric acid is 1.09 equal to 7 grams ($\frac{1}{4}$ oz). Add 1.09 to the 2.50 p.p.t. already recorded from titration and the total is 3.59. Reference to section B again shows that 3.5 p.p.t. sulphuric is equivalent to approximately 5 p.p.t. citric acid. This is much less complicated in practice than it seems in theory.

An over-acid must may be further diluted but precipitated chalk, calcium carbonate, is usually added, especially in a rhubarb must, which may contain some oxalic acid. 7 grams ($\frac{1}{4}$ oz) chalk in a demijohn of must will reduce the acidity by 1.5 p.p.t. sulphuric acid.

It is interesting to note some typical acidities of certain well-known commercial wines.

PORT varies from 4.15 to 6.12 p.p.t. tartaric acid.

SHERRY	4.2	5.1	p.p.t.
BURGUNDY	5.3	7.0	p.p.t.
CLARET	4.2	6.1	p.p.t.
MOSELLE	6.75	9.2	p.p.t.
CHAMPAGNE	5.0	10.7	p.p.t.

The precise quantity of acid in a wine, however, is rather less important than the actual taste or degree of the acidity. Some acids taste more sharp than others and in wine it is this taste that really matters. The degree of acidity is measured by the hydrogen ion concentration which is the active acidity of a solution. The letters *p*H followed by a figure indicate the degree of acidity. For wine a *p*H of 3.4 is regarded as the optimum within a range 3.1 to 3.6. The neutral point, neither acid nor alkali, is *p*H7. Reducing down from 7 and a solution becomes rapidly sharper to the taste. Above 7 the solution becomes more alkali.

Some winemakers are critical of testing wines by *p*H on the grounds that certain musts contain a complex of different acids, pectins, salts, sugars, tannins etc., which act as buffers, causing only a small change in the *p*H, with a comparatively large change in the quantities of acids present. This is a theoretical argument however, and in practice if a *p*H test is conducted before the addition of pectic enzymes, acid, tannin, nutrients, sulphites, sugar and so on, a sufficiently accurate result can be obtained. The process is simple in the extreme. A piece of a *p*H indicator paper covering the range 2.5 to 4 is dipped into the liquid to be tested, the colour of the paper changes and is compared with a colour chart supplied. The approximate *p*H of the liquid is read off the chart instantly. For the general run of making wine at home this is quite adequate. For any reading around 4 or above, acid must be added. For any reading below 3 the acid should be reduced with some powdered chalk. What is important to remember is that acid is essential within a reasonable range, but the precise quantity is not critical. If the wine has rather more acid than necessary the wine will just take longer to mature and be better for it. Some quite splendid dessert wines are being made with relatively high quantities of tartaric acid – 8 to 9 p.p.t. – and are then left to mature for up to 10 years.

Titration is a simple way of determining acidity, but it needs to be accurate, so do not hurry the operation

Sugar content

The amount of sugar in a must varies between different ingredients and between the same ingredients from year to year. For this reason it is always advisable to check the sugar content of every must prior to the addition of any extra sugar. It may well be that the must has much more sugar than originally thought, or much less. An hydrometer is the instrument used to test the sweetness of a must. It records the specific gravity of a must, *ie* the weight of the must relative to the same weight of pure water at a precise temperature – usually 15°C (59°F). The difference is the weight of the sugar in the must. An hydrometer reading is sometimes distorted at the lower and upper ends of the scale by dissolved and unfermentable suspended solids other than sugar. Some authorities believe that these can cause a variation of up to 8 units of specific gravity and some allowance for their presence is therefore made in the Sugar Content Tables (*No. 4*).

In addition to the specific gravity hydrometer, there are hydrometers which measure the potential percentage alcohol present in a must or the percentage sugar present. All of them are graduated at a precise temperature and any variation in temperature of the must will reflect an inaccuracy in the hydrometer reading. Due allowance for this must be made.

An hydrometer is usually in the form of a graduated plastic or glass tube weighted at one end. It is used by placing it in a tall narrow jar and filling the jar with the liquid to be tested. A reading is taken at eye level and by reference to the tables provided, the relative information can be read. By means of an hydrometer one can tell at a glance:

1 The quantity of natural sugar present in a must.
2 The potential alcohol content of that must.
3 The amount of additional sugar required to produce a wine of a given strength.
4 The progress of a fermentation.
5 The quantity of residual sugar present in a finished wine.
6 The alcohol content of a wine to which additional doses of sugar have been added during fermentation.

Alcohol is less heavy than water, being only about 70% of its weight. When alcohol is formed in a wine it therefore slightly dilutes the water. Accordingly a reading of 1.000 in a finished wine does not mean that all the sugar has been fermented. To achieve this, and allowing for the dilution of the water, a specific gravity reading of at least 0.990 would be necessary.

The hydrometer is the most important instrument a winemaker can possess and it should be used several times in the making of every wine. It is, for instance, far more important than the kind of sugar used.

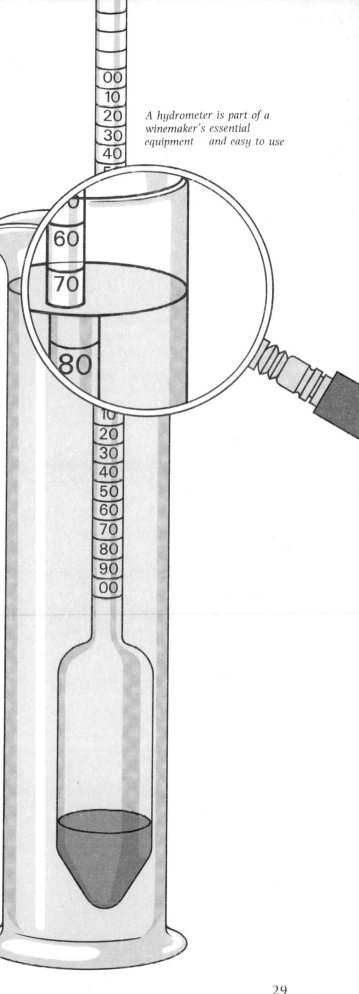

A hydrometer is part of a winemaker's essential equipment and easy to use

29

Racking

The process of removing wine from its sediment is called racking. The wine may be poured carefully into another jar, in a manner similar to decanting, and as soon as the sediment reaches the mouth of the jar, pouring is stopped. The most common way, however, is to siphon the wine.

The jar containing the wine and sediment is stood on a table and an empty sterilised jar is placed on the floor directly beneath it. The bung is removed from the wine jar and one end of a siphon inserted into the wine in such a manner as not to disturb the sediment. The siphon is then pumped, or the end of the tube is gently sucked until the tube is full. The end is squeezed between thumb and forefinger, and placed in the empty jar. Pressure is released and the wine flows from the upper jar to the lower jar. By careful tilting of the upper jar, all the clear wine can be removed, leaving only the sediment behind to be discarded.

The sediment from fermentation contains mostly organic pulp debris and dead yeast cells. If these are not removed their decomposition taints the wine. It is essential, therefore, to rack a wine as soon after fermentation as a sediment appears. Precipitation of the sediment is encouraged by a lowering of the temperature. Frequent racking helps to clarify a wine quickly and avoid off flavours. After racking, light sulphiting at the rate of 50 p.p.m. (1 Campden tablet per gallon) prevents oxidation and infection.

It is unwise to rack a fermenting wine, even if a substantial sediment can be seen, unless the fermentation has been going on for longer than six weeks. To do so may remove so much nutrient and living yeast as to terminate the fermentation.

When a wine has been racked the jar should be topped up to exclude the air.

Fining and Filtering

Occasionally a wine is slow to clear. The most common cause is simply suspended solids and these can be precipitated with several remedies. Isinglass is the one most widely used and is available in a number of proprietary wine finings which usually include some sulphite and tannin. The appropriate quantity recommended by the manufacturer is mixed with a little of the wine and then stirred into the bulk. After a few days, sometimes only hours, the wine can be seen to be clearing and the deposit forming. As soon as the wine is bright, rack it into a clean jar or bottle.

Bentonite, a finely ground volcanic clay, is also easy to use, and effective. The powder is mixed to a paste with some wine, left for 24 hours and then stirred into the bulk.

White of egg well beaten with some wine and stirred into the bulk is an old remedy that is still popular; so too, is gelatin and tannin.

Experience over more than 30 years, however, indicates that very few wines need fining and most

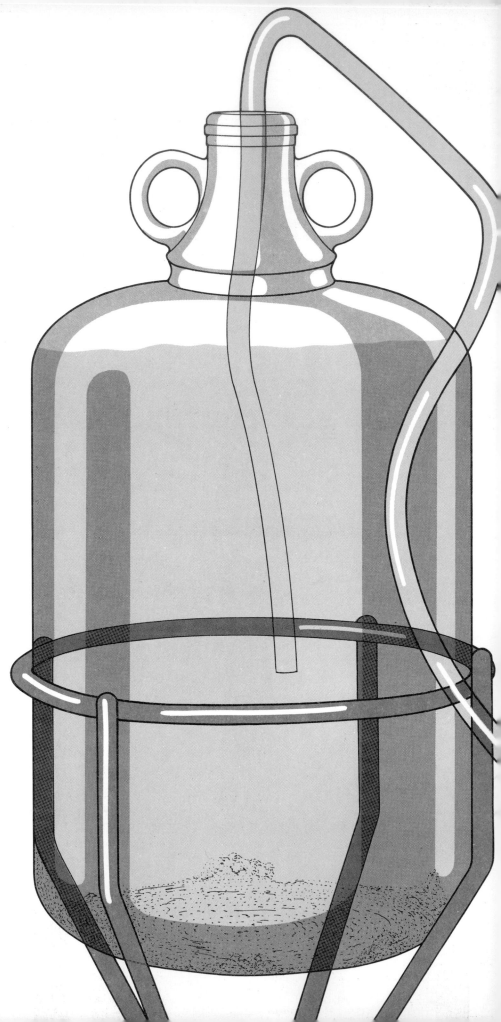

wines clear naturally, simply by racking them from precipitated deposits.

A clear wine that is not star-bright may be filtered, and there are now some very useful filter kits available. Immediately after filtering it is advisable to add sulphite at the rate of 50 p.p.m. to prevent oxidation of the wine. Always follow the instructions provided with the kit purchased, since these vary with the filter media used. Filtering is rarely necessary and should be used as a last resource rather than as standard practice.

Racking and filtering. The jar of wine to be racked or filtered must always be well above the reception jar

Essential & Desirable Equipment

Preparing the must

The first essential is a mashing bin. Choice ranges through a plastic bucket, an unchipped enamel or a stainless steel pail, a glazed earthenware vessel, a ceramic bowl, a wooden tub, a plastic dustbin, even a polythene bag in a carboard box, but best of all is a high-density, natural polythene mashing and pulp fermentation bin. These come in a wide variety of sizes up to 25 litres (5½ gallons) with a tight fitting lid that often contains grommets for an air-lock and/or an immersion heater that can be attached to a thermostat. They are light and easy to clean, are graduated in gallons and litres, and are well worth their cost.

Some kind of crusher is desirable in preparing hard fruit. An Italian model in three sizes will handle up to one ton in one hour. It is surprisingly difficult to crush gooseberries, damsons, currants and even grapes without some assistance. A small mill with a single roller does the job perfectly and effortlessly and ensures that no fruit is wasted by not being crushed.

Anyone making a reasonable quantity of fruit wine at a time will certainly be glad of a press. The choice, from small to large, is finely graded. With the intelligent use of a press, up to 80% of the weight of fruit can be extracted in juice. This ensures a fuller flavour and better use of all the natural goodness in the fruit.

A wide selection of sizes in polypropylene and wooden spoons, and natural polythene funnels, will be found most useful, as well as some nylon sieves and straining bags complete with a wire framed stand.

A preserving pan, stock-pot or large alluminium stewpan will be needed for vegetables and sometimes for fruit or honey. A steam or electric juice-extractor is also a useful piece of equipment to have in the home.

Fermentation needs

The essential equipment is a fermentation jar or — better still — several of assorted sizes. The most popular is the colourless demijohn of the 1 gallon size, but larger glass carboys in a wicker frame can be obtained and polythene fermenters holding 10 gallons (45 litres) are well worthwhile. They have a wire frame support and are sometimes used by garages for containing distilled water.

The assortment of air-locks and bored bungs to take them is wide and inexpensive. Their help in making good wine far outweighs their cost of a few pennies. The plastic ones may be more durable than those made of glass, but the latter will last well if handled with care.

An hydrometer and trial jar is the most useful instrument the winemaker can possess. It is essential in controlling the alcohol content and sweetness of a wine. The quality of home-made wine improves considerably if an hydrometer is used intelligently. They are available both in glass and in plastic, are

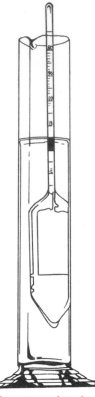

Hydrometer and trial jar

Left: Basic equipment for making wine

clearly calibrated and show both specific gravity and potential alcohol content.

A thermometer is also of great value in checking the temperature both of a must, a fermenting wine and a wine about to be served.

For the technically-minded, acid-testing equipment is well worth-while. Small but complete kits can be bought that include a pipette, a beaker and small bottles of sodium hydroxide and phenolphthalein. A pH meter would be equally useful but a simple acid-testing paper is quite effective in giving you some idea of the acidity of a must or wine.

Storage

It is essential to mature every wine, certainly for some months and possibly even years. In a cool dry atmosphere a wooden cask, not smaller than 25 litres (5½ gallons) capacity, is most helpful, especially for red wines. In a humid atmosphere they are less useful, since the alcohol tends to evaporate, rather than the water. Earthenware jars, though heavy, are perhaps best. They keep the wine dark and at an even temperature. Sizes range from 5 to 30 litres (1 to 6 gallons) and they can be obtained complete with a tap for drawing off the wine. Glass storage jars may be used but plastic or polythene vessels are not recommended. Whilst inert to acid and alkali, they are not totally inert to alcohol. Polythene vessels are not always vapour-proof, either. They are useful for short term purposes but not for long term storage.

Wide-necked mashing jar

Simple boiling pan

Boiler with draw-off tap

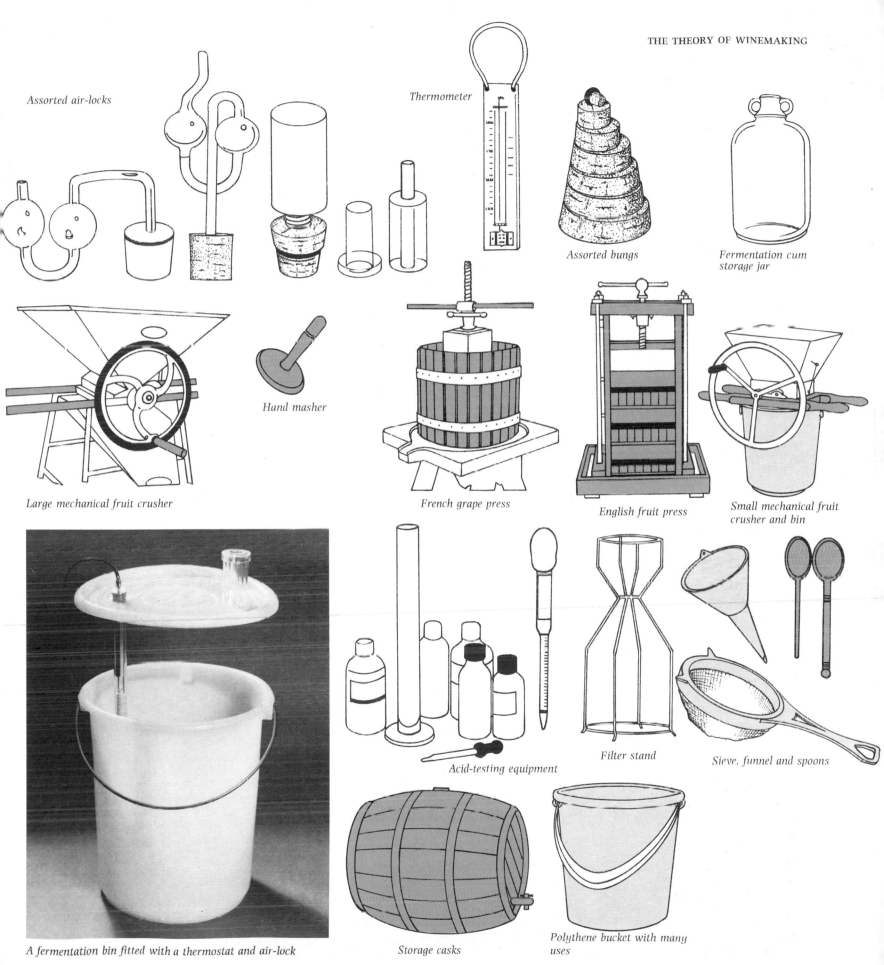

Assorted air-locks

Thermometer

Assorted bungs

Fermentation cum storage jar

Large mechanical fruit crusher

Hand masher

French grape press

English fruit press

Small mechanical fruit crusher and bin

Acid-testing equipment

Filter stand

Sieve, funnel and spoons

A fermentation bin fitted with a thermostat and air-lock

Storage casks

Polythene bucket with many uses

A siphon is almost essential. Although wine can be poured from one vessel to another, it is so much easier to siphon clear wine from a deposit of sediment without disturbing it. Siphons are available in several designs, some with a pump, some with a tap, some with a U-tube, some with a solid end and bored holes. The tubing is usually made from polythene but rubber is equally good.

Wine bottles are essential too, preferably the punted variety in green glass, to protect the wine from fading in the light. A bottle brush is essential to clean them thoroughly – and storage jars too. The selection includes mechanical and rotary brushes and machines, in addition to a simple cylindrical brush. Corks and bungs should be the best you can buy. Poorer qualities weep and admit too much air to the wine. Long cylindrical ones are best for storage, short flanged stoppers for exhibitions and short term use. Sparkling wines need hollow plastic stoppers and cages, with a pair of pliers to help twist the wire. A pair of proper champagne pliers is especially useful in easing the stoppers out of the bottles.

A corking aid is essential – you cannot push cylindrical corks in by hand alone. A simple flogger is a possibility but an Italian corker or a Sanbri mechanical cork press are much better. A bench model is even easier to use. Metal foil or plastic caps and decorative labels provide the professional finish. The colours and designs are varied and attractive.

A storage bin or bottle rack is more of a necessity than a luxury. The range of designs and sizes should fit most needs and available spaces.

Before a wine is bottled, however, it may need filtering. An effective air-excluding filter is now available, together with filter pads that polish a wine to star-brightness. Easy and effective to use, the filter is a useful piece of equipment for the perfectionist.

At opening time a wide selection of corkscrews and cork removers are available. The best again come from Italy and are lever-type and dual screw, automatic corkscrews.

ASSORTED ADDITIVES

Sulphite

The most important chemical always to keep in the winery is sulphite. Buy it either in tablet or in powder form. The tablets are called Campden tablets and the powder sodium metabisulphite. A slightly more expensive but superior product is Bio-Sulphite Jaquemin, a product of the research carried out at the Institute of that name in France. Jacquemin was a contemporary of Pasteur. This product not only releases sulphur dioxide into the must but also bi-ammonium phosphate, a nutritive for the yeast. A somewhat similar product, without the yeast nutrient, is Conservateur Jacquemin for post fermentation use. It is a good stabiliser and sterilising agent.

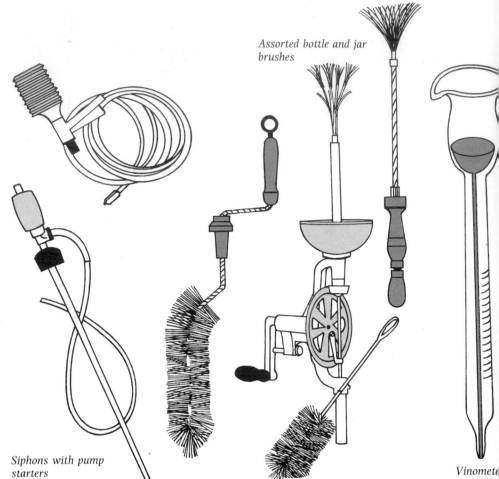

Assorted bottle and jar brushes

Siphons with pump starters

Vinomete

A third product of the Institute is Fluotone Jacquemin for cleaning and sterilising equipment of all kinds. Chempro SDP, a chlorine-based product, is another good cleaning and sterilising product although ONLY for equipment. It must NOT be added to the wine.

Fining

Sanocol Jacquemin is a quick action clarifier for cloudy wines. But there are also liquid wine finings, isinglass made from powdered fish bladders and gelatin products, all for the same purpose. Bentonite, a powdered red volcanic clay from Wyoming USA, is also excellent.

Pectic Enzyme

Pectic enzyme comes in varying qualities both in powder and liquid form. The liquid does not keep effectively and should be used *soon* after buying it. In an air-tight container the powder will keep for several years. How much to use depends on the quality. It is available under a variety of trade names. Rohament 'P' Enzyme is also recommended by some authorities for use in extracting the maximum flavour and goodness from fruit. It is not necessary to use this with other pectic enzymes.

Acids

Acids readily available include citric, tartaric, malic and succinic, and sometimes also an acid blend. Keep the crystals air-tight and cool, and they will

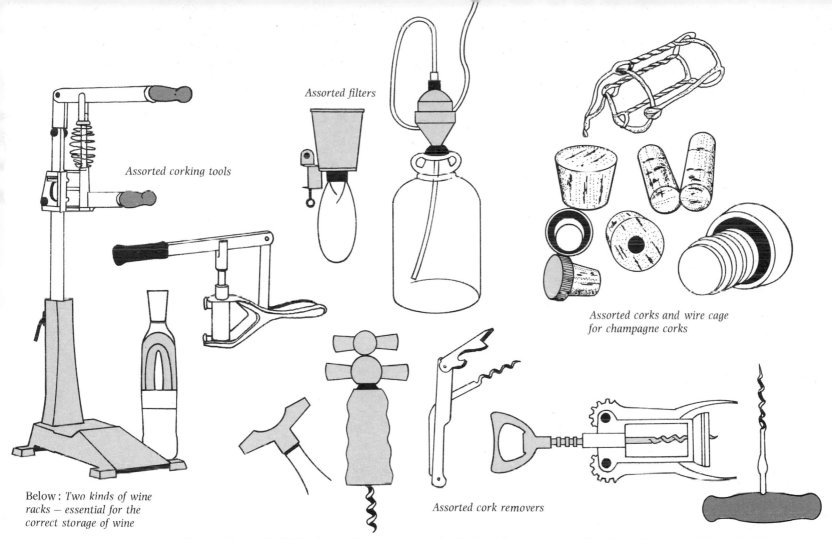

Assorted corking tools

Assorted filters

Assorted corks and wire cage for champagne corks

Assorted cork removers

Below: *Two kinds of wine racks – essential for the correct storage of wine*

have a long shelf-life. A tiny balance is available for measuring small quantities such as 5 or 10 grams.

An acid-reducing solution, as well as powdered chalk, calcium carbonate, is available to reduce the excess acidity sometimes found in rhubarb or in under-ripe fruit. Glycerine is also available to mask excessive acid in a finished wine.

Tannin
Grape tannin, too, keeps well and should always be in stock. It is too rarely used by many winemakers and their wines lack character as a result.

Yeasts
Sufficient has already been written on yeast, but some dried yeasts should always be kept in stock. Keep yeast dry and cool. Liquid yeasts and yeast cultures are best used soon after buying them; there is no knowing how long they have been in the shop.

Nutrient
Nutrient in the form of ammonium sulphate or phosphate is the minimum essential, but a better balanced nutrient including a range of vitamins is more useful. Sometimes the combination of nutrient and vitamins is called a yeast energiser or booster.

Sugar
In addition to ordinary granulated white and brown sugars, invert sugar, candy sugar, glucose and fructose are offered to the winemaker. Each has its supporters but the majority of winemakers use only granulated sugar. Glucose is helpful in the making of sweet wines since it ferments more slowly than fructose. Invert sugar ferments quickly and is best used in beer. Candy sugar is sometimes used in feeding a fermentation. For sweetening a finished wine there is both lactose, a non-fermentable sugar, and saccharin in both liquid and powder form.

Beware of ascorbic acid or sorbate when offered as a wine stabiliser, for although it kills yeasts and other minor organisms effectively, it has chemical side effects which create off smells and esters in the wine.

Beware
The craft of making wine is constantly developing and new chemicals are regularly being offered that are said either to be superior to something already in use or to improve the wine. A certain reserve is worth observing unless you regard yourself as a master winemaker. There is no doubt that some winemakers are able to improve their musts or wines marginally by the addition of a certain acid or enzyme, but it is unlikely that the majority of people tasting that wine could tell the difference.

The essentials are household sugar, citric or tartaric acid, grape tannin, ammonium sulphate, a good yeast and the wise use of sulphite. There is a touch of 'gimmickry' about many other additives.

Basic Methods of Winemaking

THERE are only a limited number of ways of making wine and once the basic processes have been mastered you can adjust the ingredients to suit the type of wine you wish to make.

LIQUID MUSTS

Dry

The simplest way is what one might call the all-liquid method. This includes those musts in which the ingredients are all liquid, for example grape juice concentrates, other fruit juices, either bought in jar or can, or expressed by juice extractor, or boiled ingredients where the solid is not used, as with vegetables.

The concentrate, fruit juice or vegetable liquor is poured immediately into a fermentation jar, sugar syrup is added together with acid, tannin, nutrient and active yeast. An air-lock is fitted and the must is fermented in a warm place 21°C (70°F) until all the sugar has been converted and the finished product is a dry wine.

The initial specific gravity should be checked and if necessary adjusted to between 1.086 and 1.090 which, when fully converted, produces a wine containing 12% alcohol by volume. The finished specific gravity is likely to be around 0.996. This wine will keep well and is quite strong enough to serve as a table wine.

German style light wines should be less strong, 1.066 to 1.070 is a sufficient original gravity. These wines are meant to be light in body, often for drinking cold on a warm evening out of doors, on a picnic, or for lunch when one has subsequently to return to work. The lower alcohol content is balanced by the lighter body and in the right circumstances is, therefore, more attractive.

In musts entirely fermented in a fermentation jar some head room should at first be left in case there is a tumultuous initial ferment. As soon as this dies down, the jar may be topped up.

A steady temperature will ensure a speedy fermentation which may be finished in anything from 2 to 4 weeks. Always use a good quality yeast, activated in a starter bottle before adding it to the must. Make sure too, that sufficient acid and nutrient are included, without overdoing either.

When fermentation is finished move the jar to a cooler position for a few days while the sediment settles. Rack into a clean jar, just rinsed with a sulphite solution, add sulphite at the rate of 50 p.p.m. for red wines and 100 p.p.m. for white wines. This will prevent oxidation, infection and re-fermentation. The wine should clear to brightness naturally, but if a haze remains after three or four months then, fine and filter.

Bottle when the wine is six months old, four months for light wines and keep for a further two to three months.

Sweet

Moderate alcohol wines of the same kind, but required to be sweet, are made in the same way. The initial specific gravity should be a little higher, though no more than 1.110. When the gravity has fallen to 1.020, fermentation should be terminated. This is done by adding sulphite at the rate of 100 p.p.m. and some wine finings. Move the wine to a cold place to encourage precipitation of the sediment and as soon as the wine begins to clear, rack it into a clean jar. Top up with similar wine or with cold boiled water and refit the air-lock. No further action should occur but the air-lock will soon show if there is any further fermentation. If there is, some more sulphite – at the rate of 100 p.p.m. – should be added, and after 24 hours the wine filtered. All the yeast cells should now be dead. Remove them from the wine, which should be star-bright, stable and sweet.

Keep it in bulk in a cool store for six months, add sulphite at the rate of 50 p.p.m., bottle and keep till the wine is one year old.

Fermentation can be terminated this way at any specific gravity you choose. 1.020 is usually high enough for a sweet wine and 1.010 to 1.006 for a medium sweet wine. The great advantage that home winemakers have is that the sweetness can be adjusted to whatever degree is required.

An alternative method is to make a dry wine and to sweeten it with saccharin. Great care should be taken not to use too much saccharin and it is best to add this drop by drop, frequently tasting the wine until the right amount of sweetness has been attained.

A third way is not to sweeten the dry wine until it is about to be served. Sufficient sugar may be dissolved in a little wine and mixed with the remainder in a decanter or carafe.

Pulp Fermentation

Many wines are best made by fermenting the juice in the presence of the fruit. The small amount of alcohol formed in the early stages helps to extract the colour and to leach out all the goodness. Many substances are more soluble in alcohol than they are in water.

The fruit should be mashed up after the removal of stalk and stones, placed in a mashing bin, and water poured over it. If several different fruits are being used, all should be included. Immediately, if cold water is being used, or as soon as cool, if hot water has been used, add sulphite at the rate of 50 p.p.m. but if the fruit is less than perfect the rate should be 100 p.p.m. A pectin-destroying enzyme should be added, at the manufacturer's recommended quantity, and also any acid or tannin required. The whole should be well stirred, covered with a well-fitting lid, a closely woven linen cloth or a sheet of polythene secured with a rubber band. The

Crushing small berries with a spoon

Adding granulated yeast to a must. Better to use an activated yeast from a starter bottle and leave more headroom in the bin

purpose is to exclude micro-organisms of every kind. Clearly a muslin cloth is not adequate.

The mashing bin should be left in a warm place for 24 hours for the pectic enzyme and sulphite to effect their necessary actions. Next day grape juice concentrate may be added and the specific gravity checked. From this the amount of sugar to be added can be easily calculated by reference to the Sugar Content Tables (No. 4).

Nutrient and an active yeast should now be stirred in, the bin re-covered and left in the warm, 21°C (70°F), for from 4–8 days. At least once and preferably twice, each day the bin should be uncovered and the must stirred. The objective is to mix into the liquid, the cap of fruit lifted above the must by the carbon dioxide gas released during the fermentation. If this is not done, acetobacter may settle on the fruit and taint the wine with acetic acid.

Fermentation on the pulp begins when visible signs of fermentation are evident and not from the moment the yeast is stirred in. There is sometimes a lag phase of 12 to 24 hours while a sufficiently large and strong yeast colony is built up.

After the recommended number of fermentation days has elapsed, strain the wine from the pulp and press this to extract the remaining juice. If fruit is left too long in a pulp fermentation it breaks down into fine particles which can be very difficult to clear.

The additional sugar should now be added to the must and the whole transferred to a fermentation jar, fit an air-lock and continue as already described.

Strong Sweet Wines

Wines of a higher alcohol content are made by continuing the fermentation with extra sugar. If the initial amount of sugar in a must is too high, the yeast cells are unable to admit the sugar molecules or expel the alcohol and carbon dioxide molecules. In effect they are unable to move because of the weight of the sugar upon them. Therefore, always start a fermentation between 1.086 and 1.090 and never higher than 1.110. Indeed to make a really strong wine the lower you start, the better it is, for in this way the alcohol tolerance of the yeast can be built up steadily.

Calculate in advance with the aid of Table No. 5 just how much additional sugar you will require. It is the difference between the original sugar content of your must and the alcohol content you desire. Plan to add this amount in small doses, sufficient headroom for the sugar, remembering time. Wait until the previous dose of sugar has been fermented before raising the gravity again. Leave sufficient headroom for the sugar remembering that the sugar will occupy about half its weight in volume. 1 lb of sugar will require about half a pint of space. 1 Kg of sugar requires about 0.6 of a litre.

Always remove some wine in which to dissolve the sugar and return it slowly, since frothing frequently occurs. Check the specific gravity regularly and keep a note of the dates and the readings. From this information you will be able to see when fermentation is slowing down. Such a long fermentation does require a constant temperature, a yeast with a suitably high alcohol tolerance, plenty of acid and sufficient nutrient, including vitamins. Additional acid will be required to balance both the extra alcohol and the final sweetness. In such a fermentation it is a practical hint to use a small excess of tartaric acid. Strong wines require longer maturation and the extra acid not only helps to protect the wine from infection, but also gets precipitated by the alcohol in the form of potassium tartrate — small glass-like crystals — during maturation.

At the end of fermentation the number of units of gravity fermented can be added up and the total compared on the hydrometer Table No. 4 with the alcohol equivalent. In this way you have a reasonably accurate record of the amount of alcohol in your wine.

Although a final specific gravity of 1.020 is normally enough to make a wine taste sweet, a higher figure may be necessary to balance the extra alcohol, depending, of course, on your palate. The additional sugar may be added after fermentation has been completed and the wine has been racked. Because the limit of the alcohol tolerance has been reached, no more fermentation will occur.

Strong Dry Wines

Wines that you wish to ferment on and finish dry are made in exactly the same way as strong sweet wines. Great care must be taken, however, to ensure that the must ferments down to S.G. 1.000 each time, before extra sugar is added and that only 100 grams (3½ oz) of sugar per gallon are added at a time.

Special Wine Types

Sparkling Wines

Ever since that Benedictine monk Dom Perignon perfected his method of making sparkling wine in the 17th century it has been a source of special happiness to men and women. Indeed the happier the occasion, the greater is it enhanced by sparkling wine. This is an established *must* for celebrating weddings, christenings, anniversaries and all new ventures. It is increasingly popular for receptions of countless kinds, and it can be equally enjoyable at home. It can be still more enjoyable if you have made it yourself!

Many ingredients are suitable for making sparkling wines, though probably the best are grapes, apples, pears and gooseberries. Redcurrants make a pretty pink 'champagne', and damsons a red one.

Start the wine with the intent to make it sparkle. Don't make it too strong! If you do, you may not get a second fermentation in the bottle. An initial S.G. of 1.080 to 1.086 is quite adequate. Use a good champagne yeast; it improves the flavour and facilitates racking. Don't make the wine too strong in flavour either, otherwise the champagne flavour will not be sufficiently noticeable.

Method

1 Make the wine as already described. Ferment it to dryness, rack it and store it for six months to mature and fall star-bright. If necessary fine and/or filter out any haze.

2 Dissolve $2\frac{1}{2}$ oz (70 grams) sugar per gallon in the wine. $2\frac{1}{2}$ oz of sugar per gallon is the ideal quantity. In no circumstances should more than 3 oz. be used in case the pressure of carbon dioxide produced in the secondary fermentation becomes so high as to burst the bottle.

3 Prepare an active champagne yeast and when fermenting vigorously add it to the wine and fit an air-lock. It is very important to use a champagne yeast to obtain the correct flavour and a firm deposit. Other yeasts give an off flavour and are difficult to remove.

4 Prepare enough proper champagne bottles by washing them clean, sterilise them with a sulphite solution and drain them dry. No other bottle is strong enough to withstand the pressure of a secondary fermentation. Do not use chipped or scratched bottles in case they have been weakened.

5 Soften sufficient hollow plastic stoppers in hot water and have them ready.

6 Have some wire cages, known as 'muselet', ready to fasten down the stoppers.

7 As soon as the wine is fermenting, siphon it into the champagne bottles.

8 Shake any surplus water from the stoppers, press them tightly home and fasten each one down with wire.

9 Label the bottles, including also the date of bottling and secondary fermentation.

10 Place the bottles in a warm situation for one week, while the sugar syrup is fermented, then remove them to a cool store for *at least six months and preferably for one year*.

11 It is effective in this period to store them upside down in a crate or wine bottle carton, so that the yeast deposit settles in the hollow stopper.

12 It is necessary to leave the wine on the yeast for *at least six months and preferably for a year*, to absorb the flavour. Champagne yeast in these circumstances does not produce off flavours.

13 Shortly before serving the wine, chill the neck of each bottle in some crushed ice mixed with salt, until a small block of ice is formed in the stopper, encapsulating the sediment. While this is happening prepare some sugar syrup and some clean stoppers and wires. Some winemakers dissolve caster sugar in Vodka, others use 3 drops of saccharin or one Sweetex tablet per bottle.

14 When the bottles are ready, take them one by one and hold them at an angle of $45°$ facing a clean and sterilised bucket.

15 Remove the wire and ease out the hollow stopper with the yeast sediment adhering to the inside of the dome.

16 Quickly add the saccharin or syrup to the bottle, insert a clean stopper and rewire until the wine is wanted. It is ready for serving as soon as the cold wine has warmed up a little.

17 Serve it at about $8°C$ ($46°F$) in a tall flute shaped glass accompanied by the food of your choice – from oysters to rich fruit cake.

Sparkling wine makes a splendid aperitif before a meal and has sufficient character to be served throughout a meal. It also makes an ideal mid-morning tonic. It can be served to young and old – and all the others in between!

Once the knack of sparkling has been learned you will find yourself making more and more sparkling wines to serve in festive mood on many occasions.

A plastic stopper has been marketed, called a Vintrap, which has a short tube or blister above the dome. The wine is stored so that the sediment falls into this blister which can be cut off just prior to serving the wine. A bung is provided to fit into the hole made when the blister is cut off. The sediment can be seen in the blister and the whole process is made that little bit easier. With a Vintrap, it is sufficient to chill the wine hard and it is not necessary to freeze the neck.

Sherry-type wines

An amateur winemaker would have to be extremely fond of sherry to go to the trouble of setting up a solera system. The commercial sherry that we so much enjoy in all its different styles is expensive to produce because of the long period which must elapse before wine can be sold from a solera, and

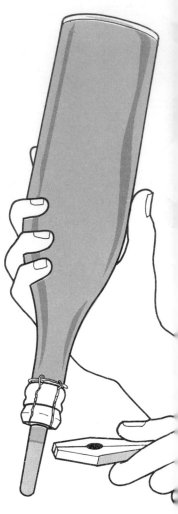

A Vintrap enables the sediment from a sparkling wine to be removed without difficulty. Just snip off the tube or blister prior to serving the wine

38

The solera system in operation

because of the amount of work involved in its preparation.

In the first instance a sherry-type wine would have to be laid down in a cask. Each year for the following several years at least, a similar wine would have to be prepared. After 3, 5, 7 or 14 years, one-third of the wine could be taken from the first cask and bottled for use. The cask would then be topped up from the second cask, the second topped up from the third, the third topped from the fourth and so on until the last cask was topped up with new wine. As a result the old wine quickly imparts its flavour to the new wine, so that from the first cask comes a wine of remarkable constancy, free from the irregularities of varying vintages. For the home winemaker with much else to do, the prospect may be daunting beyond acceptance.

An attractive sherry-like wine can however be made at home if certain care is taken.

Fermentation

In the first instance a suitable must should be prepared from Victoria plums, oranges, prunes, rosehips, figs etc. Some suitable grape juice concentrate of the appropriate sherry-type should be included. Fermentation should be with the aid of an active sherry yeast. For pale dry wines a 'Sherry Flor' yeast is recommended, for medium and sweet sherry-type wines an ordinary sherry yeast is most suitable.

During fermentation, the jar should not be completely full. For example, make a 10-bottle quantity in a 12-bottle jar. Use a plug of cotton wool instead of an air-lock. This acts as a filter to micro-organisms but allows a small quantity of clean air to come into proximity to the wine and so encourages the formation of acetaldehyde.

When making a sherry type wine it is important to use an hydrometer. The initial specific gravity should be about 1.080 and the must should contain an adequate quantity of yeast nutrients and mixed acids. Fermentation should be conducted around a steady 24°C (75°F). To this end an immersion heater fitted with a thermostat may be desirable, or a heated pad on which to stand your jar, or a fermentation cupboard. The important factor is to maintain a constant and unfluctuating temperature, just slightly higher than usual.

The S.G. of the must should be checked frequently and as soon as it falls to 1.000 a further quantity of sugar should be stirred in. Either some wine may be taken from the jar, the sugar stirred into it and the sweet wine returned to the jar, or an invert sugar syrup may be poured straight in. Enough to raise the S.G. 12–14 points at a time is sufficient, ie about 170 gms (6 oz.) for a 6-bottle quantity.

This process should be repeated as often as possible, a record being kept of the total number of points actually increased. From this can be ascertained the approximate alcohol content. For dry wines care should be taken with the later additions. If fermentation is clearly slowing down, a smaller quantity of sugar should be added so that it can all be fermented. For a dry sherry the final S.G. should be about 0.996. For a medium sherry about 1.008 and for a sweet sherry about 1.020.

When fermentation is quite finished, move the jar to a cool place to encourage the suspended particles to settle. Rack the wine into a sterile jar, leave it not quite full and plug the neck with cotton-wool, not a bung. Because of the high alcohol content of the wine it is unlikely to become infected and so, providing all the equipment is quite sterile, no Campden tablets will be necessary. Any oxidation of the alcohol will improve the flavour of the wine.

If the wine does not soon fall bright, it may be fined with isinglass or Bentonite. At this stage the flavour of the wine may be enhanced by the addition of some real sherry of a similar type, but it is hardly worth buying the most expensive. One bottle of sherry to five bottles of wine is enough.

Alternatively a bottle of sherry brandy such as *Fundador* or *Sobrani* may be added and left to homogenize for about a year before bottling. This has the effect of increasing slightly the alcohol strength of the wine as well as improving the sherry flavour. For best results, this wine should be kept in bulk for at least one year and preferably two, then bottled and kept for another six months or so.

By these methods some remarkably good, sherry-type wines can be produced. They are well worth the little extra trouble required.

Dessert wines

These wines may be of the cream-sherry, port, madeira or tokay styles, but they do not have to be imitations of these well-known wines. Many fruits and some vegetables, can be made into dessert wines that are most attractive in their own right.

The common factors are being full-bodied, strong and sweet.

The body is best obtained by using a number of different ingredients so that the flavour of any single one does not become overpowering. The addition of some dried apricots, ripe bananas, broad beans or parsnips, or some flaked rice, will improve the body of a wine without affecting the bouquet and flavour of the main ingredient. Something in excess of 2 kg (4½ lb) of base ingredients for a 6-bottle quantity is essential. The acid quantity needs to be higher than usual – somewhere about 0.7% or 7 parts in 1000 on titration, pH3.1 on acid-testing papers. Tannin too needs to be increased up to a total of a level 5 ml spoonful for ingredients low in tannin.

A strong wine can be easily produced by starting fermentation with an S.G. of about 1.080 and adding sugar in doses to the limit of fermentation of the yeast used, as already described.

For very strong wines a madeira or a tokay yeast should be used. If you are trying to capture something of the flavour of a port for example, use a port yeast at first and when some 8 or 10% alcohol has been formed, *ie* after the S.G. has fallen from 1.080 to 1.000, rack the wine into a clean jar and add sugar and an actively fermenting madeira or tokay yeast. The strong colony of the new yeast should then be able to take over the fermentation of the additional doses of sugar.

For madeira-style wines use soft brown sugar and store in a warm, instead of a cool, place.

For tokay-style wines use as much grape juice concentrate as possible instead of sugar.

In these circumstances a heavy yeast deposit will form and the wine should be racked as soon as fermentation is quite finished. Some proprietary wine fining should also be added to help clear the wine before the next racking, which should be as soon as another deposit appears. One crushed Campden tablet should be added to inhibit the growth of any unwanted micro-organisms and to prevent oxidation.

Some of these wines require extra sugar at the end of fermentation to obtain a good balance and the resultant S.G. may be as high as 1.030. Your palate must be the final arbiter.

The hardest part of making these superb wines is waiting for them to mature. They need at least two years and will improve still further in bottle. They should possess a deep and attractive bouquet, be rich, full and mellow, very smooth and evenly balanced. Not easy; but possible and very well worth the effort.

Fortified wines

In the early days of winemaking, before wine yeasts were available to the home winemaker and before the principles of fermentation were understood, it was customary always to add a bottle of brandy to each brew. The resultant wine must have reeked of brandy for its smell and flavour is almost impossible to overpower.

With modern techniques it is mostly unnecessary to fortify a wine, but there is no difficulty in fortifying a wine to whatever alcohol content is required, if one so wishes. Care must be taken to ensure that the wine still remains well-balanced and that one is not conscious of the extra alcohol. There is no point in fortifying a wine unless it is going to improve the overall standard of the bouquet and flavour.

The spirit to use

Only a flavourless alcohol should be used, since all other spirits alter the flavour of a wine. Vodka at 70° Proof or Polish Spirit at 140° Proof are the only spirits that can be recommended. Before the process begins it is desirable to have some idea of the alcohol content of the wine to be fortified. This information may be available from the records kept when the wine was being made and can be calculated from the starting and finishing specific gravity readings.

A little instrument called a vinometer may be of some help with a dry wine, but is of no use with a sweet wine.

Knowing the strength of an existing wine or must, next determine the strength of the wine required after fortification. With these two figures it is easy to calculate how much Vodka or Polish Spirit to add, to increase the alcohol content of the existing wine to the required strength.

Pearson's Square

The calculations are made with the aid of the diagram that follows:

$$A \qquad\qquad D$$
$$C$$
$$B \qquad\qquad E$$

In the corner marked A write down the alcohol content of the spirit being used. If only a Proof figure is printed on the label divide this figure by 7 and multiply by 4. This gives you the percentage alcohol.

In the corner marked B write down the present alcohol content of the wine to be fortified. In the centre marked C write down the alcohol content that you require in the fortified wine. In the corner marked D write down the difference between B and C. In the corner marked E write down the difference between C and A.

The ratio of D to E is the ratio of spirit to wine that you will need to add to obtain the required fortification.

The only important factor is to work exclusively in Proof Spirit or percentage alcohol. Always convert one to the other if necessary, so that you can use the same basis throughout.

Example 1

Assume the wine to be 15% alcohol at present, the spirit to be 40% alcohol (70° Proof) and the wine when fortified to be 18% alcohol.

Three bottles of Vodka of 70° Proof must therefore be added to 22 bottles of wine of 15% alcohol to increase the alcohol content to 18%.

then: $A = 40 \qquad D = C - B = 18 - 15 = 3$

$$C = 18$$

$$B = 15 \qquad E = A - C = 40 - 18 = 22.$$

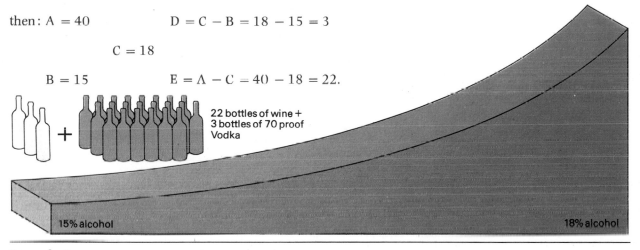

22 bottles of wine +
3 bottles of 70 proof
Vodka

15% alcohol

18% alcohol

Example 2

Assume the wine to be 14% alcohol at present, the Polish Spirit to be 140° Proof (divide by 7 and multiply by 4 = 80% alcohol) and the wine when fortified to be 20% alcohol.

One bottle of Polish Spirit of 140° Proof will be required to increase the alcohol content of 10 bottles of wine of 14% alcohol to 20% alcohol.

Then: $A = 80 \qquad D = C - B = 20 - 14 = 6$ or 1

$$C = 20$$

$$B = 14 \qquad E = A - C = 80 - 20 = 60$ or $10$$

10 bottles of wine +
1 bottle of 140 proof
Polish Spirit

14% alcohol

20% alcohol

Wines from Grape Juice Concentrate

Some of the wide range of grape juice concentrates and yeasts that are now available

A few countries, notably Spain, have been concentrating their surplus juice for many years. In England this was used to produce 'British Wines' – inexpensive drinks much enjoyed on special occasions by those who normally drank beer and tea. At the end of the 1950s some amateur winemakers used it to make their wine. It was generally regarded as being inferior to the country wines then made. A few years later as the craft of winemaking developed, it was found to make an excellent additive to country wines in place of raisins and sultanas.

More and more people were being attracted to winemaking and the purchase of grape juice concentrates increased. This substantial demand attracted competition for the importers and as a result manufacturers began to blend different grape juices and flavourings to form new and very attractive concentrates. France, Italy and Germany at first declined to sell their grape juice for this purpose but supplies were forthcoming from Eastern European countries trading with the West.

By the early 1970s several manufacturers in England and others in America were offering a wide range of blended concentrates designed to make wine of a type similar to the traditional commercial types at something like one quarter of the cost, and with but the minimum of equipment, effort and expertise.

In America the situation is even better. Vast quantities of grapes are grown and a great deal is known about viticulture and viniculture. The Californian Institute of Technology has done wonderful work in this connection and the English-speaking world owes a great debt to Professors Amerine and Cruess, among others, who have contributed so much through their research and publications. American manufacturers of grape juice concentrate endeavour to buy the best grapes available, not merely those not required for making into wine immediately. As a result the quality of American grape juice concentrate, though expensive by British standards, is very high. Furthermore, because of the more even seasons, the grapes tend to remain of a similar quality year by year. As a result there is probably more wine made from grape juice concentrate in America than in other countries.

These concentrates contain all the flavour, acid, tannin and nutrient required. Only water, some additional sugar, and, of course, yeast have to be provided. Some manufacturers now produce ranges which require no sugar — only water and yeast. The resulting wine is certainly of a high standard and worth the extra cost. These wines have more body than some others made from concentrates.

Although the bulk concentrates are imported into England from the wine-producing countries, the finished product, mostly in 1 kg cans with attractive labels and detailed instruction for making the wine, are then exported to a great many countries — not only to Canada, the USA, Australia and New Zealand but also to Iceland, Libya, Denmark, Sweden, Eire and South Africa, as well as to the Middle East.

The instructions supplied with each can are so simple that they can be followed by anyone who has never made wine before, and within a few months they produce a drinkable wine. The process of concentrating the grape juice certainly causes the wines to mature early, but even so, all these wines do benefit from a period of bulk maturation as well as a few months in bottle.

The average concentration seems to be 39/40° Beaume and this is said to be adequate for making into 6 bottles of wine. At least 5 cans full of water are required, however, and this dilutes the concentrate to about 1.056 specific gravity, hence the need to add extra sugar. The amount usually recommended for a table wine is 280 grams (10 oz.), more for a dessert or sweet wine. Larger quantities of concentrate are available in 3 kg and 6 kg polythene containers with screw top sealing. These are a little less expensive, pro rata than the 1 kg cans and are ideal for using as an additive to fruit and other wines. When you have taken out as much as you need for a recipe you can screw on the stopper and store the concentrate in a cool dark place until it is next required. In these conditions the concentrate will remain perfectly good for up to two years. The concentrate tends to darken, however. The red develops a touch of brown and the white a darker shade of gold.

For simple winemaking with the very minimum of effort, modern grape juice concentrates cannot be surpassed. There is no tedious or hard work in the preparation of the must. Less equipment is required and therefore less storage space. A very wide range of wines can be made at the same time and within a year one can have a very useful cellar, say a dozen bottles each of as many as ten different types of wine. At the time of writing the range includes Beaujolais, Bordeaux, Burgundy, Chablis, Chianti, Claret, Hock, Liebfraumilch, Moselle, Port, Riesling, Rosé, Sauternes, Sherry and Vermouth. It must be emphasised however, that these concentrates cannot and do not produce the real wine bearing these names, but only good wines similar in *type* to the real wines. There are also some interesting fruit and grape wines in combination. These include grape and bilberry, grape and elderberry, grape and gooseberry, grape and morello cherry, with more to come.

All that is required is to open a can and pour the contents into a fermentation jar. Wash out the can with tepid water and make up to the specified quantity. The recommended quantity of sugar is then stirred in, followed by the yeast. An air-lock is fitted and the jar stood in a warm place.

Fermentation is usually over within a few weeks and the wine begins to clear. It is then racked into a clean jar, a Campden tablet is added to stabilise the wine and prevent both oxidation and infection. A good bung is pushed well home and the jar is labelled and stored in a cool place for a month or two. After this it should be star-bright, but if it is not then it may be fined or filtered or both. The wine is now poured or siphoned into 6 bottles, corked and labelled, and stored. The temptation to try a bottle is intense, use half bottles as well as the full-size bottles. In this way half a bottle is saved every time temptation becomes irresistible. Light wines come on first, with heavy and strong wines taking rather longer. Serve the whites, and rosé wines well chilled, about 10°C and the reds free from chill, about 20°C.

Wines from Fresh Fruits

APPLES

Many different wines can be made from apples, either by themselves or in combination with other fruits. No one variety is known to be outstanding on its own but cooking varieties make better wine than dessert varieties. Experience over many years has shown that a combination of cooking, dessert, crab apple, pears and quince make the most attractive wine of all. Apples respond well to most yeasts but especially to champagne yeast.

Although perfect fruit is desirable for most wines, windfall apples make excellent wine. The apples do not need to be peeled or cored, but naturally any badly bruised parts that have turned brown should be cut away, with any parts infected by a maggot.

Apples are sometimes hard to crush but various answers have been found to this problem. Perhaps the easiest is to wash the apples in a sulphite solution of about 100 p.p.m., so removing dust, leaves and grass at the same time as killing off unwanted micro-organisms. Next, drain off the surplus water, pack the apples into polythene bags and place them in a freezer for 48 hours. When thawed they should be soft enough to crush with your hands.

If a freezer is not readily available, place the washed apples – a few at a time – in a polythene bag and hit them with a mallet, wooden rolling pin or steak hammer. When each bagful is crushed, drop the contents into water containing sulphite and citric acid to prevent oxidation.

A third method is to place the apples in a strong polythene or wooden bin and to ram them with a 10 cm. (4 in.) cube of wood on the end of a broom handle.

Another way is to liquidise them, and yet another is simply to cut each apple into about 16 pieces. Coarse mincing is not recommended unless it is known for certain that the metal from which the mincer is made, does not react to acids.

Apples should always be fermented on the pulp. If you lack a big enough bin for this purpose, a heavy gauge, large polythene bag inside a cardboard container may be used very effectively. The neck can be gathered and fastened with a rubber band or a wire tie – not so tightly, of course, that the carbon dioxide cannot escape.

After pulp fermentation a press is needed to extract all the juice. Bale the pulp out of the bin into a freshly sterilised hessian, linen or nylon bag placed inside the press. At first the juice will run free, and then a little shaking-up of the bag will encourage even more to do so. When pressure is applied, do so intermittently rather than steadily; a better run is thereby obtained. When you are satisfied that no more juice can be extracted, the apple cake can be used to make a second-run wine.

Often elderberry, or blackberry, or damson, or plum, wine is being made at or about the same

The pulp is contained in a nylon bag within the press and the juice runs straight into the jar

time. The addition of the applecake to the other fruit improves the body and flavour of that wine. Alternatively, the two pulp residues may be mixed together and added to a grape juice concentrate wine to improve its body and flavour. Spent apple and elderberry pulp mixed with a white grape juice concentrate can make an attractive rosé.

It is always worth making the maximum amount possible of apple wine. It blends well with other wines, is useful for topping up jars, that are not quite full – no matter what the wine they contain – and it makes an excellent base for liqueurs.

APRICOTS

This tangy fruit is related to the peach but is somewhat smaller. If cooked or dried, the colour of the flesh becomes an attractive orange. When making wine from apricots, the fruit should be just ripe: soft enough for the stone to be easily released when the fruit is cut in two, but not over-soft and mushy. The stone taints the wine unpleasantly if it is not removed.

BANANAS

Over-ripe bananas are best for making wine. The outside skins can be almost black while the fruit inside is still quite sound. The bananas should be peeled and boiled for $\frac{1}{2}$ hour to extract the flavour and goodness. Some thinly-pared lemon rind helps to improve the flavour. Only the liquid is used and that needs pectic enzyme treatment when cold and before yeast is added. Best made into a sweet wine.

BILBERRIES

After the grape these are one of the best fruits for making wine. They can be used for both table and dessert wines and will blend well with other fruits. Use fully ripe berries picked free from stalk. In some places this fruit is known as the Whortleberry. The family name is *Vaccinium myrtillus*. The parent plant is a small shrub which grows to a height of only 50 cm (about 20 in).

BLACKBERRIES

There are two sources of blackberry for the amateur winemaker. The cultivated variety is large and juicy but lighter in flavour than the wild blackberry which is usually smaller in size. Both make into excellent wine although the cultivated berry is more suitable for table wine and the wild berry is better for dessert wine. They should be fully ripe and dry when picked, and free from stalk.

BLACKCURRANTS

These are a strongly flavoured and highly acidic fruit, best made into a dessert wine. Pick the currants fully ripe so that the sugar content is at its highest and the acid at its lowest. Remove all the stalks and wash the fruit clean. The skins are very tough and it is best to mash the fruit and break every currant before water is added.

BLUEBERRIES

This fruit, sometimes called Blaeberry, is more widely available in America than in the UK. Its family name is *Vaccinium corymbosum* and it grows to a height of $2\frac{1}{2}$ metres (about 8 ft). It is a close relation of the Bilberry and makes a similar good red wine. It needs no tannin or pectic enzyme.

BULLACE

This small red-black, plum-like fruit has plenty of acid and tannin. After stalking and rinsing the fruit in cold water, it should be washed in near-boiling water containing a little washing soda to remove the waxy bloom. Rinse again in cold water then mash the fruit and remove the stones. Make into a dessert type wine.

CHERRIES

Use cooking cherries, sometimes called sour cherries, either red or white or both. Remove the stalks and stones and make a table wine.

CHERRY PLUM

This creamy-red, cherry-shaped plum will make a white or rosé table wine. Remove the stalks and stones when the fruit is fully ripe.

CRANBERRIES

This small red fruit similar in shape and size to a bilberry makes into a rosé table wine. Stalk and stone the berries first.

DAMSONS

This small, blue-black, plum-like fruit makes excellent table and dessert wines. After removing the stalks and rinsing the fruit free from leaves and grass, wash it in near-boiling water containing some washing soda crystals to remove the waxy bloom. Rinse again in cold water, then mash the fruit and remove the stones before adding the water.

ELDERBERRIES

There are several varieties of this small, red-black berry, which grows on shrubs up to 4 metres ($13\frac{1}{2}$ ft) high. The berries should not be gathered until they have all turned black and the stalks have become red. The weight of the fruit should be so heavy for the stalks, that they hang upside down. Gather the berries from as many different bushes as you can, choosing a warm, dry day on which to do so. Remove each berry from its stalk with a fork or your fingers. Use rubber gloves to do this since dye in the fruit stains everything it touches. The colour and goodness is best obtained by boiling the fruit for 20 minutes in half the water. After cooling and pressing, use the pulp to make a 'second run rosé'. Alternatively it may be boiled again for another 10 minutes to remove the remaining colour and goodness. The flavour is very strong and bitter, and this fruit makes a better dessert wine than a table wine. It blends very well with other fruits and vegetables to make table, social and dessert wines. The secondary fruits or vegetables make up the body lost by using a smaller quantity of elderberries to reduce the flavour. In all such blends 1 lb (454 g) of elderberries is sufficient to make 6 bottles of wine.

GOOSEBERRIES

There is no doubt that gooseberries make one of the best white wines available to the amateur wine-maker. They will make a light Hock-like wine, a sparkling wine, or a sweet table wine. Use the gooseberries when just ripe, whilst still green but with a full, soft feeling. Top, tail and wash them before crushing each berry.

GRAPEFRUIT
Great care must be taken in making wine from this fruit. Only the very thinly pared and chopped yellow skin and the fruit juice should be used. The white pith and flesh should be discarded. Make a dry table or aperitif type wine.

GRAPES
If possible, use only grapes known to be suitable for making wine, rather than dessert grapes. Whether home-grown or bought-in, grapes should be stalked and washed in a sulphite solution before crushing them to release their juice. Each berry must be broken, but in such a manner as not to break the pips. Several grape varieties should be mixed in. When the juice is expressed, a specific gravity check should be made and if necessary some additional sugar added. Similarly, an acid check should be made in case the grapes are too low or too high in this essential ingredient.

Whether black or white grapes are being used, the must should be sulphited, covered and left for 24 hours. White grape pulp may then be pressed to remove the skins and pips. The juice should be poured into a fermentation jar together with an active yeast. Fit an air-lock and ferment to dryness.

Black grapes should be fermented on the pulp and an active yeast should be added 24 hours *after* the sulphite. After 10 days the skins and pips should be removed and fermentation continued in the usual way.

A rosé wine can be made from black grapes by removing the skins 24 hours after fermentation has started. It can also be made from a mixture of white and black grapes in the proportion of nine measures of white to one of black, fermented on the pulp for 7 days.

Grapes may be made into sparkling wines; into

The traditional ingredient of wine

sherry-type wines, by feeding the fermentation with grape juice concentrate or sugar; or into sweet table wines, by terminating the fermentation at S.G. 1.016.

Fresh grapes may be added to any other fruit when preparing a must. The spent skins and pips may also be added to another must to provide some additional nutrient, tannin and trace elements.

When fermentation is finished, grape wines should be sulphited and matured as for any other fruit wine.

GREENGAGES
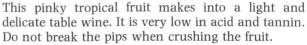
This greeny, golden fruit can produce an excellent table wine. The fruit should be fully ripe, and soft enough to permit the stone to be easily removed.

GUAVA
This pinky tropical fruit makes into a light and delicate table wine. It is very low in acid and tannin. Do not break the pips when crushing the fruit.

LEMONS
Only small and very ripe lemons are suitable. Use the thinly-pared rinds and the juice, not the flesh. The acid must be ameliorated with glycerine.

LIME

Although rich in vitamin C this fruit is too high in acid and flavour to make into wine.

LOGANBERRIES

The strong flavour of this raspberry-like fruit can be overpowering if too many are used. Because of the full flavour, it is best made into a sweet dessert wine.

LYCHEE

Also known as *Litchi* or 'Chinese gooseberry'. This fruit has a husk and stone, both of which have to be removed. It has a delicate but pleasant flavour and makes a light table wine.

MANDARINS

This small, loose-skinned orange originated in the Orient although it is now grown in other areas of the world. Only the flavour from the skin and the juice may be used. The skin can be very thinly pared, so that no white pith is removed, or rubbed with sugar lumps which absorb the zest. Cut the oranges in two to express the juice, and ferment all the ingredients in a fermentation jar. Remove any particles of skin after 7 days.

MEDLARS

These small, hard, green fruits must be ripened and mellowed until the green has turned to gold and the fruit feels soft without being mushy. They have a delightful bouquet and flavour, and make up into an attractive table wine. They also blend well with apples and pears.

MELON

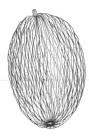

The large yellow water melon is best for making wine, but the flavour is very delicate. It can be sharpened with a little ginger and then makes a light wine for drinking cool on a hot day. Use all the melon — skin, pulp and seeds. Cut up the skin and pulp into small pieces and place in a bin with the seeds and bruised ginger.

MORELLO CHERRIES

These bitter/sour cherries should be black and soft when used for making wine. Remove the stalks, wash the cherries, extract the stones and make a rich dessert wine of magnificent colour and flavour.

MULBERRIES

This large raspberry-shaped, dark mauve-coloured fruit grows prolifically on a mature tree. Gather the berries each day as they fall, or pick them if they come free from their stalk at the slightest touch. This is when they are fully ripe. The flavour is extremely strong and makes a dessert wine.

NECTARINES

Similar to the peach but a little smaller and with a smooth skin, this delicious fruit makes an attractive sweet table wine. Remove the stalks, wash the fruit and cut in halves to remove the stones, then chop into small pieces.

Oranges also make good wine

ORANGES

There are many varieties of the orange and they make wine of different flavours and qualities. An excellent aperitif-type wine can be made from a mixture of bitter marmalade oranges from Seville and the sweet orange from Navel. The fruit must first be washed and then most thinly pared to ensure that no white pith is removed. The fruit is then cut into two and the juice expressed. Wine is made by fermenting all the ingredients together for 7 days and then removing the skins. Some wine-makers lightly roast the skins for 20 minutes before using them. Makes a strong dry wine.

ORTANIQUES

This is a new fruit which is a cross between the orange and the tangerine. As big as a very large orange, it has a fairly tough skin and flesh that is a very bright orange in colour, extremely juicy and well flavoured. Prepare exactly as for orange wine.

PASSION FRUIT

The greyish, brown-green, apple-like fruit of the passion flower can be made into a white table wine, dry or sweet. Passion fruit have no effect on the passions or emotions! The name comes from the resemblance of the flower to the 'crown of thorns' placed on the head of Christ during His Passion.

Left: *Peaches make the perfect sweet table wine*

Above: *Plums make all types of fine wines*

PAW PAW
This fruit is sometimes written as Paupaw. It grows to about 25 cm (10 in.) long, is rectangular in shape and a dull orange in colour. Small black seeds are embedded in its flesh. It is low in acid and tannin. Wipe the fruit clean, mash into pulp with a potato masher and pour on boiling water. Makes a sweet table wine.

PEACHES
Wait until the fruit is fully ripe so that the stones can easily be removed. Chop the halves into pieces and make into a sweet table wine.

PEARS
Only hard or cooking pears are suitable for making wine. Soft or ripe dessert pears are quite useless. The skin contains much tannin but the flesh is low in acid and flavour. Pears make excellent sparkling wine and blend well with apples, medlars and quince. Prepare in the same way as apple wine.

PINEAPPLE
This popular fruit is widely available and makes into an attractive sweet table wine. The top leaves and root stump must be removed but it is not necessary to peel the fruit. Simply wash free from dust, chop up into small pieces, place in a bin and pour boiling water over it.

PLUMS

There are many varieties of this fruit suitable for making wine. 'Early Rivers' and 'Pershore Yellow Egg' have excellent flavour and each makes a light, dry table wine. 'Czar' and 'Monarch' are two larger plums that are also good, especially for dessert wines. Victoria plums make a superb aperitif-type wine. But there are many others.

After removing the stalks rinse the fruit in cold water and then wash in very hot water containing some washing soda to remove the waxy bloom. Rinse again in cold water, then remove the stones and crush the fruit. Pour on boiling water.

With 'Early Rivers' use red grape juice concentrate and a Burgundy yeast.

With 'Pershore Yellow Egg' use a white grape juice concentrate and a Chablis yeast.

With 'Czar' and 'Monarch' use a rosé grape juice concentrate and a Sauternes yeast. Finish the wine at S.G. 1.006.

With Victoria plums use a white grape juice concentrate and a Sherry yeast. Feed the fermentation to maximum alcohol and finish nearly dry at S.G. 1.002.

With so many culinary plums available to the amateur winemaker there is no need to use dessert plums which do not make such good wine.

QUINCE

This greenish yellow fruit has a crude pear shape. Two varieties are suitable for wine. The large apple-sized type, a rich golden yellow when ripe and with a texture similar to an apple, has a fragrant bouquet and makes a delicious golden wine. It is not easy to come by. The other variety, and more widely available, is the Japanese Quince. It is the fruit of the *Cydonia japonica*. At first very hard and green, this small crab-apple sized fruit slowly mellows, softens a little and turns an attractive yellow. The fruit is still relatively hard to cut and contains a large number of small brown/black seeds, similar to apple seeds. It has a very strong bouquet that is most attractive and distinctive. It makes a good wine by itself but is at its best mixed in with apples, the bouquet and flavour of which it improves substantially.

RASPBERRIES

This strongly flavoured and acid fruit makes a better sweet dessert wine than a table wine. It blends well with other soft fruits. Berries should be fully ripe and easily parted from their stalks. Rinse in clean cold water before mashing them. Cold water may be used with this fruit.

REDCURRANTS

Another high acid fruit with a delightful flavour. It makes an excellent dry table wine and an even better medium-sweet rosé-type wine. Remove the fully ripe berries from their stalks, wash in cold water, mash and pour on cold water.

RHUBARB

The best time for making wine from rhubarb is in the late Spring when the sticks are well developed but before they become old. Red varieties have a better flavour than the green stalks. Oxalic acid is present in the leaves which are poisonous so cut them off about 2.5 cm (1 in) down the stem. Also cut off the white foot of the stem. Then wipe the sticks clean with a sulphited cloth and chop into small pieces. Place in a bin and pour boiling water over them.

Rhubarb makes a white table wine, but blends well with other fruits especially those low in acid. The thinly-pared rind of a lemon improves the rhubarb flavour.

SLOE

This hedgerow fruit is blue/black, the size of a small grape and grows on a prickly shrub to a height of 3 metres (10 ft). It contains a small stone which is best removed, though this is not easy to do. It makes both table and dessert wines and marries well with gin to make a liqueur. Although blue/black in colour the sloe does not make good red-coloured wine, but more often gives a tawny. The berries should be gathered when they feel soft and easily come free from their stalks.

STRAWBERRIES

None of the many varieties make a particularly good wine but strawberries can be mixed in with other soft fruits.

TANGERINES

This is a small loose-skinned orange similar to the Mandarin. Make wine from it in exactly the same way as for the latter (see page 47).

UGLI

This ugly-looking(!) fruit is a cross between an orange and a grapefruit. It has a rough, greenish yellow skin but a good-flavoured flesh. Use only the very thinly-pared skin and the juice; avoid all white pith.

WHITE CURRANTS

An excellently flavoured fruit more closely related to the red currant than the black. It makes a good dry white table wine and blends well with other soft fruits.

WHORTLEBERRIES *See* Bilberries, page 45.

YOUNGBERRIES

A modern cross between the blackberry and the raspberry. They are not so bitter as the former nor so sharp as the latter. Make into a red table wine.

Wines from Dried Fruits

Always keep a wide selection of dried fruits in reserve

FOR the winemaker living some distance from available fresh fruit or whose summers are busy beyond words, dried fruits enable him or her to make wine just whenever it is convenient to do so. The range of dried fruits available for making wine at home is impressive: apples, apricots, bananas, bilberries, currants, dates, elderberries, figs, muscatels, peaches, pears, prunes, raisins, rosehips, sloes and sultanas. Indeed, in some parts of the world there may even be locally grown fruit specially dried for use in the area. The dried fruits listed above are all readily available in the United Kingdom and the U.S.A., and can also be obtained by mail order from suppliers in both countries.

The fruits are sulphured during the drying process and this, coupled with the concentration of sugar, keeps the fruit in good condition almost indefinitely if stored in air-tight containers. Dried fruits may, indeed, be used to make all types of wines, sweet or dry, table or dessert. As with fresh fruits, rather more is required in dessert and full-bodied wines than in light table wines. Dried fruits contain up to two-thirds of their weight in sugar and account of this should be taken when preparing a must for fermentation. The use of an hydrometer is strongly recommended.

Acid Needed
Most dried fruits need additional acid, nutrient or tannin but this varies from one to another. Bananas, dates, elderberries and figs for example are almost devoid of acid. Some details about each fruit are given in the text and in Table 15.

Dried apricots and figs, in particular, are very strongly flavoured and should be used in relatively small quantities.

Wash Them First
Although dried fruits are able to resist infection, there is no way to prevent micro-organisms of all kinds from settling upon them. Furthermore, they are often left lying around in the open or in half-filled bags and sacks. Thus, it is always important to wash them thoroughly in a sulphite solution before use. The amount of dust and other particles left behind in the solution is always surprising. Some fruit is lightly rinsed in liquid paraffin (a colourless, harmless mineral oil) before packaging. This imparts an attractive, fresh-looking gloss to the fruit but needs to be removed by washing the fruit in fairly hot water before use.

Other Uses
Apart from their value in making good wines in their own right, dried fruits make excellent additives to other musts. Raisins and sultanas, in particular, give not only vinosity but also body and sugar. Bananas, too, are very popular for giving body to a wine. Elderberries are widely used for the addition of good colour and fruitiness.

Methods
It is not possible to give one basic recipe suitable for *all* dried fruits. In preparing them, one of the two popular methods should be followed. The first is to mince the fruit or to cut it up into small pieces, place in a mashing bin, pour on boiling water leave to cool, then ferment on the pulp. The second is to soak the fruit overnight in sufficient water to cover it, then gently boil in the same liquor for 15–20 minutes until the fruit is tender, then use only the liquor to make the wine.

Either method, or a combination of both, may be safely followed.

APPLES
Dried apples are mostly processed in California. The fruit is hand-picked but peeled, cored and sliced by machinery. It is exposed to sulphur fumes to prevent oxidation before drying. One measure of dried apples is equal to six–nine measures of fresh fruit, depending on the loss in peeling and coring.

A light dry table wine is produced.

APRICOTS
Dried apricots are produced in Mediterranean

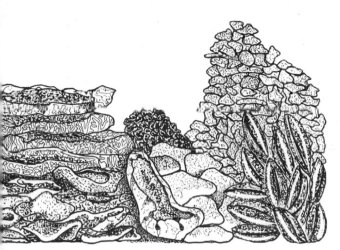

countries as well as in California. The varieties chiefly used are 'Blenheim' and 'Moorpark'. They are hand-picked when fully ripe, cut in half, the stone removed then placed in trays, cut side up. Sulphur fumes prevent oxidation and the fruit is then sun dried for several days. One measure of dried apricots equals five-and-a-half of fresh fruit.

BANANAS
Dried bananas are available mainly from 'Home Brew' centres. They contain a little citric and malic acid but two-thirds of their bulk consists of fermentable sugars. Dried bananas do not make a particularly attractive wine by themselves but make an excellent additive to other wines where additional body is required. One measure of dried bananas is equal to three measures of peeled fresh bananas.

BILBERRIES
Widely grown in Poland and Eastern European countries as well as in North America and Canada, this fruit dries well but needs to be used within six months or so. It is more prone to infection than sweeter fruits. The sugar content is only about 18%. Of excellent colour and flavour for wine, it can be used by itself or in conjunction with other fruits. One measure of dried bilberries is equal to four measures of fresh fruit. This makes an attractive red table wine, worth making in quantity.

CURRANTS
Few people realise that the best currants are grown on the slopes of the southern shore of the Gulf of Corinth, from which they take their name. They are tiny seedless grapes which grow on vines little more than half a metre high (20 in). The best varieties are 'Vortizza' and 'Gulf'. After cutting, the best bunches are hung on the vine in the shade of the leaves to dry. Poorer quality currants are either dried on wire mesh trays or laid out on the ground in the sun. Australia also produces excellent currants.

Currants are not often used in winemaking and are best used to provide body and vinosity for other fruits. Two-thirds of the dried currant consists of fermentable sugar. One measure of dried currants equals four of fresh currants.

DATES
This fruit grows at the top of palm trees and was used for making wine by the Ancient Greeks. It appears all along the Mediterranean coastline and indeed throughout the sub-tropical areas of the world. It has a high sugar content but is low in acid.

For winemaking it is best to use the loose, newly-dried dates, rather than the packaged varieties available in the UK and other temperate-zone countries. The stones should be removed and discarded before using the fruit.

ELDERBERRIES
Dried elderberries are regularly imported into the UK mainly from Poland and Eastern Europe. Like bilberries, they are relatively low in sugar and equally prone to infection. They should always be well washed in a sulphited water solution before use. The sugar content is about 15%. One measure of dried elderberries equals four of fresh fruit.

FIGS
Although figs are grown in many countries with sub-tropical climates, the finest quality figs in the world are exported from Smyrna — perhaps better known today as Izmir — in Turkey. The fruit grows directly from the wood of the tree and there are both male and female forms. The flowers, hundreds of them to each fruit, bloom on the inner surface of the hollow receptacle reached only by a tiny 'Fig wasp'. The male figs are threaded on strings and hung on the branches of the female tree to facilitate fertilisation. The emerging insect with pollen on its wings and feet has, therefore, only a little journey to the female flowers.

The fig is not picked like other fruit — when fully ripe, it drops off the tree on to a mat placed for it to fall upon, and where it will remain for a few days to dry. Farmers collect the figs and take them into the towns where they are sterilized and graded. Women then press then into shape and pack them for distribution all over the world. More than half the dried fig consists of sugar but it also has more than the usual quota of calcium, iron, magnesium, phosphorous and potassium.

Figs have a very pronounced flavour and should therefore be used in moderation. One measure of dried figs is equal to three-and-a-half of fresh figs.

MUSCATELS
These large dried black grapes exported from Southern Spain, have a distinctive and unique bouquet and flavour. They contain large pips and are often packed with their stalk. Muscatels are used

more for dessert than culinary purposes. Because of the fragrant bouquet, this fruit is best used for making a sweet flavoured wine. Two-thirds of the dried fruit consists of sugar. One measure of dried muscatels is equal to four measures of the fresh fruit.

PEACHES

Although grown in many sub-tropical and even some near-temperate climates, and exported fresh from Israel, Italy and Spain, dried peaches are mostly exported from California, USA. The fruit was taken there by Spanish missionaries in about 1770 and some 1,500 varieties have recently been recorded. The most popular for drying are the 'freestone' peaches as opposed to 'clings' (which are mainly used for canning).

Like apricots they are hand-picked, split in two, the stone removed, the peaches placed in trays, cut side up, sulphured to prevent oxidation and slowly dried. Just over 40% of the dried peach consists of sugar. One measure of dried peaches is equal to five-and-a-half measures of fresh fruit.

PEARS

Dried pears, like dried peaches, are exported from California, where the fruit was taken by Spanish missionaries. The well-known Bartlett pear is used both for drying and for canning. It is a dessert variety and is picked, peeled, dried and packed in the same way as apples. The sugar content nearly reaches 40%. One measure of dried pears is equivalent to three measures of fresh fruit.

PRUNES

These blue/black plums were taken to California in about 1850, but they have since 'spread' to Australia and South Africa. They are not picked but are left hanging on the trees until they are so ripe and full of sugar that they fall to the soft ground beneath, rather like the harvesting of figs. They are then collected and dipped in hot soda water for 15 seconds to remove the wax bloom and allow the moisture to escape through the skin. The lye solution (possibly slang for alkali) is then washed off under a fine spray of water and the plums are graded and placed on trays for drying, first in the sun and then in the shade. Next they are placed in large bins called 'sweat boxes' for 2/3 weeks to equalise the moisture content. The prunes are again washed and sterilised by passing them through near boiling water. They are then drained, cooled and packed. About 44% of the prune consists of sugar. One measure of dried prunes is equal to at least three of fresh plums. Finish the wine dry as an excellent aperitif wine.

RAISINS

Raisins are dried black grapes and are grown for export in Victoria (Australia), California (USA), Valencia (Spain) and South Africa. California and South Africa are famous for their seedless raisins.

The fruit is picked when fully ripe, placed in a string bag, dipped in boiling soda water for just a second or so, then laid out on straw mats or cane trays in the sun. If the weather is bad, the cane trays are stacked in hot-air drying sheds, but this is an expensive process and avoided whenever possible. After six days natural drying in the sun, the fruit is cleaned from stalks and cap stems by revolving screens of fine mesh. The raisins are then graded, exposed to sulphur fumes to improve the colour, and packed for despatch. 66% of the fruit consists of fermentable sugar.

One measure of dried is equal to four of fresh.

ROSEHIPS

Arguably a dried fruit rather than a flower, rosehips and rosehip shells are available from Home Brew Centres. They are rich in Vitamin C. Like bananas they do not make a distinctive wine by themselves but together with dried figs make an excellent sherry type wine.

SULTANAS

The main difference between sultanas and raisins is that sultanas are made from white grapes.

After picking, the bunches of grapes are dipped into hot water containing some soda and olive oil. This wrinkles and cracks the skin so that the moisture can begin to evaporate when the fruit is laid out in the sun. After about a week they are dry enough to be shaken from the main stalk and graded. The grapes are then spun in a wire mesh to remove the tiny cap stems, and washed clean. As soon as they are dry they are sprayed with a thin mineral oil, such as liquid paraffin, to prevent the berries sticking together and forming lumps. Next the berries pass through a chamber in which sulphur is being burned, and then through a chamber in which hot air evaporates the remaining moisture. Finally the sultanas, now with an attractive shiny golden hue, are packed for despatch. Before being used they should be washed in hot water to remove the oil. Sultanas make an excellent additive to all white wines. They affect the flavour of delicate wines less than raisins and yet still give vinosity and body.

The sultana has a 68% sugar content and is rich in mineral salts and vitamins A, B1 and B2. One measure of sultanas equals four of fresh fruit.

SLOES

The dried version of this small, blue/black berry comes mainly from East European countries. Although it has a good flavour, the sugar content is similar to the elderberry, and dried sloes sometimes arrive in less than perfect condition. They should always be thoroughly washed in a sulphite solution. One measure of dried sloes is equal to three of fresh fruit because of the weight of the stone in both.

Wines from Canned Fruits, Juices & Jams

The keen winemaker is always on the look-out for new ingredients for making wine, and the supermarket can therefore be a veritable Aladdin's cave. From all over the world comes an exciting range of canned fruits.

All the various types of wine can be made from these ingredients. Relatively small quantities of fruit are required depending on the flavour of the fruit and type of wine being made.

To make six bottles of wine you will need to use:

1 can A1 size, 15½ oz, 440 grams
of strongly flavoured fruit for table wines.

1 can A2 size, 19 oz, 540 grams
of moderate and lightly flavoured fruit for table
and sparkling wines.
or
of strongly flavoured fruits for dessert wines.

2 cans A1 size
of moderate and lightly flavoured fruits for
dessert wines.

Strongly flavoured fruits are not recommended for sparkling wines.

All wines made from canned fruits need some additional body to give them substance and vinosity. Raisins or sultanas or grape juice concentrate may be used. 225 grams (½ lb) of dried fruit or 250 grams (½ pint) grape juice concentrate, is sufficient for six bottles of table and sparkling wines. Increase this quantity by half for aperitif and social wines and double it for dessert wines. The amount of sugar to use, again depends on the type of wine being made:

Light, dry table and sparkling wines	750 grams in 5 litres	1½ lb per gallon
Robust, dry table wines, light aperitif and social wines	1 kg in 5 litres	2 lb per gallon
Sweet and strong wines	1.5 kg in 5 litres	3 lb per gallon

Although the sugar syrup in the can may mask the acidity of the fruit, it is best to include 2 level 5 ml spoonsful of acid crystals per six bottles in every wine – unless it is made from black and red currants, cherries, gooseberries, grapefruit, oranges, raspberries and rhubarb, when in each case one spoonful would be sufficient. Half a level 5 ml spoonful of grape tannin is needed, to give bite and character.

Whilst it is not essential to use pectic enzyme with every fruit, doing so helps with flavour extraction, as well as in the prevention of haze.

Nutrient and an activated yeast are, of course, essential ingredients.

The method of preparing the must is the same for all canned or bottled fruit.

1 Open the can or bottle, pour off and save the syrup, and mash the fruit.
2 Place the fruit pulp in a bin together with the chopped raisins or sultanas (if these are being used), and pour on ½ litre (1 pint) boiling water for each bottle of wine being made. Cover and leave to cool.
3 Stir in some pectic enzyme and sulphite at the rate of 50 p.p.m. Cover and leave in a warm place for 24 hours.
4 Pour on the syrup from the can or jar, the grape juice concentrate if being used, the acid, tannin, nutrient and an active yeast.
5 Cover and ferment on the pulp for four days, stirring twice daily.
6 Strain out the pulp through a fine sieve or cloth, rolling the pulp around rather than pressing it. Stir in the sugar, pour the must into a fermentation jar, top up with cold boiled water, fit an air-lock and ferment in a warm place.

Wines from canned and bottled fruits are little trouble to make. They produce some delightful wines especially if you enjoy a light wine, gentle in flavour and light in texture. They mature very quickly and may be ready for drinking in 3 or 4 months.

Cans of pie fillings can be used in the same way. The fruit is already mashed and may therefore be placed immediately in the mashing bin.

Canned or bottled fruit juices are even easier to use, in that they may be poured immediately into a fermentation jar. Natural and unsweetened fruit juice is best.

The cans and bottles vary somewhat in size but the precise quantity is not critical.

Grape juice concentrate is needed for body and vinosity in the same proportion as for canned fruit; sugar, acid, tannin, nutrient and active yeast too. Finally, top up with water, fit an air-lock and ferment.

Some concentrated syrups are available that are well worth making into wine. The actual amount to use depends upon the concentration, but you will need 12 fl oz to make into six bottles of wine.

Jams are another source of useful ingredients. Almost half their weight is in fermentable sugar, so less granulated sugar is required. Because of the pectin in jam (required to give a good 'set'), double the normal quantity of pectin destroying enzyme is required. Jam containing only fruit and sugar is best for winemaking. Some contain preservative and pectin as well. 7 lb (3 kg) of jam is sufficient to make twelve bottles of wine. Fine-cut marmalades may be used, but coarse-cut varieties contain pith that causes bitterness.

The lovely colours and the fragrance of their bouquet is enough to tempt any winemaker into using flowers. Some of them, notably red roses, May-blossom and elderflower, make most attractive wines. Because of their fragrance, flower wines should be served medium sweet; neither dry, which contradicts their fragrance, nor sweet, which when added to their fragrance makes them cloy the palate.

Flowers to be used in making wine should be gathered in warm sunshine when the flower is well-developed and free from moisture. All trace of green, whether of stem, leaf or calix must be discarded since this causes a most bitter taste in the finished wine. Once gathered flowers should be used without delay, unless they are properly dried.

Sadly, however, flowers (like herbs) contribute nothing but bouquet and flavour to a wine. Everything else must be added. For this reason it is a practical idea to make a straight white grape juice concentrate wine and to flavour it with different flowers. By adding lactose the wine can be fully fermented and will still taste sweet.

BASIC RECIPE

White grape juice concentrate	1 kg (1 quart)
White sugar	285 g (10 oz)
Lactose	100 g (3½ oz)
Water	to 4½ litres (1 gallon)
All-purpose yeast	
Flowers	

Adjust S.G. to 1.086 and ferment out.

The essence from the flowers is always extracted in the same way. Place the florets or petals in a mashing bin or bowl, pour on boiling water, cover and leave to cool. Add 1 Campden tablet, stir daily for three days, then strain and press. Use only the liquor. To make six bottles of wine use:

Bramble: 5 lb young bramble leaves and shoots from first pruning.
Broom: 2 quarts yellow broom flowers.
Carnations: 2 quarts white garden 'pinks'.
Clover: 2 quarts of purple clover.
Coltsfoot: 2 quarts yellow flowers.
Dandelion: 2 quarts yellow flowers.
Elderflower: 1 quart creamy florets.

Tapping a mature birch tree. Plug the hole afterwards

Geranium Leaf: 2 quarts small green leaves, rinsed free from dust. (*Pelargonium quercifolium* only. No other variety.)
Golden Rod: 1 pint golden florets.
Hawthorn (May) Blossom: 2 quarts pink or white florets.
Lime: 2 quarts of bracts with flowers.
Marigold: 2 quarts marigold heads.
Primrose: 2 quarts creamy yellow flowers.
Oak Leaf: 2 quarts green leaves, gathered when just mature.
Rose Petal: 2 quarts dark red petals.
Vine Leaves: 5 lb of young vine leaves and tendrils from first pruning.
Walnut Leaf: 1 large handful of green walnut leaves gathered when just mature.

* Exceptionally lactose may be omitted and the wine served dry.

Sap wines are quite widely made in small quantities. Only the sap from birch, sycamore and walnut trees are known to be suitable. Sap should be taken from a well-developed tree about 20 cm (8 in) in diameter. It should be taken just when winter turns into spring and the sap begins to rise.

A small hole about 1 cm in diameter, should be bored about 2 cm deep, some 40 cm from the ground. Into the hole push one end of a polythene or rubber tube of similar external diameter. Place the other end in a demijohn or polythene container with a narrow neck. Plug the neck around the tube with non-absorbent cotton wool and cover all the equipment with a clean sack or blanket.

After 24 or 36 hours about 4 litres of sap should have flowed from the tree to the jar and this is enough for any one tree to give at a time. Remove the tube from the tree and plug the hole with a cork of suitable diameter. It is most important that you do this, otherwise the tree may 'bleed' to death. Take the sap home, pour it into a pan and bring it to the boil. Simmer the sap gently for 15 minutes and then leave to cool.

The sap will need some body and this is best provided from the grape. Either chop up 500 grams of raisins or sultanas and add them to the hot sap when simmering is finished or, more simply, as soon as the sap is cool mix it with 500 grams of white grape juice concentrate.

Sugar	450 g (1 lb)
Tartaric acid	15 g (½ oz)
Tannin	½ level 5 ml spoonful
Lactose	50 g (2 oz)
Nutrient	
All-purpose yeast	

Adjust to S.G. 1.090 topping up with cold boiled water if necessary.

Wines from Grains

The selection of suitable grains is not wide, but some interesting wines can be made from wheat, oats, rye, barley, maize, millet and rice. They mostly have a subtle but distinctive flavour and plenty of body.

Adequate acid and tannin must be added. Always wash grains free from dust before use.

They must then be cracked, crushed or flaked so that the goodness can be extracted. Soak them for an hour in enough warm water to cover them. This softens them and they can then be crushed with a rolling pin or in a coarse-grind coffee mill or the like.

Place in a mashing bin, pour boiling water over them, cover and leave to cool. Add some diastase or fungal amylase in accordance with the supplier's instructions and leave covered for a further 24 hours. Stir in acid, tannin, white grape juice concentrate, nutrient and an activated cereal yeast. Ferment in the warm for four days then strain out the solids, stir in the sugar, pour into a fermentation jar, fit an air-lock and continue fermentation.

Cereal wines are preferred by most people to be of the strong dessert type, and so the fermentation should be fed with additional sugar to the limit of fermentation, and the wine sweetened to at least S.G. 1.020 when finished.

These wines usually require two or three years to mature, but can be very smooth and attractive. Herbs make excellent additional flavouring if required.

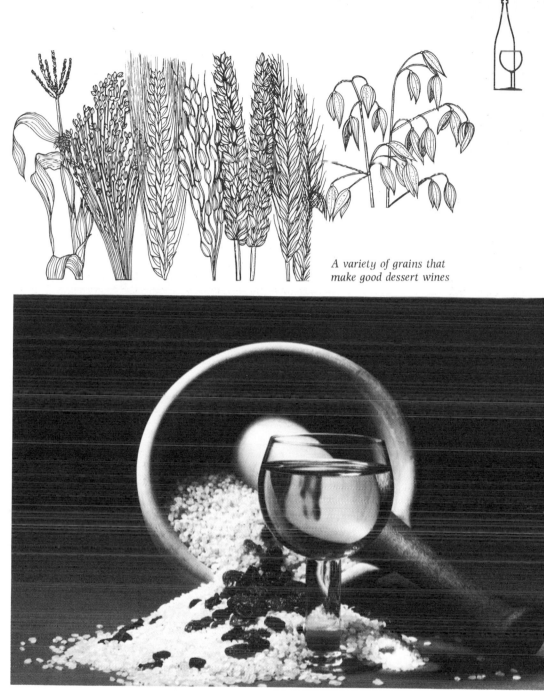

A variety of grains that make good dessert wines

After long maturation, grain wines are very smooth

BASIC RECIPE

Cereal	1.5 kg (3½ lb)
White grape juice concentrate or	1 kg (1 quart)
Sultanas or raisins	500 g (1 lb)
Sugar	1 kg (2¼ lb)
Tartaric acid	15 g (½ oz)
Tannin	½ level 5 ml spoonful
Water	to 4½ litres (1 gallon)
Diastase	
Nutrient	
Cereal yeast	

Sake is a rice wine made from a variety of rice grown specially for the purpose. After polishing, it is soaked in water and steamed, then cooled and left for two days. About one fifth of the amount of rice used is then sprinkled with the mould *Aspergilles oryzae*. After a few days the now mouldy rice (called 'Koji') is mixed with the rest of the rice and changes the starch into sugar. Water and a *sake* yeast are added to convert the sugar into alcohol. The fermentation lasts for three to four weeks and produces about 20% alcohol by volume.

The *sake* is filtered, pasteurised and matured for a month, diluted to 17% alcohol or less, bottled and sold. *Sake* does not keep well, probably because of its low acid and tannin content. It is, therefore, best consumed within six months of making. It has a transparent, colourless appearance and a very subtle bouquet and flavour. It is usually served at blood heat from a small ceramic cup holding about 30 ml (1 fl oz).

A kind of *sake* can be made at home using a long grain rice, diastase and a cereal yeast. Follow the same method recommended for other cereal wines. The flavour is improved if some sultanas or raisins are included, in the proportion of 3 measures of rice to 1 of sultana or raisin. Serve it as a social wine preferably with salty biscuits.

The best of the cereal wines are wheat, barley, maize and rice. Oats, rye and millet are less attractive.

Wines from Vegetables

It is well-known that some soils are better for cereals or vegetables than for fruit. If fruit is not available man turns to what *is* readily at hand to be used in making an alcoholic beverage. Vegetables have widely been employed in this way, and some have given very good results. The best known is parsnip, followed by beetroot, carrot and potato, but broad beans, pea pods, runner beans and celery also produce good wines. The Jerusalem artichoke, celeriac, lettuce, mangold, marrow, spinach, sugar-beet and swede-turnip have also been used with varying success.

Vegetables can be made into any type of wine. Parsnip and beetroot make excellent dessert wines. Broad beans, celery and pea pods make good table wines. The others are best as social wines.

The time to harvest vegetables for winemaking is as soon as they are fully mature. Parsnips are best after they have been frosted, as this concentrates the sugar and flavour. Celery, carrot and beetroot should be used in the Autumn, parsnips in the winter and mangold left until March. Broad beans are left until the husk is inedible, pea pods are used when the peas are mature. Spinach and lettuce – outdoor grown, cos variety, not hot-house salad lettuce – should be fully grown; so too, the marrow, swede, sugar-beet and artichoke.

Vegetables lack acid and tannin but have adequate body except for lettuce and spinach. These two need some cereal or raisins added. Some vegetables have a high starch content and so a cereal yeast is recommended.

The method is the same for all vegetable wines. Top and tail, wash and scrub all the roots until there is no trace of earth, mould or blemish. Cut into dice-like cubes and simmer gently until they are just cooked. Use no salt in the cooking, but if you subsequently wish to serve the vegetable as part of a meal you may do so. It is the liquor alone which is used for making wine. Frequently spices, such as cloves and ginger, and dried fruit, such as raisins or sultanas, are used to improve the flavour and vinosity.

ARTICHOKE

Jerusalem Artichoke	2 kg (4½ lb)
White grape juice concentrate	250 g (½ pint)
White sugar	1 kg (2¼ lb)
Tartaric acid	15 g (½ oz)
Tannin	½ level 5 ml spoonful
Lactose	50 g (2 oz)
Water	to 4½ litres (1 gallon)
Nutrient	
Cereal yeast	

Cut up into dice-sized pieces and boil for half an hour, strain, cool, add other ingredients and adjust S.G. to 1.090.

Make into a social wine.

BEETROOT

Beetroot, scrubbed and diced	2 kg (4½ lb)
Red grape juice concentrate	500 g (1 pint)
Sugar	1.5 kg (3¼ lb)
Tartaric acid	25 g (1 oz)
Tannin	1 level 5 ml spoonful
Water	to 4½ litres (1 gallon)
Nutrient	
Cereal yeast	

Boil the beetroot for up to 1½ hours, strain and cool. Adjust the S.G. to 1.090 at first then add extra sugar and continue fermentation to maximum alcohol tolerance of the yeast. Finish the wine sweet and mature for about two years, to make a strong dessert wine of superb colour.

BROAD BEAN

Shelled broad beans	1.5 kg (3¼ lb)
White grape juice concentrate	250 g (½ pint)
Sugar	1 kg (2¼ lb)
Tartaric acid	15 g (½ oz)
Tannin	½ level 5 ml spoonful
Water	to 4½ litres (1 gallon)
Nutrient	
Cereal yeast	

Boil the beans for 1 hour, strain and cool. Adjust the S.G. to 1.086 and ferment to dryness. Serve as a white table wine.

CARROT

Carrots, scrubbed and diced	2 kg (4½ lb)
White grape juice concentrate	500 g (1 pint)

Other ingredients and method as for Beetroot wine, but half an hour boiling is sufficient. Serve as a social wine.

CELERIAC

Celeriac	1.5 kg (3¼ lb)

Top and tail the celeriac, cut into bean-sized pieces and boil for half an hour. Other ingredients and method as for broad bean wine.

CELERY

Celery	2 kg (4½ lb)

Use no leaf or root, only stalk, cut into bean-sized pieces and boil for half an hour. Other ingredients and method as for broad bean wine.

Celery wine was once thought to be beneficial to people suffering from arthritis or rheumatism. It was made by country housewives specifically for this purpose. Perhaps it had a diuretic effect and removed some of the uric acid. The alcohol would at least have eased the pain.

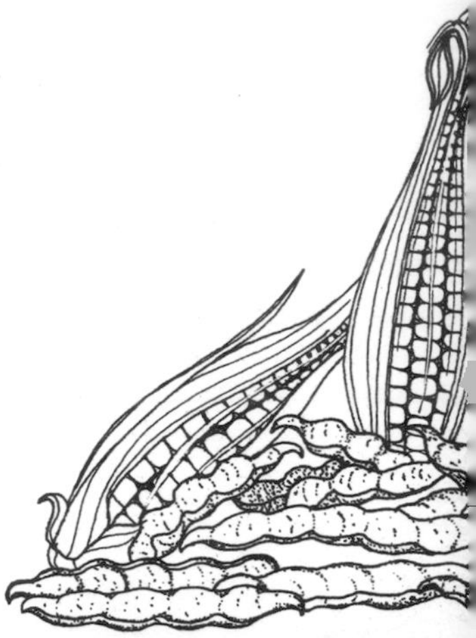

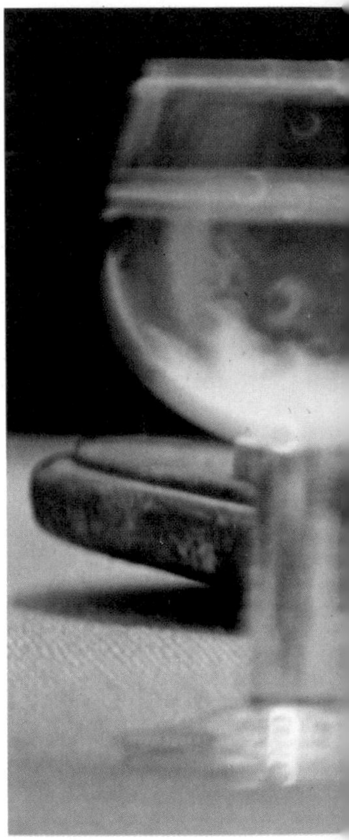

Vegetables are great favourites with country winemakers

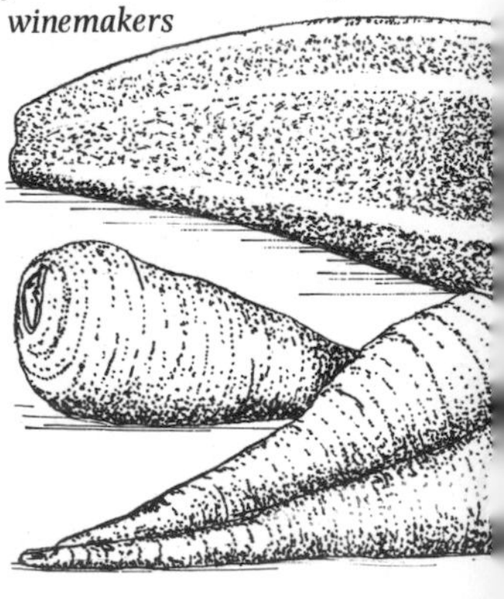

LETTUCE

Cos lettuce (chopped)	1 kg	(2¼ lb)
White grape juice concentrate	500 g	(1 pint)

Other ingredients and method as for artichoke wine.

MANGOLD

Mangolds, scrubbed and diced	2 kg	(4½ lb)

Other ingredients and method as for artichoke wine, but boil for one hour.

MARROW

Marrow	2 kg	(4½ lb)

Use all the marrow, skin and unbroken seeds as well. Other ingredients and method as for artichoke wine. Like many other vegetables, marrow has little flavour and you could add some thinly pared and chopped orange and lemon rind (excluding all white pith), or some ginger, even flowers or indeed any other flavouring you choose.

PARSNIP

Parsnips, scrubbed and diced	2 kg	(4½ lb)
White grape juice concentrate	500 g	(1 pint)

Other ingredients and method as for beetroot wine but boil for only half an hour.

PEA POD

Pea pods, shucked	2 kg	(4½ lb)
White grape juice concentrate	250 g	(½ pint)

Chop up the clean pods to bean-sized pieces and boil for half an hour. Other ingredients and method as for broad bean wine.

SPINACH

Spinach, washed and prepared	1 kg	(2¼ lb)
White grape juice concentrate	500 g	(1 pint)

Other ingredients and method as for artichoke wine — but boil for only twenty minutes.

SUGAR-BEET

Sugar-beet	2 kg	(4½ lb)

Other ingredients and method as for artichoke wine, but boil gently for 1½ hours. This is another lightly-flavoured wine, like marrow, that benefits from the addition of lemon, orange or ginger.

SWEDE-TURNIP

Swede-turnip, scrubbed and diced	2 kg	(4½ lb)

Other ingredients and method as for artichoke wine but only boil for forty-five minutes. The orange swede is less bitter than the white turnip.

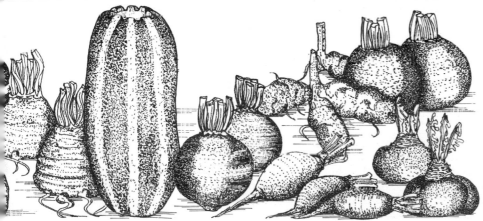

57

Wines from Herbs & Spices

BEFORE the development of modern medicine herbs had a great reputation for their properties of healing. This lingered on in the countryside, where doctors were scarce and herbs were plentiful, until the middle of the 20th century. Indeed, the growth in recent years of the number of Health Food and Herbalist shops is an indication that many people still have faith in the concept that 'nature's cure' is best.

Herbs used in making wine may be bought dried from a Herbalist shop, grown in the garden, or gathered from the hedgerow. The time to harvest the herb depends on the part being used — flower, leaf, seed or root. Flowers should be gathered in warm sunshine just before they are fully out and 'blown' and when their scent is at the peak. Leaves should be gathered just before the flowers appear, for that is when their aromatic oils are most abundant. Seeds should be gathered by harvesting the flower at 'petal fall' and hanging the plant upside down in a paper bag to catch the seeds as they are released from the plant. Roots are harvested during the plants resting time, when they are full in their food. Because of their very nature herbs should always be handled gently so as not to bruise them and lose their volatile goodness.

Herbs may be used to make any type of wine — aperitif, table, social or dessert. Because most of them have a pronounced flavour, they are perhaps best used for aperitif or social wines, with the exception of parsley which produces an attractive table wine.

It must be remembered that, like flowers and leaf wines, herbs and spices provide only bouquet and flavour and that body (and indeed everything else) must be added. Accordingly, herbs can be used to give bouquet and flavour to vegetable, cereal or fruit wines that may be lacking in these qualities. For simplicity, a plain grape juice concentrate wine is suggested as the base in the following herb and spice recipes. Lactose will ensure a sweet finish to the wine.

BASIC RECIPE

White grape juice concentrate	1 kg	(1 quart)
Sugar	500 g	(1 lb)
Lactose	100 g	(3½ oz)
Water	to 5 litres	(1 gallon)
Herbs		
Activated All-purpose wine yeast.		

Adjust S.G. to 1.090.

AGRIMONY

This wine has a flavour akin to apricots.

Use 1 quart of fresh leaves lightly pressed down. Wash them in clean cold water, shake off the surplus water, measure and pour 3 litres of boiling water over them. Cover and leave for three days, stirring twice daily. Strain out the leaves, press gently and use only the liquor.

BALM

The smell of lemon is exuded by this plant which has been a popular culinary herb for centuries. Use 1 quart measure of the leaves, stripped from their stalks. Continue as for agrimony.

CHAMOMILE

Has a flavour akin to apple and banana.

Use 1 heaped teaspoonful of flower heads, placed in a Pyrex jug or similar. Pour on boiling water, cover and infuse till it is cool. Strain out the flowers and use the liquor.

CLARY

Has a sage-like smell, yet imparts a muscatel-like flavour. Use 3 pints of the blue flower heads. Continue as for agrimony.

COFFEE

Use 225 g (½ lb) freshly-ground coffee, simmer it gently for twenty minutes in 2 quarts of cold water, leave to cool, then strain into the must.

GINGER

Use 60 g (2 oz) whole root ginger, which should be well bruised so that the flavour can be leached out. Boil it in a quart of water for 20 minutes, together with the thinly pared rind of two or three lemons and/or oranges, depending on their size. A pinch of cayenne pepper emphasises the ginger flavour and should also be added, but *don't* overdo this. Leave the essence to cool, then strain and add the liquor only to the must.

MINT

There are many varieties of this herb, of which the best known are spearmint and peppermint, as well as the common garden mint. Use only the leaves pulled from their stalks and wash them clean. A litre measure or about 1¾ pint (USA 1 quart) is ample. Continue as for agrimony.

NETTLE

The well known stinging nettle has been used for thousands of years to flavour beers and wines. Use the tops of young plants. They are rich in minerals and vitamins, especially iron and vitamin C, and have a somewhat bitter taste. You may prefer nettle beer to nettle wine. Use 2 quart measures of nettle tops excluding tough stalk. Wash them in cold water and then boil gently for half an hour in 3 quarts of water. Leave to cool and then strain into the must.

PARSLEY

Another herb rich in minerals and vitamins. Pick the leaves of a mature plant in June but exclude the stem base. As always, wash the leaves and then simmer 1 lb of them in 3 quarts of water for 20 minutes. Leave to cool, then strain into the must.

The lactose should be omitted since Parsley makes a light table wine that is especially enjoyable when served with fish.

TEA

Every variety or blend of tea makes a brew of a different flavour so use your favourite. Twelve tea bags (10 g) are enough to flavour six bottles of wine. They contain much tannin, so if you use another base recipe than the one mentioned, omit tannin.

Place the tea bags in a large pot, pour on boiling water, leave for no more than 10 minutes. Strain out the tea bags, leave the tea to cool and then add it to the must. You may if you wish omit the lactose from this wine, but most people prefer it to be slightly sweet, rather than dry.

THYME

This is a very popular herb used frequently in most kitchens for flavouring stuffing for poultry, pork, lamb and the like. There are several different varieties of which the best known is lemon-flavoured. However there is an orange-flavoured thyme and a common garden thyme which are equally attractive. Use one pint of flowers and leaves stripped from their stalks. Continue as for agrimony.

YARROW

This herb is widely used for flavouring beverages in many different parts of the world. It is rich in minerals and salts and has a hot, bitter taste which 'grows' on you. Use 3 quart measures of flowers and leaves stripped from their stalks. Continue as for agrimony.

Wines from your Freezer

MANY winemakers own freezers. If you are among them, during the summer months when picking soft fruit, put some aside in the freezer, earmarked for wine. The crop never comes all at once and picking is often spread over three weeks. Rarely is there enough at one picking to make wine, but with a freezer the whole crop can be saved.

Packing

When freezing fruit for winemaking it is sufficient, after cleaning, to pack it dry, free from sugar or syrup, although this may be used if available. For the soft fruits such as loganberries, mulberries, strawberries, raspberries, blackcurrants, redcurrants, gooseberries, elderberries, blackberries and bilberries, flat plastic cartons are especially suitable. Place the carton, labelled with the name of the fruit and the date, in the coldest part of the freezer.

Larger or harder fruits such as apricots, damsons, apples, pears, peaches, pineapples, plums, nectarines and the like need only be washed, stoned and packed into polythene bags, the necks fastened tightly, and placed in the freezer. Damaged fruit must, of course, have the offending parts removed and then be soaked for a minute or two in water containing a Campden tablet and a little citric acid. This prevents oxidation or browning which would taint the finished wine.

Crushing facilitated

Fruit will keep well in a good freezer for at least one year and often longer. That some fruits become pappy when thawed is a positive advantage for winemaking. One of the difficulties in making wine from certain fruits is the inability to crush them easily and so enable the juices and flavours to be fully extracted. Freezing does this job perfectly for the winemaker and facilitates a juice extraction of between 75% and 80% of the weight of the fruit.

Convenience

The other great advantage of a freezer to the amateur winemaker is that wine no longer HAS to be made on the same day that a quantity of fruit is received — which was often inconvenient and sometimes impossible, for one reason or another! The freezer has therefore become the winemaker's friend, and stores the fruit in a perfectly fresh condition until it is convenient to make the wine. Because of this particular problem, before the advent of freezers home winemakers turned to canned or dried fruit and to fruit concentrates for making wine at their convenience. But there is no substitute quite as good as fresh fruit, and with a freezer the winemaker can now always use the best.

New recipes

Having frozen and stored the fruit until it is convenient to turn it into wine, the next step is a most interesting one. Instead of using only one kind of fruit at a time (because that is all that is available), the freezer now makes it possible to make new and different wines from unusual blends of fruit. Blackberry and apple is an old favourite, but now you can try apple and blackcurrant; elderberry and blackcurrant; apple and raspberry — that sets the taste buds watering! And countless other wines of your choice. Use the same quantities as for fresh fruits. N.B. A crushed vitamin C tablet added before freezing maintains the colour.

Faults: Cause & Remedy

THERE are not many ailments a wine can suffer if it is correctly made, and it is much easier to prevent disorders than to cure them. The wise and generous use of acid and sulphite, coupled with the exclusion of air, can prevent almost every problem. Clean, sterile, natural polythene mashing bins, fermentation and storage vessels; good quality, sterile bungs and corks; regular racking; well-filled jars and bottles — these are the factors that can prevent disorders.

The most common fault found in a variety of wines is an off-putting smell and taste. This may be caused by:

1 Putrefaction Yeast cells and fruit pulp decompose in the same way as all vegetable matter. If they are not removed in good time, the wine absorbs the putrefying flavours. Once present in a wine these cannot be removed and the wine should be discarded. Prevention is achieved simply by racking the clearing wine from its sediment as soon as it appears.

2 Mousiness This smell and taste — reminiscent of mice — is caused by bacteria, probably of the *lactobacillus* group. It occurs only in wines low in acid that have not been adequately sulphited. Sufficient acid should be included in the preparation of every must and sulphite should be added immediately after fermentation. There is no cure for an infected wine.

3 Vinegar taint Although a wine may not have turned completely to vinegar the unpleasant smell and taste may be present. This could be due to infection by *mycoderma aceti* which floats invisibly in the air or are carried by the tiny fruit fly. Certain species of wild yeast, especially *Hansenula*, if present in a wine cause the vinegar smell, ethyl acetate. *Lactobacillus* also produce acetic acid from the dextrins that may be present. Finally, acetobacter will produce the vinegar taint. There is no cure and the wine should be discarded.

The must and wine should be protected by keeping them well covered at all times. Ingredients to be used should be washed and any infected or damaged portions removed. The mashing bin must be kept well covered with a lid or sheet of polythene secured with a rubber band, or a thick cloth tied down. Fermentation should be under an air-lock, sulphite should be added when the wine is racked, jars and bottles should be kept full and tightly stoppered.

4 Bad-egg smell Should a wine smell of bad eggs (hydrogen sulphide) it is because there was a lack of pantothenic acid in the must. This is a vitamin in the B1 group and essential to promote healthy yeast. Many winemakers include a 3 mg Benerva tablet with the nutrient. The addition of grape in one form or another is the best nutrient but Tronozymol is a well-balanced artificial nutrient and will prevent what is an incurable condition.

5 Pear drops This smell — amyl acetate — also occurs because of insufficient nutrient. The yeast needs nitrogen to function effectively and this it obtains from the ammonium in the nutrient salts or from the grape. Without it, this unpleasant smell and taste can spoil the wine.

6 Bitter almonds This smell and taste come from the kernels of crushed pips and fruit stones, and is due to prussic acid. It cannot be cured and could be dangerous to health. It will not occur if care is taken to exclude large fruit stones and not to crush small pips.

7 Geranium smell This unattractive smell has occasionally been noticed in wines that have been treated with sorbate to inhibit fermentation. The precise doses required for this are not yet certain, and until more information is available, it is better to use only racking and sulphite to terminate fermentation.

8 Sulphur The use of too much sulphite can taint a wine with the smell of sulphur. Up to 100 p.p.m. is perfectly safe, since commercial wines sometimes contain up to 300 p.p.m. Aeration of the wine by pouring it into another container frequently drives the smell away.

9 No bouquet Acid is the cornerstone of bouquet and flavour. If a finished wine has little or no smell, the cause is almost certainly due to lack of acid in the must. It is too late to add any when the wine is finished and the only cure is to blend the wine with one in which the flavour is too strong.

10 Medicinal taste Due to lack of acid in the fermentation. Blending is the only remedy.

Other ailments are:

Plum 'Bloom'

Sometimes plum and damson wines develop a 'bloom' which detracts from their appearance though not from their bouquet or flavour. This is possibly due to the sticky wax, sometimes very pronounced, on the skin of the fruit. It has been described as a hydrophillic wax, but other waxy fruits such as quince do not develop this bloom in the wine. Another possibility is suspended protein molecules. No adequate answer has yet been found, though thoroughly washing the fruit in hot water — to which has been added a handful of washing soda — will help.

Hazes

Before trying to remedy a haze it is always best to diagnose the cause. This saves much time since filtering alone is not always effective.

Pectin can easily be detected in a finished wine that appears hazy. Pectin-testing reagents can be purchased but ordinary methylated spirit will do. Simply pour some methylated spirit into a small bottle and add a 5 ml spoonful of the wine to be tested. Shake the bottle vigorously and then leave it to settle. If the haze is caused by pectin, jelly like clots or strings will appear, although this may take up to an hour.

The treatment is to mix the appropriate quantity of a pectin-destroying enzyme with a little of the wine to obtain a smooth paste. Stir in some wine — about a pint — and leave it in a warm place (25°C) for an hour, shaking the bottle gently from time to time. Stir this into the hazy wine until it is well mixed, then replace the cork and air-lock and stand the jar in a warm place for three or four days. When the wine begins to clear, move it to a cold place to encourage precipitation. As soon as the wine is quite clear rack the wine into a clean jar or bottle it.

In wines prepared from grains or vegetables, a possible cause of haze is starch. Starch is a polysaccharide not fermentable by wine yeast until it has been reduced by enzyme action to the monosaccharides: dextrin and glucose. Starch in a wine may be in the form of a protective colloid like pectin or simply in micro-particles. A testing reagent may be bought but ordinary iodine does just as well. Place a small quantity of wine in a bottle or test tube and add 5 drops of iodine. If starch is present the wine will turn blue or blue/black.

The remedy for this condition is the enzyme diastase sometimes sold as a fungal amylase. Use it in the quantities and method recommended by the manufacturer. They vary but are equally effective.

Metal hazes can usually be detected by a metallic taste and brownish colour in the wine. The remedy is too technical for use in the home and such wines are best discarded.

Ropiness

Very occasionally a wine will develop an oily or slimy appearance, due to infection by a member of the family of lactic acid bacteria. It is variously called *Leuconostoc* or *Streptococcus mucilaginosus, var. vini*. The bacteria form a long string or rope of a polysaccharide containing galactose, mannose, arabinose and galacturonic acid. The remedy is to add sulphite at the rate of 100 p.p.m. and to beat the wine well with a wooden spoon.

This breaks down the long chain of molecules and after a few days a sediment is formed and the wine returns to normal. It should be racked into a clean and sterile jar or bottles and may safely be consumed. But prevention is better than cure and adequate sulphite immediately after fermentation prevents this disorder.

Malo-lactic ferment

Another member of the same family originally called *Bacterium gracile* but now regarded as a member of the *Leuconostoc* species is the cause of the malo-lactic fermentation which occurs in inadequately sulphited fruit wines.

It has already been indicated that malic acid is a major constituent of many fruits and, therefore, remains in the wine after fermentation. If the wine is not properly sulphited this bacteria can convert the malic acid into lactic acid and carbon dioxide during the period of maturation. As a result the wine tastes less sharp and has an attractive *petillance* or sparkling appearance. This probably accounts for apparently dry wines beginning to ferment even after bottling and especially when the weather begins to warm up. Whilst a malo-lactic fermentation is not necessarily a disorder in so far as the wine does not become undrinkable or unattractive, nevertheless it can cause blown corks or burst bottles which can be the source of inconvenience and danger. Far better to control your wine totally by using sulphite.

GREEN punted bottles of 75 cl capacity are best for wine since these exclude light, but colourless Sauternes bottles may also be used, and indeed are stipulated for exhibitions. All previous labels should be removed and the bottles should be scrubbed clean with a bottle brush (some staining is quite difficult to remove except with the aid of a brush). Hold the bottle up to the light to ensure that it is quite clean, then rinse in cold water and dry the outside, before sterilising it with a sulphite solution.

Bottles should be filled to just above the neck so that the gap between the top of the wine and the bottom of the cork is about 2 cm ($\frac{3}{4}$ in).

New cylindrical corks of the best available quality should be used if the wine is to be stored for more than a few months. Corks removed from other bottles are unsuitable since they will have been pierced in some way when being removed. Cork stoppers, such as those used in sherry bottles, are not suitable for long storage but may be used for wines that will soon be consumed. Plastic stoppers rarely fit well enough although improvements in them are being made. The one exception is the hollow-domed plastic stopper used for sparkling wines.

A corking machine of one of the types illustrated should be used to insert the corks into the bottles. The corks must first be softened by soaking them in a sulphite solution for 24 hours, or in hot water for half an hour followed by a sulphite rinse. Keep them under the water all the time by placing a plate or the like upon them. Shake the loose water off the cork, insert it into the corker, place the corker on to the mouth of the bottle and press the lever. A firm base is required for the bottle and if a flogger is used to drive home the handle of the corker then it is advisable to stand the bottle on a wad of absorbent material such as a folded towel or a sponge.

The cork should fit flush with the edge of the bottle mouth. Some winemakers use a plastic adhesive cap to ensure that the bottle does not leak or the cork come out. Others wire across the mouth of the bottle just to secure the cork. Unfortunately the quality of the corks available to the home winemaker is rarely good enough to risk laying a full bottle of wine on its side without fear of the cork giving way sooner or later. By laying a bottle on its side the cork is kept moist and swollen by the wine, and is thus prevented from drying out and admitting air through the pores.

After corking, each bottle should be briefly labelled with its name and date before being put away in a cool store.

A purpose-built bottle rack is illustrated and is the ideal, but in the absence of such storage facilities, bottle cartons make excellent substitutes. Indeed, these are particularly useful for sparkling wines in that the bottles can be stored upside down, so that the sediment from the secondary fermentation can collect in the hollow domes of the stoppers.

Always use well-softened corks, shaken free from surface water. Better still, give them a final soak in wine! These corkers are quite inexpensive and well worth using even for as few as six bottles at a time. Sterilise them before and after use.

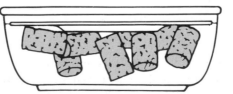

If the storage place available is not of a cool, even temperature, cover the cartons with some insulating material, old blankets or sacks, so as to protect the wine against substantial changes in temperature.

It is a good idea always to keep some half bottles, so that from time to time one can be tried to see how the wine is developing. In this way, the main stock can be saved until the wine is fully matured.

Blending

Even when all possible care has been taken in the preparation, fermentation and maturation of a wine, it can occasionally turn out to be a disappointment. The reason probably lies in the quality or flavour of the base ingredient used. In general, the better the fruit or other ingredients, the better the wine. However, one variety of a fruit may produce a better wine than another variety of the same fruit. Almost nothing is known about this subject. Experienced winemakers always try to use a blend of different varieties or to blend together a number of different base ingredients. There is room for enormous experiment here and no two wines are ever the same.

It can happen that although a wine is free from all fault, its flavour is not attractive. The answer is not to throw the wine away, but to blend it with another. It is not possible to provide firm instructions for blending, but there is little success to be gained by putting a little of this with a little of that, and then tasting it! After blending wines together, further chemical changes occur which can entirely alter the wine. Frequently deposits are thrown, and often a re-fermentation will occur. In any case, it takes some little time for a blend of wines to homogenise.

When the wine appears ready for bottling, taste it and try to assess its quality and character. If you are satisfied then bottle it. If you are not — and don't be too easily satisfied — then put it on one side for blending. As soon as you have several such wines, think about them. Guide lines for blending are to mix opposites. Thin wines with thick wines, too dry with too sweet, too acid with too bland, too astringent with too flabby, too strong with too weak, those with no flavour with those with too much. More than two wines may be blended and red may be blended with white.

Pour all the wines to be blended into a bin, and give them a good stir. Wash out and sterilise the jars and then refill them. Check the specific gravity and if there is any sugar present decide whether you want a sweet wine or a dry. If there is some sugar present and you want a dry wine, then fit an air-lock and stand the jar in a warm place. If you want a sweet wine, then add crushed sulphite tablets at the rate of 100 p.p.m. — i.e. 2 per standard demijohn. Keep blended wines in bulk for a month or two before bottling them, and then think of a suitable name for them.

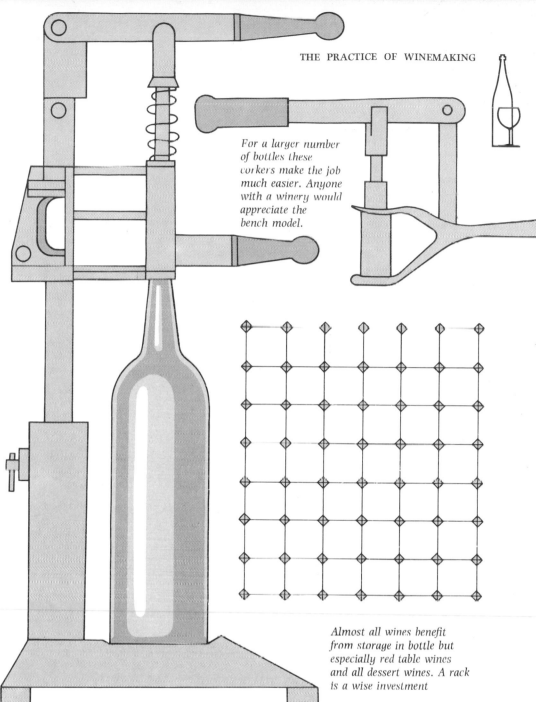

For a larger number of bottles these corkers make the job much easier. Anyone with a winery would appreciate the bench model.

Almost all wines benefit from storage in bottle but especially red table wines and all dessert wines. A rack is a wise investment

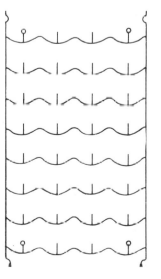

An excessively sweet wine can only be reduced by blending it with a drier wine. A dry wine, however, may be sweetened by the addition of sugar just prior to serving, by the addition of lactose when bottling, or by the addition of saccharin at any time. Always add too little at first so that more has to be added. It is so much easier to add than to take away.

Blending is only for sound wines, the flavour of which is not to your standard. No wine that suffers from any disorder should be blended, because it will infect the sound wine. You can't get rid of a vinegar taste by blending, nor can you get rid of any taint caused by bacterial infection. There is no alternative but to cut your losses.

Blending is an art which can improve considerably the quality of average wines. There is no shame in blending. It shows, instead, an awareness of quality and a refusal to be satisfied with less than the best.

How to serve Wine well

Without wine in the bottle it is hard to have guests
OLD CHINESE PROVERB

Maturity

BEFORE selecting a wine to serve make sure that it is in fact ready for it. It should be absolutely star-bright and adequately mature, free from rough edges, astringency, overstrong flavours, yeastiness, vinegar taste — indeed from all imperfections. Too many wines are drunk before they reach their prime.

Taste buds start tingling at the sight of wine served on a silver salver

Suitability

Some experience with wine can show you that different wines accompany different foods with more success than others. A sweet peach wine, for example, makes a perfect accompaniment to the sweet dessert course of a meal but tastes almost sickly with roast meats. Conversely, a dry elderberry, black-berry or bilberry tastes quite splendid with roast beef or a grilled steak but most unpleasant with a sweet dish. In the same way, a dry gooseberry or parsley or pea pod wine tastes excellent with fish and white meats. Each wine will be found to have its mate and the search to match the two is indeed worth the effort.

Before taking a wine from stock then, consider the purpose for which it is to be served. Is it to be an aperitif? Then it should be especially clean and tangy, perhaps dry or nearly so, preferably light with sufficient alcohol to calm the stomach nerves and relax them for the meal to come.

Is it to accompany a meal? Then choose a wine to complement the food. Rosé wine will accompany a light meal very elegantly. A sparkling wine will add vivacity to any meal, but especially with pork and poultry. The tannin in red wine balances the heavy texture of red meat and game. The dry crispness of a white wine enhances the flavours of salmon, sole and skate as well as cold chicken and the like.

After dinner serve a sweet and strong dessert wine, either red or white. If friends have just dropped in for a chat, then choose a medium-dry-cum-semi-sweet wine, a little stronger than a table wine but not as strong as a dessert. Serve it in a fair-sized, friendly glass and offer some savoury biscuits or nuts.

There are suitable wines for every occasion. Make sure that the wine you serve is quite fitted for its purpose.

Temperature

White and rosé wines benefit from being chilled for an hour or two in the refrigerator to make them crisp and fresh. Sparkling wines should be disgorged beforehand and served quite cold — around 8–10°C (45–50°F). This helps to retain the bubbles for longer and prevent the wine from becoming prematurely flat.

A red wine should be served free from chill to soften the harshness of the tannin. At least a couple of hours in a warm room is necessary.

Serving wine at the temperature appropriate to its type is not a foible of the wine snob. It is an intelligent application of the knowledge gained from making wine and knowing something of its chemistry.

Decanters and Carafes

Because chemical reactions continue in wine throughout its life, many wines throw a further deposit during their storage in bottle. Accordingly the bottle should be stood upright a day or two so that the sediment can slip to the bottom. Before serving, the clear wine should be carefully poured into a decanter or carafe, leaving the sediment behind. Hold the bottle firmly in one hand in such a position that you can see the sediment clearly as it slides up the inside of the bottle. Take a decanter or carafe in the other hand and pour the wine slowly down the inside of the decanter, watching the sediment all the time. As the sediment nears the neck raise up the bottle and cut off the flow. This process is called decanting. The sediment need not be thrown away because it can be added to a gravy sauce to improve the flavour.

Apart from enabling the wine to be served clear, decanting helps the wine to absorb a little oxygen in the process, and improves the bouquet. The wine also looks much better in a decanter than in a bottle, no matter how pretty the label.

All wines, with the exception of sparkling ones, seem to benefit from a period in a decanter just prior to serving. Older wines need less time than young wines simply because they are more mature. Reds need longer than whites because of their extra tannin.

After use, a decanter should be washed immediately and drained dry. Stained decanters are easily cleaned by filling them with tepid water containing Chempro or a bleach. After an hour or so they should be emptied and rinsed several times, until all trace of smell has gone. Lead shot, sand, chain, or similar abrasives only aggravate the situation by making the inside of the decanter even rougher than at first.

Glasses

A glass is to wine what a frame is to a picture. It should isolate the wine and concentrate one's gaze upon it free from every distraction. The glass should be colourless and consist of an incurved bowl to retain the bouquet. An almost spherical bowl is best for table wines but thinner and longer bowls are best for sparkling wines. The bead is then concentrated and elongated and adds considerably to the appearance of a sparkling wine — which, by its very nature, has to be served straight from the bottle, without the aesthetic aid of a decanter.

Aperitif glasses are often a smaller version of the tulip-shaped glass and are epitomised by the sherry *copita*. Liqueurs need smaller glasses because only smaller, often highly-coloured, quantities are served.

A glass should also have a stem with which to pick it up, and a base by which to hold it, with the thumb on the top of the base and the fingers spread out beneath it. In this way the highly-polished bowl is never touched by hand and so obscured by finger prints.

After use, glasses should be washed in a warm detergent water, rinsed in clean cold water, *drained* dry and polished. Before use they should always be repolished with a clean dry cloth free from lint, to remove any dust, either inside or outside the glass.

A decanter and glasses look best on a polished silver tray which reflects every hint of hue and brilliance. A coloured tray distracts from the wine and should never be used. It is better to cover it with a white cloth.

Food

Consider very carefully the food that you serve with wine, so that the one enhances the other. Nearly all wines need a biscuit at the very least.

Company

Consideration must also be given to the people who are to drink your wine. If someone only enjoys sweet wine it is discourteous to serve them a dry wine which they will not like. The converse is equally true. If a person really prefers beer then you may be wasting an excellent wine on a non-discerning palate. If some prefer tea or coffee, then save your wine for other guests. Serve your best wine to your best friends on occasions to be remembered. Serve your ordinary wines within the family.

Drinking

Glasses should be just over half filled but never more than two-thirds filled. This enables the bouquet to collect on top of the wine and leaves room for the nose to get into the glass and so savour the bouquet. A completely full glass is not only difficult to move without spilling, but also looks greedy and lacks aesthetic appeal.

The glass should be lifted by the stem and held by the base. First raise it to the light to inspect the clarity and hue of the wine. It should, of course, be absolutely star-bright. Red wines should wear a rich robe, devoid of blue or brown tints; the white or golden wines may have a hint of green or straw but should look clean, fresh and attractive. Rosé wines should be a pale but pretty pink and not a light red or a pale tawny. Sparkling wine should be almost colourless, to enhance the vision of the dancing bubbles. Liqueurs should have a jewel-like quality and look smooth, highly polished and rich.

Raise the glass to your nose and take a deep breath. The volatile esters and aldehydes should be free from taint, clean and appealing. They may possess fruitiness or vinosity, but the experience should be so enjoyable that you feel encouraged to go on smelling the wine.

When you taste the wine take a good mouthful, not a tiny sip. Swirl the wine around your gums, your cheeks and your tongue, so that all the taste buds can react. Astringency will be quickly spotted by your gums and set them tingling. Excess acidity will be tasted on the front of your tongue, whilst the excess tannin will show up on the sides of your tongue and cheeks. Sweetness will be evident on the top of your tongue and alcohol at the very back. All should be in harmony. When you swallow wait quietly for the farewell to show up on the elbow of your tongue, just where it enters your throat. Some wines have no farewell; others linger deliciously.

All of these different sensations of sight, smell, taste and farewell add up to a full appreciation of the wine. Get the utmost out of it.

After a few moments of silent concentration, share your thoughts with those about you. There is still more pleasure to be had from the wine by talking about it with like-minded friends — everyone an oenophile.

Exhibiting Wine

PREPARATION

THERE is great satisfaction in making good wine that an experienced judge publicly proclaims to be the best in its class. To attain this kind of success in exhibiting there are a few rules to follow. When you hear of a Show in which you contemplate exhibiting wine, first get a schedule of classes and read this carefully. Some schedules include definitions of wine styles. Make sure that you understand them and that you comply with them when presenting your exhibits. Here is such a list of definitions:

Aperitif A wine that can be drunk by itself before a meal and stimulates the appetite.
Table wine A wine that is suitable for accompanying a meal, Generally not too strong in bouquet and flavour, with an alcohol content of only 10–12%. Usually lighter in body and drier than social and dessert wines.
Dessert wine This wine can be white, golden, red or tawny. It needs to be rich in bouquet and flavour, medium to sweet, full bodied and of high alcohol content. It should be served at the end of a meal.
Social wine Widely made and drunk. This wine is intended for drinking other than with a meal. It is usually less strong and rich than a dessert wine, though with more flavour and sweetness than a table wine.
Rosé wine NOT necessarily made from rose petals, this wine should be pink, delicate in bouquet and flavour, light in texture and alcohol and dry to medium dry. It is suitable for serving at any time.

Select the classes in which you think you have suitable wines. If you are in any doubt as to the meaning of a class, ask for clarification; don't assume anything.

Having decided on the classes in which you propose to enter, look over your wines and make sure you have some really worthwhile entries. When you have made your selection, complete your entry form and send it off to the Entries Secretary at once.

Set about preparing your wines without delay and do not wait until the night before the Show. The schedule usually demands colourless wine bottles of the Sauternes type. All cork stoppers are normally specified, also the position where labels are to be fixed. Wash your bottles inside and out, rinse thoroughly, drain dry and wipe the outside with a cloth. Fill each bottle, preferably with the top half of two bottles of the same wine. In this way there can be no question of sediment being transferred. If the wine is not star-bright, filter it. Fill the bottle to that position in the neck that is about 2 cm ($\frac{3}{4}$ in) from the bottom of the cork when it is inserted. Insert a clean, preferably new, cork stopper, tie on a temporary label and stand the bottle in a cool place till the entry labels arrive.

Be especially careful not to enter a sweetish wine in a dry class nor a dryish wine in a sweet class. Dessert wines need to have an S.G. of 1.020 or thereabout. Dry wines should be 1.000 or below. Rosé wines are pink – not red, yellow or brown!

When the labels do come, stick them on to the correct bottles in the precise place indicated, *ie* slap between the seams and not nearer to one than the other nor across one of them, and the correct distance from the bottom of the bottle as prescribed in the schedule. Wipe the bottle free from paste, gum and fingermarks and wrap it in tissue paper till the entry day. Take the wine to the Show in good time and sit back knowing that you have done your best.

To the visitor to the Show, the hundreds of bottles will superficially look most attractive. The judge sees each separately and is looking for trouble. He will first check that each bottle has been placed correctly in the class by the stewards and that he has no 'foreigners' in his group. Then the bottles are counted and the individual registration numbers are entered on his mark sheet.

JUDGING

Presentation
Each bottle is first scrutinised individually to see that it is of the style specified by the schedule; also the cork. Next, that the bottle is free from stains, chips, cracks, scratches and manufacturer's descriptive indentations and engravings. The cork is inspected for cleanliness and correct positioning and the label also. 2 marks are awarded for perfection.

Clarity and colour
The wine is then inspected in the bottle for clarity and colour. Marks are deducted for the slightest haze or sediment, or some piece of cork or other matter floating in the wine. Sweet wines are checked for late sweetening, for sometimes the sugar can be seen swirling around on its own. Clarity must be star-bright, the colour according to the schedule. A red must have a rich robe, free from blue or brownish tints. A white or golden wine must be what it says and not tawny or pinky. Perfection attracts 4 points.

The wine is inspected by eye and nose

Bouquet

When all the bottles have been so checked, one by one, the steward starts with the first bottle, removes the stopper and pours a small quantity into one of the judge's tasting glasses. The judge inspects the wine in the glass, gives it a swirl, notes what he sees and inhales the bouquet deeply. He may do so several times whilst evaluating its quality: freedom from off-putting smells; the depth or shallowness of the bouquet; its fruitiness or vinosity; any acidity or sweetness. All these he notes and eventually evaluates with 4 points for perfection – rarely, alas, achieved!

Flavour faults

But now comes the real test, for the judge takes a mouthful of wine, swirls it round his mouth several times and over his uvula before spitting it out. Then he sits quietly waiting for the farewell, while he evaluates the greeting, the texture, the balance, the flavour and so on. Imperfections in balancing a must stand out; lack of acid or tannin; too much of one strongly flavoured ingredient; the wrong kind of sugar e.g. a brown sugar in a Moselle type wine; too much sugar resulting in too much alcohol. Imperfections in fermenting or maturing the wine; a too-long fermentation on the pulp; a too-long storage on a sediment of dead yeast, resulting in off flavours; too much air admitted and with it *mycoderma aceti*, the vinegar bug, or some other spoilage organism. Too long left badly corked or the jar not filled so that oxidation has occurred and the wine has gone flat. These are the sort of faults the judge is looking for and deducts points from the perfection of 20. But who makes perfect wine? A very good wine might get 16 or even 17 points, an average wine 12 or 13 points. A poor wine 8 or 10 points or, if diseased, none at all.

Adjudication and palate renewed

The steward empties the glass and washes it before preparing to pour the second wine into a clean glass. The judge adds up the points, writes a few comments or remarks and cleans his palate with a piece of dry biscuit, a piece of cheese, a piece of apple, some dry bread or clean cold water.

The wine is 'chewed' in the mouth and evaluated

Adjudication Marks

Bottle No	Presentation	Clarity Colour	Bouquet	Balance Flavour and Quality	Total	Remarks
2	4	4	20	30	. . . . .

Some judges work entirely in silence, concentrating exclusively on the task in hand. Others talk to their steward, share a wine with him, explain the merits and faults of a wine. In this way the skill of judging is passed on and others are encouraged.

Placing the finalists

When all the wines have been assessed six or eight are selected for reassessment. Many judges place a clean glass in front of each bottle and have some wine poured into it. The wines are then compared one with another and placed in an order of merit. No mean task this and in a big class of more than 100 entries it is customary to have three or more judges sorting out the best wines for a fresh judge to come along and adjudicate. It can easily take as long to place 6 or 8 wines in an order of merit as to sort out those 6 or 8 wines from the rest of the class.

Judges agree

Details of the placings are written up and taken to the Show Secretary, together with the judges' comments on the class as a whole. The judge still has no idea who has entered any given bottle and usually has no wish to know. It is the more interesting then, that a good winemaker, who has entered wines in several different classes, may get placed in each one. It says much for their competence that different judges can all spot the same good quality of wine in different classes.

Questions to the Judge

Stewards stick on the prize-winning labels and when the exhibitors attend to see the Show, the judge may be called upon to answer questions about the wines he has adjudicated. There is often a splendid opportunity here to assist exhibitors. When different factors are pointed out to them they realise where they went wrong. In other Shows individual written comments are placed under the bottle for the exhibitor to read at his leisure.

The Guild of Judges

In Great Britain there is a group of some 200 trained judges qualified by a difficult examination. They are held in very high esteem and their services are in constant demand. It is counted an honour to be a member of the Amateur Wine and Beer Maker's National Guild of Judges.

Emblem of the Amateur Winemakers' National Guild of Judges

Liqueurs

THE very word 'liqueur' conjures up a vision of luxury. Liqueurs have always been expensive and used to be associated with a life-style exclusive to the rich. In recent years the situation has changed in two ways. A sophisticated life-style is now enjoyed by a great many more people, and means have been developed for the making of liqueurs in the home at a modest cost. Very little expertise is required, and very pleasant liqueur-like drinks can be made in a very short time.

A liqueur is defined as an alcoholic beverage containing spirit, sugar and flavouring. It can be of a very high or a relatively low alcohol content, either very sweet or quite dry, and of any colour or of no colour at all.

Liqueurs are made commercially in several different ways. Firstly there are the fruit brandies such as *Calvados* (known as *Apple Jack* in North America and Canada) and *Slivovitz*, the fiery plum brandy made in Yugoslavia. A wine is first made from the fruit juice and this is then distilled and refined in much the same way as grape brandy. Fruits so used include apples, bananas, blackberries, blackcurrants, peaches, pears, plums, raspberries and strawberries. They are sometimes described as *Eaux de Vie* and always have a high alcohol content of 40%, sometimes described as 70° Proof. They are usually unsweeted. Because of the large quantity of fruit that has to be used, these liqueurs are always very expensive.

Another style of liqueur is made from steeping the fruit in a grape brandy for some months so that the flavour of the fruit is absorbed by the brandy. Sugar is usually added to emphasise the fruit flavour. A well-known example is *Apricot Brandy*. The alcohol content is much lower, between 24 and 28% alcohol, or 40 to 50° Proof. Almost any fruit may be used, including those just mentioned.

The third way of making liqueurs is by mixing spirits – such as brandy, rum, whisky and vodka – with essences derived from coffee beans, cocoa beans, fruits, herbs, honey and seeds. Such liqueurs include *Anisette, Benedictine, Chartreuse, Crème de Menthe, Drambuie, Kirsch, Tia Maria* and so on. Recipes are frequently secret and are carefully guarded. Most are very strong and some are very sweet.

Ingredients to use in the home

Although brandy, rum and whisky may be used to make liqueurs at home, good results have been, and can be, obtained by using just Vodka, a colourless and tasteless spirit which only adds alcohol and some water to the liqueur. Clearly the stronger you want your liqueurs, the more expensive they will be. Experience has shown that a liqueur-like drink of about 18% alcohol, 31° Proof, is quite acceptable and very reasonable in cost.

It is not necessary to follow the same methods as the commercial manufacturers in obtaining the required flavourings as a wide variety of flavourings can now be bought in tiny bottles ready for adding to a spirit. The flavourings vary, however, in quality and accuracy, and you may find that you prefer certain flavourings from one manufacturer and others from another. Each bottle is supplied with the manufacturer's recipe, but great care should be taken with it. Frequently they are much too strong and experience over a wide variety of flavourings suggest that it is wiser never to use more than two thirds of the essence in the first instance. More can be added if required, but once included it is extremely difficult to diminish and

These beautiful, antique, cordial glasses, between 6 and 7 inches high, were created about 1750. They indicate that the making and drinking of what we now call liqueurs was well-established more than 200 years ago.

Wine, too

Strong wine is almost universally recommended to provide the bulk of the liquor. It is important that this be as bland as possible with no pronounced flavour. A Sauternes-type grape juice concentrate fermented for as long as possible with extra sugar, in conjunction with a Tokay yeast, makes an excellent base. The wine should, of course, be similar in colour to the finished liqueur, e.g. a morello cherry wine should be used for *Cherry Brandy* and a blackcurrant for *Cassis*.

Basic recipe

Vodka	$\frac{1}{4}$ bottle approx 185 ml (6$\frac{1}{2}$ fl oz)	
Caster sugar	6 tbs approx 170 g (6 oz)	
Strong wine	$\frac{2}{3}$ bottle approx 480 ml (17 fl oz)	
Flavouring of your choice		

Put all the ingredients in a jug and stir well but gently, to mix them thoroughly and dissolve the sugar completely. Taste and if necessary adjust the sweetness and/or flavouring. Pour into suitably shaped and sterile bottles, cork and label.

Although the liqueur-like drink may be consumed immediately, it is best to leave it for about a week for the ingredients to homogenize.

This simple recipe may be varied to suit your own palate. The vodka may be increased up to one third of a bottle, with a consequent reduction in the amount of wine required and possibly an increase in the sugar used.

Variations

If you wish rum may be used with the coffee-flavoured essence that produces a Tia Maria-type liqueur. Similarly whisky may be used with a 'honey-smoke' flavouring that makes a Drambuie-type liqueur. Brandy is not suitable with essences and flavourings, since its flavour is too pronounced. But apricots, peaches, plums, raspberries, strawberries and the like may be washed, dried, cut up and steeped in brandy for three months to produce an expensive but very attractive liqueur. Discard the stones at the outset and eat the fruit at the finish. The more fruit used the stronger the fruit flavour. Start off with 110 g (4 oz) of fruit to a bottle of brandy. If the flavour is not strong enough, more fruit may be used. Remember that the flavour of the fruit used varies in location, time and variety. The French colourless brandy 'Eau de Vie pour les Fruits' is best for this purpose.

Gin may be used with sloes or orange skin, but is not successful with other fruits. Wash and stone the sloes or thinly peel or grate the orange skin, avoiding any white pith. Steep the fruit or rind in the gin for three months. Sugar may be used to suit your palate but start with 170 g (6 oz) in the bottle and increase as necessary.

in excess could have a somewhat artificial taste.

Ordinary white sugar is used for sweetening and many of the manufacturers again tend to recommend too much. Two thirds of their recommended quantity is often found to be a more acceptable amount. In any case more can be added if required. Liqueurs can become sickly if too sweet. Some recipes recommend the use of sugar syrup based on the formula of 2 lb sugar dissolved in 1 pint of water but the water dilutes the alcohol and it is far better to dissolve the sugar in the spirit. If a finely ground sugar is used it will dissolve with very little effort. Stir gently in a dry atmosphere so as not to dissipate the alcohol from the spirit.

Cooking with Wine

For many people the very thought of cooking with wine is off-putting, another trouble, too difficult, the creation of new flavours to which the family are not accustomed. The latter alone is true, but the new flavours are most interesting and enjoyable. They are not difficult to create. Very little wine is needed and often the last few drops in a bottle can be used most successfully.

As with so many other ingredients, the first principle is not to use too much. During cooking the alcohol will be vaporised by the heat and so no one need fear intoxication. Wine may be used in the preparation of almost any dish, often only as much as a tablespoonful or so being required. Red, white or rosé, sweet or dry, all may be used. The home wine-maker has a special advantage of a great variety of wines from which to choose.

The following list of recipes is not intended to be comprehensive, rather to point the way and suggest ideas that can be followed up with the wines available.

Stewed fruit
Whenever you cook apples, apricots, blackberries, blackcurrants, greengages, pears, prunes or rhubarb, put wine instead of water into the pan. The flavour is enhanced and the juice is delicious.

Fresh fruit salad
A glassful of wine poured over pineapple, melon or grapefruit, raspberries, strawberries or mixed fruits, then sprinkled with sugar and left for an hour in a cool place, emphasises the flavour.

Marinading
Coarse meats and fish soaked in wine over-night are tenderised, and the flavour is greatly improved. Meat for goulash, or casserole, or pie; fish for baking or kedgeree; poultry for casserole; all benefit from soaking in wine.

Try kipper fillets marinaded in red wine for 24 hours. Drain and skin the fillets, cut them into finger-sized pieces and serve on crisp buttered toast with a dry white wine.

Shrimps or prawn for 'cocktail' *hors d'oeuvres* are much improved if soaked in wine for an hour or two beforehand.

Cherry pie, plum pie and similar dishes improve considerably if the fruit is marinaded overnight in wine.

Roasts, casseroles and stews
All of these dishes can be additionally enjoyed if a glass of wine is poured over them five minutes before serving.

Sauces
Almost every sauce, sweet or savoury, becomes more sophisticated with the addition of a tablespoonful of an appropriate wine – sweet or dry as the case may be. Red wines tend to make sweet white sauces somewhat muddy in appearance, and white wines are therefore recommended. It's the obvious which sometimes gets overlooked!

In place of wine, mead may be used and in many instances beer also. Try sausages poached in beer. Cider and vinegar also help to improve flavours, especially with pork and fish, however cooked. Liqueurs should not be forgotten when ice-creams are made or served. Even a small quantity is deliciously discernible.

Home-made wines, meads, liqueurs, beers, ciders and vinegars are every bit as good in the kitchen as their commercial counterparts.

Note on the Recipes

Nearly all the recipes that appear in the Calendar make six bottles of wine. If greater quantities are required, increase all the ingredients *pro rata*, except the yeast, which remains constant up to 10 gallons – 60 bottles.

The quantities given in metric and Imperial do not always equate precisely. The variations often compensate one another, but in any case are too small to be discernible in the finished wine. Basic ingredients vary so much from place to place and from year to year, that no two wines can ever be quite the same. The specific gravity of concentrated grape juice also varies from one manufacturer to another. An average quality has been assumed and allowed for in the total fermentable sugar content of each recipe. An alcohol content appropriate to the wine will be produced, varying from around 10% for light table wines, to 12% for red table wines, 11–13% for social wines and some 15–16% for dessert wines. Subsequent sweetening is usually left to the differing palates of individual winemakers. Weight watchers may use saccharin.

The Home Winemaker & Brewer's Calendar

January

PARSNIPS and oranges dominate this month's wine making: lager and barley wine are the beers to make. They all need long storage and should be nicely matured by next Christmas.

Wines made in the autumn should be inspected and those that have thrown a new sediment should be racked. Gooseberry wine made last July may now be sparkled. Make sure that you have sufficient champagne bottles, hollow-domed plastic stoppers and wire cages before you begin refermentation. No other bottles are safe and both cylindrical and flange corks are quite unsuitable.

If stocks have been depleted by the recent Christmas festivities make a few 'quickies' to be ready by Easter, or at least Whitsun. White wines mature more quickly than red.

RECOMMENDED RECIPES

White table wine I

Unsweetened orange juice,		
2 cans,	each 1.34 litres	(43 fl oz)
Concentrated grape juice,		
(Chablis type)	1 kg	(1 quart)
White sugar	2.25 kg	(5 lb)
Tartaric acid	3 tsp	
Grape tannin	1½ tsp	
Water	to 13.6 litres	(3 gallons)
Chablis wine yeast and nutrient		

1 Mix all the ingredients together and ferment under an air-lock in a warm place.

2 When fermentation is finished rack into a clean jar, add wine finings and 1 Campden tablet per gallon and leave in a cool place for 2 weeks.

3 As soon as the wine is bright, bottle and keep for a minimum of 2 months. These quantities should give 18 bottles.

White table wine II

Apricot concentrate	1 kg	
Sugar	900 g	(2 lb)
Water	to 4½ litres	(1 gallon)
All-purpose 'Super' wine yeast and nutrient		

Instructions accompany each can. In general make as just described. The quantities indicated should give six bottles.

'Fino Sherry'

Frosted parsnips	1 kg	(2¼ lb)
Carrots	1 kg	(2¼ lb)
Ripe bananas	1 kg	(2¼ lb)
Concentrated grape juice,		
(dry sherry type)	1 kg	(1 quart)
Sugar	2¼ kg	(5 lb)
Tartaric acid	28 g	(1 oz)
Gypsum (calcium sulphate)	56 g	(2 oz)

Cream of tartar	28 g (1 oz)
Pectic enzyme	2 tsp
Nutrient	1 tsp
Vitamin B	3 mg (1 tablet)
Water	7 litres (12 pints)
Sherry wine yeast (flor strain)	

1 Top, tail, scrub and dice the carrots and parnips; peel and slice the bananas; boil all together for 30 minutes and leave to cool.

2 Strain out the solids and make the must up to 7 litres (12 pints) with cool water. Stir in the concentrated grape juice, the pectic enzyme, the acid, gypsum, cream of tartar, nutrient, vitamin B and yeast. Ferment in a bin covered with a sheet of polythene.

3 Dissolve the sugar in $1\frac{1}{4}$ litres (2 pints) of hot water and leave to cool.

4 After 4 days, when the S.G. has fallen to 1.004, stir in about one quarter of the syrup and repeat the process each time the S.G. falls to 1.004 (every 4 or 5 days depending on the temperature) until all the syrup has been added. Then ferment out.

5 As soon as the wine begins to clear, siphon into a 3 gallon (13.6 litres) jar, so that the jar is only two thirds full. Plug the neck with cotton wool and store for 2 months.

6 If the wine is now quite bright, rack into a similar jar, re-plug with cotton wool and leave undisturbed in a cool dry place for 2 years before bottling.

7 If the wine is not bright in 2 months, stir in wine finings and rack after 2 weeks. Makes twelve bottles.

Rosehip and Orange social wine

Rosehip syrup,	340 mls (12 fl oz)
Concentrated orange juice,	340 mls (12 fl oz)
Concentrated grape juice	250 g (9 oz)
Sugar	900 g (2 lb)
Tartaric acid	1 tsp
Grape tannin	$\frac{1}{2}$ tsp
Water	3 litres ($5\frac{1}{2}$ pints)
Pectic enzyme and Campden tablets	
All-purpose wine yeast and nutrient	

The rosehip syrup and concentrated orange juice are available from many chemists and drugs stores.

1 Mix all the ingredients together in a polythene bin, pour into a fermentation jar, top up with cold water, fit an air-lock and ferment to S.G. 1.010.

2 Rack into a clean jar, add 2 Campden tablets to terminate fermentation and wine finings to clear it.

3 Leave in a cool place. As soon as the wine is bright, rack again and store for 3 months before bottling. Makes six bottles.

Serve cool and fresh.

Note: This is a favourite wine with parents of very young children who have stock of the ingredients for their use.

Parsnip and Orange 'Sherry'

Frosted parsnips	1.75 g (4 lb)
Seville oranges	4 only
Concentrated grape juice	250 g (9 oz)
Sugar	1¼ kg (2¾ lb)
Water	3½ litres (6 pints)
Pectic enzyme	
Sherry yeast and nutrient	

1 Top, tail, scrub, dice and boil the parsnips in 2¼ litres (4 pints) water for 30 minutes, then leave to cool.
2 Cut the oranges in halves, express all the juice and discard the hulks after rubbing the skins with a few sugar lumps.
3 Dissolve the soft sugar in ½ litre (1 pint) of hot water and leave to cool.
4 Mix the parsnip liquor, orange juice, grape juice, sugar lumps, pectic enzyme, sherry yeast and nutrient together and pour into a large fermentation jar. Plug the neck with cotton wool and leave in a warm place.
5 After 3 days stir in the sugar syrup, top up to 4½ litres (1 gallon) with cold water, replug with cotton wool and ferment out.
6 Rack into a sterile jar and store under a cotton wool plug for 9 months before bottling.

Parsnip and Fig 'Madeira'

Frosted parsnips	2 kg (4½ lb)
Dried figs	225 g (½ lb)
Raisins	450 g (1 lb)
Brown sugar	1.1 kg (2½ lb)
Citric acid	14 g (½ oz)
Grape tannin	½ tsp
Water	4 litres (7 pints)
Madeira yeast and nutrient	

1 Top, tail, scrub, dice and boil the parsnips in 3½ litres (6 pints) water for 30 minutes.
2 Pour the liquor on to the figs and raisins and when cool add the acid, tannin, yeast and nutrient. Cover and leave in a warm place.
3 Ferment on the pulp, pressing down the fruit cap twice daily.
4 On the fifth day stir in 225 g (½ lb) sugar.
5 On the seventh day, strain out and press the solids.
6 Dissolve the remaining sugar in ½ litre (1 pint) water and add half to the must.
7 Pour into a fermentation jar, fit an air-lock and continue fermentation.
8 Seven days later add the remaining syrup, replace the air-lock and ferment out.
9 Rack into a clean jar, add wine finings and 2 Campden tablets and leave till the wine is bright.
10 Rack again and if necessary sweeten to taste with saccharin. Store in a *warm* place for 1 year before bottling.

Parsnip 'Sauternes'

Frosted parsnips	1.75 kg (4 lb)
Ripe bananas	450 g (1 lb)
Sultanas	450 g (1 lb)
Dried elderflowers or rose petals	7 g (¼ oz)
Acid blend	20 g (¾ oz)
Grape tannin	½ tsp
White sugar	900 g (2 lb)
Water	4 litres (7 pints)
Pectic enzyme and Campden tablets	
Sauternes yeast and nutrient	

1 Top, tail, scrub, dice and boil the parsnips together with the sliced and peeled bananas in 3½ litres (6 pints) of water for 30 minutes.
2 Strain on to the chopped sultanas and dried flowers and when cool add the acid, tannin, pectic enzyme, nutrient and yeast.
3 Cover and ferment on the pulp for 6 days, then strain out and press the solids.
4 Dissolve the sugar in hot water and when cool stir it into the must. Pour it all into a fermentation jar, fit an air-lock and ferment to S.G. 1.016.
5 Rack into a clean jar and add wine finings and 2 crushed Campden tablets. Leave in a cool place till the wine is bright then rack again and store for 9 months before bottling.

Orange 'Sherry'

Seville oranges	8
Sweet oranges	8
Concentrated grape juice, (medium sherry type)	1 kg can
Sugar	2¼ kg (5 lb)
Water	6¼ litres (11 pints)
Sherry yeast and nutrient	

1 Thinly pare the oranges and place the skins in a dish in a cooling oven for 15 minutes.
2 Cut the oranges in halves, express all the juice and discard the hulks.
3 Dissolve the grape juice in 4½ litres (8 pints) cold water, add the orange juice and skins, the nutrient and sherry yeast.
4 Ferment for 4 days before removing the skins.
5 Dissolve the sugar in 1¾ litres (3 pints) water and add to the must. Plug the neck of the jar with cotton wool and ferment in a warm place.
6 When the S.G. falls to 1.006, rack the wine into a clean jar and add 2 crushed Campden tablets.
7 Store for 8 months under a cotton wool plug before bottling.

Orange 'Sauternes'

Seville oranges	4
Sweet oranges	6
Sultanas	450 g (1 lb)

Sugar 1 kg (2¼ lb)
Water 4 litres (7 pints)
Pectic enzyme and Campden tablets
Sauternes yeast and nutrient

1 Thinly pare and chop the orange skins and place them in a mashing bin with the chopped sultanas. Express the juice and discard the hulks.
2 Pour hot water on to the fruit and when cool add the orange juice, pectic enzyme, yeast and nutrient.
3 Ferment on the pulp for 6 days, then strain out and press the fruit, stir in the sugar, pour the must into a fermentation jar, fit an air-lock and ferment in a warm place.
4 When the S.G. has fallen to 1.016, rack into a clean jar and add 2 crushed Campden tablets.
5 Store for 6 months before bottling.

Sultana 'Hock'
Chopped sultanas 1.6 kg (3½ lb)
Citric acid 2 tsp
Grape tannin ½ tsp
Water 4.8 litres (8½ pints)
Hock yeast and nutrient

1 Wash and chop the sultanas, place them in a mashing bin and pour cold water over them.
2 Add the acid, tannin, nutrient, and active yeast. Cover and leave in a warm place.
3 Press down the floating fruit twice daily, until fermentation is finished.
4 Strain out and press the sultanas dry. Pour the young wine into a gallon-sized (4.8 litre) glass jar, add 1 Campden tablet, fit an air-lock and leave the wine in a cool place to clear.
5 Rack into a sterile storage jar and keep for 6 months before bottling.
Note: A 'gallon-sized' jar actually holds 4.8 litres or 8½ pints, to give a full gallon after removal of the sediment.

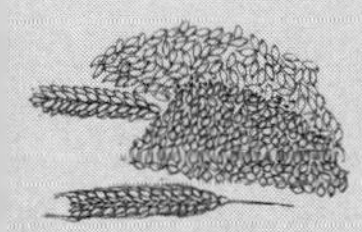

Barley wine
Malt extract 1 kg (2¼ lb)
Diastatic malt extract 14 g (½ oz)
Wheat syrup 50 g (2 oz)
Brown sugar 225 g (½ lb)
Golding hops 28 g (1 oz)
Citric acid ½ tsp
Table salt ¼ tsp
Nutrient ¼ tsp
Water to 4.8 litres (8½ pints)
Activated beer yeast

1 Dissolve the malt extract, wheat syrup, sugar, acid, salt and nutrient in half the water.
2 Boil the hops in the other half for 40 minutes and leave to cool.
3 Strain the hop liquor on to the wort and adjust the quantity to 4.8 litres (8½ pints) and the S.G. to 1.084. Pitch the yeast and ferment right out.
4 Stir in the finings and leave in the cool under an air-lock while the wine clears for a few days. If the barley wine tastes too dry for your liking, sweeten to your taste with lactose or saccharin, NOT sugar. Rack into a clean jar and wait until the wine is quite clear, then siphon into 16 half pint (¼ litre) bottles.
5 Mix 40 g (1½ oz) of sugar with 3 tablespoonsful of an active champagne wine yeast and distribute this into each bottle equally.
6 Crimp on crown caps very tightly and label the bottles with name and date. Store the bottles in a warm place for one week and then in the cool till the barley wine is one year old.
Note: Serve this 11% strong beer/wine at room temperature.

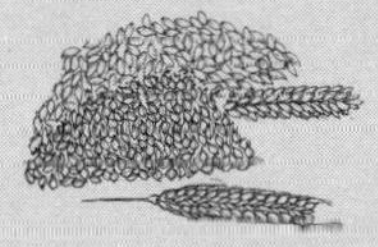

Lager – Special Reserve
Lager malt 550 g (1¼ lb)
Pale malt 56 g (2 oz)
Brumore flour 112 g (4 oz)
Invert sugar 170 g (6 oz)
Brewers' Gold hops 28 g (1 oz)
Soft water 4.8 litres (8½ pints)
Carlsbergensis yeast

1 Place the cracked grains and Brumore flour in a mashing bin, pour on cold water, heat to 62°C and mash for 2 hours.
2 Cool to 55°C and maintain this temperature for another 2 hours.
3 Increase the temperature to 67°C and maintain this to end point of conversion. Check after 30 minutes.
4 Strain off the liquor, wash the grains, add the hops and boil for 45 minutes.
5 Cool as quickly as possible, stir in the invert sugar, adjust the quantity to 4.8 litres (8½ pints) and the S.G. to 1.054.
6 Pitch an active yeast and ferment at 9°C (48°F) until the S.G. falls to 1.006.
7 Rack, bottle and store without priming since fermentation is not complete. Mature for a minimum of 3 months and serve chilled.
Note: Since carlsbergensis yeast ferments from the bottom, fermentation may be conducted in a jar plugged with cotton wool or an air-lock. All the temperatures mentioned are critical and should not be varied more than 1 degree. Make quite sure that stoppers have new rubber rings or the crown caps are very tightly crimped. Store the bottles with their name and date since some of them may be kept for up to a year.

This superb beer is very well worth making if you are prepared to take the necessary time and trouble with the mashing, fermentation and maturing.

February

THERE are usually plenty of Seville oranges still around for those who did not make wine from them last month. Early grapefruits are just reaching the market and will be plentiful and cheaper in late March. Bananas are the best of the fresh fruits. They support all the dried and canned fruits and juices.

Some of the light summer wines made last year may now be ready for bottling or blending. Taste them and give them a critical appreciation before deciding what to do. When you look over your stock, watch out for sediment and be prepared to do some racking.

RECOMMENDED RECIPES

Morello and grape dessert wine

Morello and grape concentrate (1 can)	1 kg	(2 lb 3 oz)
White sugar	450 g	(1 lb)
Water	to 4½ litres	(1 gallon)
All-purpose wine yeast		

Detailed instructions are supplied on the can's label. An attractive sweet dessert wine is produced, ready for drinking in the Autumn.

Morello Cherry 'Port'

Canned or frozen morello cherries	900 g	(2 lb)
Strong ale	2¼ litres	(4 pints)
Caster sugar	450 g	(1 lb)
Tartaric acid	2 tsp	
Grape tannin	½ tsp	
Port yeast and nutrient		

1 Split the cherries, remove and discard the stones, place the fruit in a small mashing bin.
2 Pour in the beer, stir in the sugar, acid and tannin, nutrient and active yeast.
3 Ferment on the pulp, gently pressing down the fruit daily for 14 days.
4 Strain out the fruit and roll it around a nylon sieve, then serve it in a flan with cream.
5 Pour the wine into a fermentation jar and continue fermentation as long as possible. If the S.G. falls to 1.004 stir in a little more sugar.
6 Add some wine finings and as soon as the wine is bright, rack it, sweeten it to taste and bottle it. Keep it for 12 months before serving.

Apricot table wine

Apricot pulp (1 can)	1 kg	(2 lb 3 oz)
White grape juice concentrate	250 g	(9 oz)
White sugar	700 g	(25 oz)
Tartaric acid	2 tsp	
Grape tannin	½ tsp	
Water	3 litres	(5 pints)
Pectic enzyme and Campden tablets		
Chablis yeast and nutrient		

1 Empty the apricot pulp into a mashing bin, pour on the water, add the acid, tannin, pectic enzyme and a Campden tablet, cover and leave for 24 hours.
2 Stir in the grape juice, nutrient and yeast. Ferment on the pulp for 4 days.
3 Strain out the pulp and roll it round a nylon sieve, stir in the sugar, pour the must into a fermentation jar, top up with cold water, fit an air-lock and ferment out.
4 Rack into a sterile storage jar, keep for 3 months, then bottle.

Note: This wine matures quickly and is a delightful, light summer wine worth making in larger quantities.

Gooseberry table wine

| Gooseberries (1 can) | 1 kg (2 lb 3 oz) |

All other ingredients and method exactly as for Apricot table wine. Another splendid, quick maturing, summer wine, it will be ready for drinking in December.

Rosehip wine

Rosehip purée (1 can)	425 g (15 oz)
Sugar	2¼ kg (5 lb)
Pectic enzyme	1 tsp
Water	7.4 litres (13 pints)
Tokay yeast and nutrient	

1 Empty the purée into a fermentation bin and rinse out the can.
2 Dissolve the sugar in some hot water and add to the purée.
3 Top up with cold water to the 2 gallon mark, add an activated yeast, cover and ferment for 2 days.
4 When the tumultuous fermentation has finished, strain into a fermentation jar, fit an air-lock, top up with cold boiled water and ferment out.
5 When the secondary fermentation has finished and the wine begins to clear, siphon it into a sterile jar, add 1 Campden tablet per gallon and store in a cool place.
6 After 4 weeks rack again and repeat in 8 weeks.
7 As soon as the wine is bright, bottle and store for a few weeks.

Banana 'Sauternes'

Ripe bananas	2 kg (4½ lb)
Lemons	2
Concentrated grape juice (Sauternes style)	500 g (18 oz)
Sugar	450 g (1 lb)
Dried rose petals	1 tbs
Tartaric acid	1 tsp
Grape tannin	½ tsp
Water	3½ litres (6 pints)
Pectic enzyme and Campden tablets	
Sauternes yeast and nutrient	

1 Peel the bananas, cut them into slices, boil them for 20 minutes and pour the mixture into a bin.
2 Thinly pare the lemons, chop the rinds and add this to the bananas.
3 Stir in the dried rose petals.
4 When cool add the acid, tannin, pectic enzyme and one Campden tablet and leave for 24 hours.
5 Next day add the lemon juice, grape juice concentrate, nutrient and activated yeast.
6 Ferment on the pulp for 4 days, then strain out the solids and roll them round a nylon sieve.
7 Stir in the sugar, pour the must into a fermentation jar, top up with cold water, fit an air-lock and ferment down to S.G. 1.016.
8 Rack into a clean jar and add 2 crushed Campden tablets to terminate fermentation.
9 Two weeks later, rack again and store for 2 months, then rack again.
10 Serve this sweet wine cold with the dessert course of a meal.

Banana & Fig 'Tokay'

Ripe bananas	2 kg	(4½ lb)
Dried figs	200 g	(7 oz)
Raisins	450 g	(1 lb)
Lemons	2	
Sugar	900 g	(2 lb)
Tartaric acid	2 tsp	
Grape tannin	½ tsp	
Water	4 litres	(7 pints)

Pectic enzyme and Campden tablets
Tokay yeast and nutrient

1 Peel the bananas, slice them and boil them with the figs for 20 minutes.
2 Pour into a mashing bin, add the chopped raisins and when cool the acid, tannin, pectic enzyme and one Campden tablet.
3 Next day add the lemon juice, nutrient and yeast and ferment on the pulp for 5 days.
4 Strain out the solids, stir in the sugar, pour into a fermentation jar, top up, fit an air-lock and ferment down to S.G. 1.016.
5 Rack into a clean jar and add 2 Campden tablets to terminate fermentation.
6 After two weeks rack again, and again after a further 2 months.
7 Keep for 9 months before bottling.
8 Serve this sweet and strong wine as a social wine.

Banana, Rosehip and Fig 'Madeira': Sweet

Bananas	450 g	(1 lb)
Dried rosehip shells	225 g	(8 oz)
Dried figs	125 g	(4½ oz)
Raisins	450 g	(1 lb)
Brown sugar	680 g	(1½ lb)
Water	4 litres	(7 pints)
Citric acid	15 g	(½ oz)
Grape tannin	½ tsp	

Pectic enzyme and Campden tablets
Madeira yeast and nutrient

1 Peel and slice the bananas, rinse the rosehip shells, break up the figs, chop the raisins and place them all in a stewpan with half the water. Bring to the boil and simmer for 15 minutes.
2 Empty the fruit into a mashing bin and add the rest of the cold water, then the acid, tannin, pectic enzyme and Campden tablet. Cover and leave for 24 hours.
3 Next day stir in an active yeast and nutrient, and ferment on the pulp for 5 days. Press the floating fruit down into the must twice daily and keep the must well covered meanwhile.
4 Strain out and press the fruit, stir in the sugar, pour into a fermentation jar, top up with cold water, fit an air-lock and continue fermentation as long as possible by feeding the must with additional sugar if necessary.
5 When fermentation is quite finished, siphon the wine into a sterile storage jar, sweeten to taste, add one Campden tablet and store in the cool till bright.
6 Rack the wine again and then store it in a very warm place for from 3 to 6 months while the wine develops its full Madeira flavour.

Raisin 'Madeira': dry

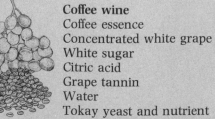

Best large raisins	1.36 kg	(3 lb)
Brown sugar	450 g	(1 lb)
Tartaric acid	1 tsp	
Water	4 litres	(7 pints)

Madeira yeast and nutrient

1 Chop the raisins, being careful not to damage any pips, place in a bin and pour hot water over them.
2 When cool add the acid, yeast and nutrient, and ferment on the pulp for 14 days, pressing down the fruit 'cap' daily.
3 Strain out and press the raisins dry, stir in the sugar, pour the must into a fermentation jar, top up with cold water, fit an air-lock and ferment out.
4 Rack into a clean jar, add one Campden tablet and when the wine is bright, store in a very warm place for from 3 to 6 months.
Serve cool as an aperitif.

Coffee wine

Coffee essence	125 g	(4½ oz)
Concentrated white grape juice	500 g	(18 oz)
White sugar	1 kg	(2¼ lb)
Citric acid	10 g	(⅓ oz)
Grape tannin	½ tsp	
Water	3½ litres	(6 pints)

Tokay yeast and nutrient

1 Mix all the ingredients together, pour into a fermentation jar, top up, fit an air-lock and ferment out.

2 Rack into a clean jar, add one Campden tablet and sweeten to taste.

3 Mature for 6 months.

Serve as a dessert wine or use as a basis for coffee liqueur.

Lemon table wine

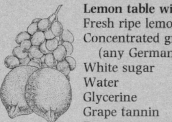

Fresh ripe lemons	10
Concentrated grape juice (any German style)	500 g (18 oz)
White sugar	565 g (1¼ lb)
Water	4 litres (7 pints)
Glycerine	1 tbs
Grape tannin	¼ tsp
Pectic enzyme and Campden tablets	
German wine yeast and nutrient	

1 Wipe over and thinly pare the lemons, then extract the juice.

2 Place the lemon parings and juice in a fermentation jar, add the grape juice, pectic enzyme, water, tannin and yeast. Leave a space of about ½ pint for the rest of the sugar. Fit an air-lock and ferment for 7 days.

3 Remove the lemon peel, stir in the sugar and glycerine, replace the air-lock and continue fermentation to S.G. 1.006.

4 Rack into a clean jar, add two Campden tablets and store in the cool for one month.

5 Rack again and mature the wine for 6 months.

6 Serve lemon wine cold on a hot day as a lunch time aperitif. It is very refreshing.

Orange Blossom mead

Honey (Californian or Spanish orange blossom)	1.36 kg (3 lb)
Tartaric acid	20 g (¾ oz)
Grape tannin	½ tsp
Tronozymol Nutrient	1 tsp
Water	to 4½ litres (1 gallon)
Maury yeast	

1 Dissolve the honey in warm water, then pour it into a fermentation jar and add cold water.

2 Stir in the acid, tannin, nutrient and active yeast, fit an air-lock and ferment out.

3 Rack into a clean jar, add one Campden tablet and store in a cool place till clear.

4 Mature for a few months in bulk, then bottle and keep a little longer.

5 Serve cold as an aperitif or with chicken or pork dishes. This is a dry mead with a delicious bouquet and flavour.

Bitter Beer I

Pale malt	2.75 kg (6 lb)
Crystal malt	450 g (1 lb)
Wheat malt	450 g (1 lb)
Invert sugar	1 kg (2¼ lb)
Golding hops	120 g (4½ oz)
Northern Brewer hops	15 g (½ oz)
Fuggle hops	15 g (½ oz)
Hardening salts	25 g (1 oz)
Water	to 23 litres (5 gallons)
Beer yeast and nutrient	

1 Crack and mash the grains at 66°C (150°F), to end point, then strain and wash the grains with hot water.

2 Boil the wort and hardening salts with the Golding and Northern Brewer hops for one hour, then leave to cool.

3 Strain through the hops and wash them, adjust the quantity of liquor to 5 gallons and the S.G. to 1.046.

4 Ferment at 15°C (39°F), skimming and rousing as usual for 3 days.

5 Add the Fuggle hops, the process known as 'dry hopping', pressing them with your hand to make them absorb the beer.

6 Continue fermentation to the end, pressing down the hops daily to keep them moist.

7 Strain into a clean bin, fine, bottle and prime as usual. Mature for 2 months.

Ginger ale

Malt extract	450 g (1 lb)
Root ginger	25 g (1 oz)
Water	4 litres (7 pints)
Large fresh lemon	1
Ale yeast and nutrient	1 sachet

1 Dissolve the malt extract in warm water, add the well-crushed root ginger and the thinly-pared rind of the lemon. When cool stir in the lemon juice and an activated yeast.

2 Ferment for 5 days, skimming off the froth on the second day.

3 Move to a cool place for 5 days while the sediment settles, then strain into 8 one-pint beer bottles.

4 Prime each bottle with half a teaspoonful of white sugar and stopper tightly.

5 Shake each bottle to dissolve the sugar and return them to the warm for 2 days.

6 Mature the ale in a cool store for 7 to 10 days.

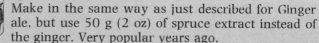

Spruce beer

Make in the same way as just described for Ginger ale, but use 50 g (2 oz) of spruce extract instead of the ginger. Very popular years ago.

March

GRAPEFRUIT, lemons and bananas are the fruits 'in season' in Britain, but there is a wide choice of canned fruits, juices and jams as well as dried fruits and grains.

Sap wine

March is also the month to make sap wine. Only the saps from birch, sycamore and walnut trees are suitable.

The sap should be gathered from matured trees some 15 cm (6 in) in diameter. Bore a hole about 45 cm (18 in) from the ground and just about 30 cm (1 in) deep. Push a piece of tubing into the hole and ensure a tight fit. Place the other end of the tube into a sterile jar and plug the neck with cotton wool. Cover the jar with a rug and leave it for two or three days while the sap drops into the jar. When the jar is about three quarters full, remove the tube and plug the hole with a tight-fitting cork pushed well home. Failure to do this may cause the tree to bleed to death, so make a good job of it.

RECOMMENDED RECIPES

Sap wine

Fresh sap	3½ litres (6 pints)
Concentrated white grape juice	250 g (9 oz)
Sugar	1 kg (2¼ lb)
Citric acid	15 g (½ oz)
Grape tannin	½ tsp
All-purpose wine yeast and nutrient	

1 Place the sap in a large pan and bring it to the boil. Stir in the acid and sugar, and simmer slowly for 20 minutes.
2 When cool, pour it into a fermentation jar, add the tannin, nutrient and an active yeast.
3 Top up the jar with cold water, fit an air-lock and ferment out.
4 Siphon into a sterile jar, add wine finings and store in the cool for 2 weeks.
5 Rack again, taste and, if necessary, sweeten to your liking. Add two Campden tablets and store for 6 months.
Serve cold as a social wine.

Grapefruit Aperitif

Large fresh grapefruit	4
Concentrated white grape juice	500 g (18 oz)
White sugar	1.35 kg (2½ lb)
Water	3½ litres (6 pints)
Tokay yeast and nutrient	

1 Very thinly pare the grapefruit, avoiding all white pith.
2 Place the chopped parings in a pan with the sugar

and half the water, bring to the boil and simmer for 10 minutes.

3 When cool, pour into a fermentation jar, stir in the grape juice, yeast and nutrient, top up with cold water, fit an air-lock and ferment to dryness.

4 Rack into a storage jar, add one Campden tablet and leave in a cool place for 2 weeks.

5 Rack again and store for 9 months before bottling.

Clover Mead: sweet

Clover honey	1.60 kg (3½ lb)
Water	3½ litres (6 pints)
Citric acid	15 g (½ oz)
Tartaric acid	15 g (½ oz)
Nutrient	2 tsp
Grape tannin	1 tsp
Maury yeast	

1 Dissolve the honey, acids, tannin and nutrient in warm water, make up to one gallon, stir in the active yeast, fit an air-lock and ferment in a warm place.

2 When fermentation is finished, rack into a clean storage jar and add one crushed Campden tablet.

3 When the mead is clear, mature for a year or longer before bottling. If necessary sweeten with honey to taste.

Note: English clover honey is the best to use.

Cyser

Apple juice, 1 can	1.3 litres (43 fl oz)
Blended honey, 1 jar	450 g (1 lb)
White sugar	450 g (1 lb)
Citric acid	10 g (⅓ oz)
Grape tannin	½ tsp
Nutrient	1 tsp
Water	3 litres (5 pints)
Champagne wine yeast	

1 Dissolve the honey, sugar, acid, tannin and nutrient in some warm water and pour the solution into a fermentation jar.

2 When cool add the apple juice, and activated yeast.

3 Top up, fit an air-lock and ferment out.

4 Rack into a sterile storage jar, add one Campden tablet and sufficient saccharin to make medium dry.

5 Store for 6 months, then bottle.

Strawberry Jam Rosé

Strawberry jam, 3 jars	1.360 kg (3 lb)
Concentrated grape juice	250 g (9 oz)
Citric acid	2 tsp
Grape tannin	½ tsp
Pectic enzyme	2 tsp
Sugar	450 g (1 lb)
Water	3 litres (5 pints)
Bordeaux yeast and nutrient	

1 Dissolve the jam in warm water and when cool add the acid, pectic enzyme and one Campden tablet, cover and leave for 24 hours.

2 Next day stir in the tannin, grape juice, nutrient and yeast. Ferment for four days then strain out the fruit through a nylon sieve.

3 Stir in the sugar, pour into a fermentation jar, fit an air-lock and ferment out.

4 Rack into a clean jar, add one Campden tablet and sufficient saccharin just to take the edge off the dryness, but not to make it sweet.

5 Store for six months, then bottle and serve chilled.

Note: Use jam that does not contain preservative and if pectin has been added, use double the quantity of pectic enzyme.

Prune 'Sherry'

Large prunes	1.36 kg (3 lb)
Grape juice concentrate (sherry style)	500 g (18 oz)
Fresh lemons	2
Sugar	700–900 g (1½–2 lb)
Tartaric acid	1 tsp
Grape tannin	½ tsp
Gypsum	4 tsp
Cream of tartar	2 tsp
Pectic enzyme	1 tsp
Water	3½ litres (6 pints)

Sherry yeast and nutrient

1 Soak the prunes overnight in hot water.

2 Thinly pare the lemons and boil the parings with the prunes for 20 minutes in the water in which the prunes have been soaking, then leave to cool.

3 Remove the prune stones and pour the pulp and liquor into a mashing bin. Make the contents up to six pints, stir in the expressed lemon juice, tartaric acid, pectic enzyme and one Campden tablet.

4 Stir in the grape juice, gypsum, cream of tartar, tannin and an activated sherry yeast. Ferment on the pulp for four days, pressing down the fruit cap daily.

5 Strain out the fruit, stir in 225 grams (½ lb) sugar and continue the fermentation in a covered bin.

6 Check the S.G. daily and as soon as it reaches 1.002 stir in another dose of sugar.

7 Repeat this process once more and if possible twice, to make the wine as strong as possible.

8 Finish the sherry either dry or medium dry.

9 Rack into a clean jar, do NOT add any Campden tablets, plug the neck with cotton wool and store in a cool place for at least one year before bottling and further storage.

With patience this wine develops a remarkable similarity to sherry. Some winemakers add one bottle of commercial sherry after the first racking, to improve the flavour.

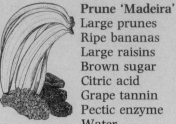

Prune 'Madeira'

Large prunes	1 kg (2¼ lb)
Ripe bananas	450 g (1 lb)
Large raisins	450 g (1 lb)
Brown sugar	700 g (1½ lb)
Citric acid	2 tsp
Grape tannin	½ tsp
Pectic enzyme	1 tsp
Water	3½ litres (6 pints)

Madeira yeast and nutrient

1 Soak the prunes overnight in hot water.

2 Peel and slice the bananas and boil with the prunes for 20 minutes in the water in which they soaked, then leave to cool.

3 Chop the raisins, being careful not to break the pips, then add them to the prunes and bananas.

4 Stir in the acid, tannin, pectic enzyme, and one Campden tablet, cover and leave for 24 hours.

5 Add the activated yeast and nutrient and ferment on the pulp for five days, pressing down the fruit cap daily.

6 Strain out the fruit and roll it round a nylon sieve, stir in 450 grams (1 lb) sugar, pour the must into a fermentation jar, fit an air-lock and continue fermentation, checking the S.G. daily.

7 When S.G. 1.004 is reached stir in the remaining sugar and continue fermentation if possible.

8 When fermentation ends, move to a cool place and four days later siphon into a clean jar, omit the Campden tablet, bung tight and store in a very warm place for 3–6 months.

9 Bottle after one year and sweeten to taste. Serve as a dessert wine.

Rice and Raisin wine

Crushed long grain rice	450 g (1 lb)
Large chopped raisins	450 g (1 lb)
White sugar	900 g (2 lb)
Citric acid	2 tsp
Tannin	½ tsp
Water	4 litres (7 pints)

Cereal yeast and nutrient

1 Place the crushed rice and chopped raisins in a bin and pour boiling water over them.

2 When cool, stir in all the other ingredients and ferment on the pulp for 14 days.

3 Strain out the solids, pour the must into a fermentation jar, fit an air-lock and continue fermentation to the end.

4 Rack into a clean storage jar, add one Campden tablet and when the wine is bright rack it again.

5 Sweeten to taste with lactose or saccharin, and bottle. Keep for a few months.

This is a very popular wine with beginners. Serve as a social wine.

Apricot Nectar

Apricot Nectar, 1 bottle	900 g (32 oz)
White grape juice concentrate	250 g (9 oz)
Sugar	700 g (1½ lb)
Citric acid	2 tsp
Grape tannin	½ tsp
Pectic enzyme	1 tsp
Water	3 litres (5½ pints)
Sauternes yeast and nutrient	

1 Empty the bottle of apricot Nectar into a fermentation jar containing 4 pints cold water, add the acid, tannin, pectic enzyme and a Campden tablet, fit an air-lock and leave in a warm place for 24 hours.
2 Dissolve the sugar and grape juice in the remaining water, pour it into the fermentation jar, add an activated yeast and nutrient, replace the air-lock and ferment out.
3 Rack into a clean jar, add one Campden tablet and when the wine is bright, rack again. Sweeten to taste with lactose or saccharin, and then bottle it.

Serve this wine cold, with the dessert course of a meal, or as a social wine. It matures in 4–6 months.

Dried apricot wine

Dried apricots	450 g (1 lb)
White grape juice concentrate	250 g (9 oz)
Sugar	900 g (2 lb)
Citric acid	2 tsp
Grape tannin	½ tsp
Pectic enzyme	1 tsp
Water	3½ litres (6½ pints)
Chablis wine yeast and nutrient	

1 Soak the apricot halves overnight in one quart of cold water and next day boil them in this water for 20 minutes.
2 Pour off the liquor into a mashing bin, add another quart of water to the apricots and boil them again for 15 minutes.
3 Add the fruit and liquor to the mashing bin and the acid, tannin, pectic enzyme and one Campden tablet. Cover and leave for 24 hours.
4 Stir in the grape juice, yeast and nutrient and ferment on the pulp for three days, stirring daily.
5 Strain out the fruit, roll it round a sieve and then discard it.
6 Dissolve the sugar in a quart of water, stir this into the must, pour it all into a fermentation jar, top up with cold water, fit an air-lock and ferment out.
7 Rack into a clean jar, add one Campden tablet and when the wine is bright, rack again.
8 Store this wine for nine months before bottling, then keep it for at least another three months.

Serve this excellent wine cold, as a dry white table wine, or even as an aperitif.

Passion Fruit wine

Passion fruit juice, 1 bottle	73 cl (24 fl oz)

All other ingredients and method as described for Apricot Nectar.
This is an unusual and delightful wine, best served cold and not quite dry.

Oatmeal Stout

Pale malt	1 kg (2¼ lb)
Black malt	100 g (¼ lb)
Flaked oats	350 g (¾ lb)
Brown sugar	350 g (¾ lb)
Goldings hops	40 g (1½ oz)
Soft water	9 litres (2 gallons)
Stout yeast and nutrient	

1 Crack the malt grains and mash with the flaked oats in half the water at 65°C (149°F) for three hours or until the end point is reached.
2 Strain the liquor, wash the grains, add the hops and boil steadily for 30 minutes. Leave it to cool.
3 Strain through the hops, stir in the sugar, top up with cold water and adjust the S.G. to 1.040.
4 Ferment at 15°C (60°F) until dry, skimming and rousing as usual.
5 Fine, rack, bottle, prime and store this distinctive stout for at least six weeks. If it is too dry for your palate, sweeten it to your taste with 170 g (6 oz) lactose or a little saccharin.

Light ale – Burton type

Pale malt	4½ kg (10 lb)
Crystal malt	140 g (5 oz)
Medium dark malt flour	140 g (5 oz)
Golding hops	100 g (3½ oz)
Hard water	23 litres (5¼ gals)
Ale yeast and nutrient	

Note: Unless you live in a hard water area, add a suitably-sized packet of hardening salts to the water.

1 Crack the grains unless they were bought already crushed, and mash all the malts in 4 gallons of hardened water for at least 2 hours or until the end point is reached. Strain into a boiling pan, wash the grains twice with a quart of hot water and add this to the pan.
2 Add 3 oz hops and boil the wort vigorously for 45 minutes, then add the remaining hops and continue the boil for a further 15 minutes.
3 Strain the wort through a sieve into a fermentation bin and wash the hops twice with a quart of hot water.
4 Top up with cold water and when the temperature has fallen to 15°C (60°F) pitch an activated yeast.
5 Skim, rouse, rack, bottle and prime as usual, then mature for at least three weeks.

April

ALTHOUGH there is nothing new in the way of fresh fruit this month, there may well be some tail-end stock about that can be obtained cheaply, especially bananas, grapefruit and lemons. Vegetable growers may find a surplus of parsnips. Any being well-frosted and freshly dug may be in perfect condition for making wine.

The flowers are coming into bloom and this is the best month to make dandelion, coltsfoot and cowslip wine. Dandelions abound on every patch of ground and are known to everyone; coltsfoot looks somewhat similar but is harder to find; cowslip, once so popular, is now very difficult to find. It may be a lot less trouble to use dried cowslips from your local Health Food shop.

Canned fruit juices, purées, pulp and whole fruit are usually in good supply. It is worth watching for any that may be on special offer at a reduced price.

RECOMMENDED RECIPES

Dandelion wine

Freshly picked dandelion heads	2 litres	(2 quarts)
Chopped sultanas	450 g	(1 lb)
Sugar	1 kg	(2¼ lb)
Citric acid	15 g	(½ oz)
Grape tannin	½ tsp	
Water	4 litres	(7 pints)
Sauternes yeast and nutrient		

1 Pick the dandelion heads only – no green – on a fine day, place them in a bowl and pour hot water over them. When cool add the acid, then cover and leave for three days, rubbing the flowers with the back of a wooden spoon daily.

2 Strain the liquor on to the chopped sultanas, add the tannin, yeast and nutrient and ferment on the pulp for seven days, stirring daily but keeping the bin covered meanwhile.

3 Strain out and press the sultanas, stir in the sugar, pour into a fermentation jar, top up, fit an air-lock and continue fermentation.

4 At S.G.1.006, rack the wine into a clean jar, add two Campden tablets to terminate fermentation and store it in a cool place until it is clear.

5 Store for six months or so, then bottle and keep a little longer.

Serve cold as a social wine.

Coltsfoot wine

Use 2 quarts of freshly picked coltsfoot flower heads and the other ingredients and methods as indicated for dandelion wine.

Cowslip wine

Use 2 quarts of freshly picked cowslip flowers or 2 oz dried flowers, and other ingredients and methods as indicated for dandelion wine.

Green Ginger wine

Root ginger	95 g (3 oz)
Chopped sultanas	450 g (1 lb)
Ripe bananas	900 g (2 lb)
Sugar	1 kg (2¼ lb)
Citric acid	15 g (½ oz)
Grape tannin	½ tsp
Water	4 litres (7 pints)

Sauternes yeast and nutrient
Green colouring

1 Break the hard ginger roots into pieces and bruise them with a mallet.
2 Peel the ripe bananas, slice them, place them in a quart of water and boil them for 30 minutes.
3 Place the chopped sultanas in a mashing bin with the ginger and strain the banana liquor on to them. Top up with hot water and leave to cool.
4 Stir in the acid, tannin, nutrient and yeast, cover and leave to ferment for five days, stirring daily.
5 Stir in 450 grams (1 lb) sugar and continue fermentation for another five days.
6 Strain out the solids, stir in the rest of the sugar, pour into a fermentation jar, top up, fit an air-lock and ferment on to S.G. 1.010.
7 Rack the wine into a clean jar, add two crushed Campden tablets to terminate fermentation, and green colouring to the colour of your choice.
8 When the wine is clear, rack again and store for eight months before bottling. Serve as a social wine.

Pineapple juice wine

Canned pineapple juice	1.3 litres (43 fl oz)
Grape juice concentrate	250 g (9 oz)
Sugar	900 g (2 lb)
Citric acid	2 tsp
Grape tannin	½ tsp
Water	approx 3 litres (5 pints)

Chablis yeast and nutrient

1 Mix all the ingredients together, pour into a fermentation jar, top up, fit an air-lock, ferment out.
2 Rack into a sterile storage jar, add one Campden tablet and when clear rack again.
3 Store for six months, then bottle.
Serve cold as an aperitif or as a white table wine.

Date and Lemon wine

Fresh lemons	6
Chopped dates	450 g (1 lb)
Chopped raisins	225 g (½ lb)
Brown sugar	675 g (1½ lb)
Grape tannin	½ tsp
Water	4 litres (7 pints)

Pectic enzyme and Campden tablets
Madeira yeast and nutrient

1 Thinly pare and chop the skins of the lemons and place them in a fermentation bin with the chopped dates and raisins.

2 Pour boiling water on to them and when cool add the pectic enzyme, lemon juice, grape tannin and one Campden tablet. Cover and leave in a warm place for 24 hours.

3 Next day add the yeast and nutrient and ferment on the pulp for seven days.

4 Strain out and press the fruit, stir in the sugar, pour into a fermentation jar, top up, fit an air-lock and ferment out.

5 Rack into a clean jar, add a Campden tablet and when clear rack again.

6 Store in a *warm* place for six months, then bottle and keep for a further six months.

This makes an attractive dry madeira-type wine that may be served cool as an aperitif or as a table wine.

Elderberry purée table wine

Concentrated elderberry purée	425 g (15 oz) can
Red grape juice concentrate	250 g (9 oz)
Sugar	1 kg (2¼ lb)
Tartaric acid	2 tsp
Water	3½ litres (6 pints)

Pectic enzyme and Campden tablets
Bordeaux yeast and nutrient

1 Mix the elderberry purée and grape juice with the tartaric acid, pectic enzyme, one Campden tablet and six pints of cold water, cover and leave in the warm for 24 hours.

2 Stir in the sugar, yeast and nutrient and ferment under an air-lock.

3 When fermentation is finished rack into a clean jar, add one Campden tablet and store till the wine is clear and bright.

4 Rack again, store for nine months then, bottle, and keep for a few months longer.

Peach and Grape wine

Peach and grape juice concentrate 1 kg (1 can)

Detailed instructions are supplied on the back of the label. Serve this wine cold as a white table wine.

Ortanique table wine

Fresh ortaniques	6
White grape juice concentrate	250 g (½ pint)
Sugar	900 g (2 lb)
Water	3 litres (5 pints)
Grape tannin	½ tsp

Chablis yeast and nutrient

1 Thinly pare the ortaniques, chop the parings and place them in a fermentation jar. Pour in the grape juice and the sugar dissolved in warm water and allow to cool to 21°C (70°F).

2 Cut the ortaniques in half, express the juice, discard the hulks and add the fruit juice, tannin, nutrient and yeast to the jar. Top up with cold water, fit an air-lock and ferment in a warm place.

3 After five days remove the fruit peel and continue fermentation to dryness.

4 Rack into a clean storage jar, add one Campden tablet and store in a cool place until the wine is clear, then rack again.

5 Store for nine months before bottling. Serve cold.

Tea wine

Tea bags	12
White grape juice concentrate	1 kg (1 can)
Sugar	450 g (1 lb)
Water	3½ litres (6 pints)

All-purpose wine yeast and nutrient

1 Boil the water and pour on to the tea bags of your choice. Cover and leave for 10 minutes.

2 Remove the tea bags, stir in the sugar and grape juice concentrate and, when cool, the yeast and nutrient.

3 Fit an air-lock and ferment to S.G. 1.006.

4 Rack into a clean jar and add two crushed Campden tablets to terminate fermentation.

5 When clear, rack again and store for six months before bottling.

Serve as a social wine with biscuits.

Pyment

Blended white honey	450 g (1 lb)
White grape juice concentrate	1 kg (1 can)
Water	3½ litres (6 pints)

All-purpose wine yeast and nutrient.

1 Dissolve the honey and grape juice concentrate in warm water, pour into a fermentation jar.

2 Top up with cold water, add the yeast and nutrient, fit an air-lock and ferment out.

3 Rack into a clean jar, add one Campden tablet and when clear, rack again.

4 Store for nine months, then bottle and serve as a white table wine.

Brown Ale: Northern Special

Pale malt	450 g (1 lb)
Crystal malt	225 g (½ lb)
Wheat malt	100 g (¼ lb)
Brown sugar	100 g (¼ lb)
Northern Brewer hops	20 g (¾ oz)
Water	4½ litres (1 gallon)

Ale yeast and nutrient

1 Crack the malt grains and mash them at 65°C (149°F) for two hours

2 Boil the wort with two-thirds of the hops for 30 minutes, then add the remaining hops and continue to boil for a further 15 minutes. Leave to cool and then strain into a fermentation bin.

3 Adjust the quantity to $8\frac{1}{4}$ pints and the S.G. to 1.032, pitch an active yeast and ferment at 15°C (60°F) to end.

4 Rack, bottle and prime as usual, then mature for one month.

Brown Ale: Southern Special

Pale malt	550 g	($1\frac{1}{4}$ lb)
Crystal malt	100 g	($\frac{1}{4}$ lb)
Flaked Barley	50 g	(2 oz)
Diastatic malt extract	50 g	(2 oz)
Wheat syrup	25 g	(1 oz)
Brown sugar	100 g	($\frac{1}{4}$ lb)
Fuggle hops	15 g	($\frac{1}{2}$ oz)
Caragheen Moss	2 g	($\frac{1}{3}$ tsp)
Water	$4\frac{1}{2}$ litres	(1 gallon)
Ale yeast and nutrient		

1 Crack the barley grains and place them in a bin with the flaked barley, malt extract and wheat syrup, add hot water and mash at 60°C (140°F) to end point. Draw off and wash the grains.

2 Boil the wort with the hops and Caragheen Moss (to help clarify the beer) for one hour, then cool and strain through a sieve.

3 Adjust the quantity to $8\frac{1}{4}$ pints and the S.G. to 1.030. Pitch an active yeast and ferment at 15°C (60°F) to dryness.

4 Sweeten to taste with lactose or saccharin, then rack, prime and bottle as usual. Mature for one month.

Redcurrant and Rosehip rosé

Redcurrant cordial	48 cls	(17 fl oz)
Rosehip syrup	34 cls	(12 fl oz)
Sugar	450 g	(1 lb)
Citric acid	5 g	(1 tsp)
Water	to $4\frac{1}{2}$ litres	(1 gallon)
Hock yeast and nutrient		

1 Dissolve half the sugar in two quarts of water and pour it into a demijohn.

2 Add the redcurrant cordial and rosehip syrup, the citric acid and an activated yeast.

3 Stir well, fit an air-lock and ferment in a warm place for one week.

4 Dissolve the rest of the sugar in one quart of water and slowly pour it into the jar. Replace the air-lock and resume fermentation.

5 When fermentation has finished, rack the wine into a clean jar and add one Campden tablet. Bung tight and store the wine until it is clear, then rack it again.

6 Store this wine for two months, then taste, sweeten if so desired with saccharin, and bottle. It should be ready for drinking in August.

Apple and Gooseberry wine

Bottled, unsweetened apple juice	75 cls	(26 fl oz)
Canned gooseberries	440 g	($15\frac{1}{2}$ oz)
Grape juice concentrate	250 g	(9 oz)
Sugar	900 g	(2 lb)
Citric acid	10 g	(2 tsp)
Water	approx 3 litres	(5 pints)
Pectic enzyme and Campden tablets		
Sauternes yeast and nutrient		

1 Pour the apple juice into a sterilised bin and add the citric acid, one teaspoonful of pectic enzyme and one crushed Campden tablet.

2 Remove the gooseberries from their syrup, mash, add to the bin, cover and leave for 24 hours.

3 Next day, add the gooseberry syrup, the grape juice and an activated yeast. Top up to $7\frac{1}{2}$ pints.

4 Ferment for four days, then strain out the gooseberries, pour the must into a fermentation jar, fit an air-lock and ferment down to S.G. 1.010.

5 Rack into a clean jar, add two crushed Campden tablets to terminate fermentation and move the jar to a cool place until the wine clears.

6 Rack again, bung tight and store for six months, then bottle and keep for another month.

Serve this light, sweet wine, well chilled, with the dessert course of a meal, or with sweet biscuits.

Blackberry and Apple wine

Canned blackberries	560 g	(20 oz)
Bottled, unsweetened apple juice	75 cls	(26 fl oz)
Red grape juice concentrate	250 g	(9 oz)
Sugar	900 g	(2 lb)
Water	3 litres	(5 pints)
Pectic enzyme and Campden tablets		
Burgundy yeast and nutrient		

Make this wine in a similar way to the previous recipe. It takes only a little longer to mature and should be ready as a red social wine by Christmas.

Black Cherry dessert wine

Canned black cherries	430 g	(15 oz)
Redcurrant cordial	34 cls	(12 fl oz)
Red grape juice concentrate	500 g	(18 oz)
Sugar	900 g	(2 lb)
Citric acid	10 g	(2 tsp)
Water	3 litres	(5 pints)
Pectic enzyme and Campden tablets		
Port yeast and nutrient		

Make this wine in the same way as the last two recipes, but add the sugar in four equal quantities at intervals of five days. Mature it for one year.

May

THE first of the home-grown fruits is available this month and traditionally rhubarb has been a great favourite among winemakers. The stalks are not usually suitable until the middle of the month, but from then until the middle of June they are at their best.

Among the flowers 'May' blossom makes a delicious wine, whilst potatoes see off the end of the vegetables.

May is also a good time to make some superb wines from multiple dried ingredients and concentrates.

RECOMMENDED RECIPES

May blossom wine

Hawthorn blossom	2 litres (2 quarts)
Grape juice concentrate	1 kg (1 can)
White sugar	349 g (12 oz)
Water	$3\frac{1}{2}$ litres (6 pints)
Campden tablets	
All-purpose wine yeast and nutrient	

1 Gather the blossom (fully out) on a sunny day. Pick out any bits of green leaf and stalk, place the petals in a measure, shake them down gently but do not press them.
2 Place the blossom in a suitable bin and pour on 4 pints of boiling water. Macerate them with the back of a wooden spoon, cover and leave to cool.

3 Add one Campden tablet and leave for three days.
4 Strain out the flowers, stir in the grape juice, top up with cold water to the shoulder of the demijohn, add the yeast and nutrient, fit an air-lock and ferment in a warm place.
5 After one week stir in the sugar, replace the air-lock and ferment on to S.G. 1.006.
6 Rack into a clean jar, add two crushed Campden tablets to terminate fermentation and then store in the cool.
7 As soon as the wine is clear, rack again and keep for a further six months before bottling.
Serve this wine cold and slightly sweet as a social wine.

Rhubarb wine

Prepared rhubarb	2.725 g (6 lb)
White sugar	1,360 g (3 lb)
Fresh lemon	1
Water	$3\frac{1}{2}$ litres (6 pints)
Pectic enzyme and Campden tablets	
Sauternes yeast and nutrient	

1 Choose best quality red stalks, wipe, top and tail them, chop into small pieces, place in a bin together with the thinly pared rind of the lemon. Pour boiling water on to them and when cool add the lemon juice, pectic enzyme and one Campden tablet. Cover and leave for 24 hours.
2 Stir in half the sugar, the yeast and nutrient and

ferment on the pulp for six days, pressing down the fruit cap daily.

3 Strain out and press the fruit, stir in the rest of the sugar, pour the must into a fermentation jar, fit an air-lock and ferment out.

4 Rack into a clean jar, add one Campden tablet and when clear rack again.

5 Store for nine months before sweetening to taste, if desired, with saccharin, and then bottling.

Note: If left without sweetening this makes an excellent wine for liqueurs, for blending and for cooking. Instead of water add one glassful of this wine to all fruits when cooking them. The fruit is greatly improved.

leave for a minimum of 24 hours.

2 Stir in the nutrient, and yeast, ferment on the pulp for four days, pressing down the fruit cap daily.

3 Strain out and press the fruit, stir in the sugar, pour the must into a fermentation jar, top up, fit an air-lock and ferment to dryness.

4 Rack into a clean jar, add one Campden tablet and as soon as the wine is 'bright', rack again.

5 Store the wine in a cool place until November or December, then prime with 70 g (2½ oz) sugar and an active champagne yeast and siphon into champagne bottles.

6 Fit hollow-domed plastic stoppers, fastened on with a wire cage. Leave in a warm place for two weeks then store the wine for at least six months.

Rhubarb sparkling wine

Prepared rhubarb	1,600 g	(3½ lb)
Chopped sultanas	250 g	(9 oz)
Fresh lemon	1	
Sugar	700 g	(1½ lb)
Water	3½ litres	(6 pints)

Pectic enzyme and Campden tablets
Champagne yeast and nutrient

1 Top, tail and wipe the rhubarb stalks, cut into small pieces, place in a bin with the chopped sultanas and thinly pared rind of the lemon. Pour on boiling water and when cool add the lemon juice, pectic enzyme and one Campden tablet. Cover and

Rhubarb and Grape rosé

Prepared rhubarb	2 kg	(4½ lb)
Red grape juice concentrate	250 g	(9 oz)
Sugar	800 g	(1¾ lb)
Lactose	100 g	(3½ oz)
Water	3½ litres	(6 pints)

Pectic enzyme and Campden tablets
Bordeaux yeast and nutrient

1 Top, tail and wipe the rhubarb stalks, chop into small pieces, place in a bin and pour boiling water over them. When cool add the pectic enzyme and one Campden tablet. Cover and leave for 24 hours.

2 Stir in the red grape juice concentrate, nutrient

and yeast, ferment for four days pressing down the fruit cap twice daily.

3 Strain out and press the fruit, stir in the sugar, pour into a demijohn, fit an air-lock and ferment out.

4 Rack into a clean jar, stir in the lactose and one Campden tablet and as soon as the wine is bright rack again.

5 Store for a further six months before bottling. Serve cool at any time.

Rhubarb, Banana and Date 'Sherry'

Prepared rhubarb stalks	2 kg (4½ lb)
Fresh lemons – small	2
Ripe bananas	450 g (1 lb)
Chopped dates	225 g (8 oz)
Grape juice concentrate (cream sherry style)	500 g (18 oz)
Sugar	900 g (2 lb)
Gypsum	28 g (1 oz)
Cream of tartar	14 g (½ oz)
Water	3½ litres (6 pints)

Pectic enzyme and Campden tablets
Sherry yeast and nutrient

1 Top, tail, wipe and chop the rhubarb stalks and place in a mashing bin. Peel and mash the bananas, chop up the dates discarding any stones. Thinly peel the lemons and add all these to the bin.

2 Pour boiling water over the fruit and when cool stir in the gypsum, cream of tartar, pectic enzyme, one Campden tablet and the expressed juice of the lemons. Cover the bin and leave for 24 hours.

3 Stir in the grape juice, activated yeast and nutrient and ferment on the pulp for five days, pressing down the fruit cap twice daily.

4 Strain out and press the solids, stir in half the sugar and continue fermentation in the covered bin.

5 One week later, stir in the rest of the sugar, pour the must into a fermentation jar, plug the neck with cotton wool and continue fermentation.

6 When fermentation stops, stir the wine, then check the specific gravity. If necessary stir in sufficient sugar to raise the reading to 1.010 or a little above.

7 Rack into a clean jar, plug the neck with cotton wool and store for at least one year before bottling. This wine will continue to improve for the next two years and is worth keeping.

Poor Man's 'Brandy' wine

Old potatoes	450 g (1 lb)
Pearl barley	450 g (1 lb)
Chopped raisins	450 g (1 lb)
Demerara sugar	1,360 g (3 lb)
Fresh lemons	2
Water	4 litres (7 pints)

Tokay yeast and nutrient

1 Scrub the potatoes thoroughly and mince or cut them into small pieces, wash the pearl barley, chop the raisins, thinly peel the 2 lemons. Place all these ingredients in a bin and pour boiling water over them. Cover and leave to cool.

2 Stir in the lemon juice, yeast and nutrient and ferment on the pulp for three weeks, pressing down the fruit cap twice daily.

3 After six days, stir in one-third of the sugar and repeat this on the 12th and 18th days. Keep the bin closely covered meanwhile.

4 About the 21st day strain out the solids, pour the must into a fermentation jar, top up if necessary, fit an air-lock and continue fermentation to the end.

5 When the wine clears, rack into a clean jar, add one Campden tablet, bung tight and store in a cool place for two years before bottling.

Note: This is a very strong wine and should be treated with respect.

Melomel

Blended honey	1,360 g (3 lb)
Blackcurrant syrup	340 g (12 oz)
Tartaric acid	15 g (½ oz)
Water	approx 3 litres (5 pints)
Nutrient	1 tsp
Maury yeast	

1 Dissolve the honey in warm water and when cool, stir in all the other ingredients. Pour into a fermentation jar, fit an air-lock and ferment out.

2 Rack into a clean jar, add one Campden tablet, stir till the melomel is clear, then rack again.

3 Store for a further six months then sweeten to taste, if desired, with saccharin, and bottle.
Serve as a social wine.

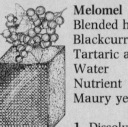

Red table wine I

Bottled bilberries	900 g (2 lb)
Dried apricots	225 g (8 oz)
Fresh bananas	225 g (8 oz)
Grape juice concentrate	250 g (9 oz)
Sugar	800 g (1¾ lb)
Malic acid	1 tsp
Water	3 litres (5 pints)

Pectic enzyme and Campden tablets
Burgundy yeast and nutrient

1 Chop the apricots, peel and slice the bananas and boil them steadily for 30 minutes.

2 When cool add the bottled bilberries, malic acid, pectic enzyme and one Campden tablet.

3 Stir in the grape juice concentrate, nutrient and active yeast and ferment on the pulp for four days, stirring twice daily.

4 Strain out the fruit and roll it round a sieve, stir in the sugar, pour the must into a fermentation jar, fit an air-lock and ferment out.

5 Rack into a clean jar, add one Campden tablet and when the wine is bright, rack again.

6 Store till the wine is one year old before bottling.

This is a superb dry red table wine worth making in larger quantities.

Red table wine II

Dried elderberries	225 g	(8 oz)
Chopped raisins	225 g	(8 oz)
Ripe bananas	450 g	(1 lb)
Grape juice concentrate (Italian style)	250 g	(9 oz)
Blended honey	225 g	(8 oz)
Demerara sugar	450 g	(1 lb)
Tartaric acid	15 g	($\frac{1}{2}$ oz)
Water	$3\frac{1}{2}$ litres	(6 pints)

Pectic enzyme and Campden tablets
Chianti wine yeast and nutrient

1 Wash the elderberries in a sulphite solution, peel and slice the bananas and boil them together for 30 minutes.

2 Add the chopped raisins and, when cool, the acid, pectic enzyme and one Campden tablet. Cover and leave for 24 hours.

3 Stir in the grape juice concentrate, the honey, the yeast and nutrient and ferment on the pulp for six days, pressing down the fruit cap twice daily.

4 Strain out the fruit and press it gently. Stir in the sugar, pour the must into a fermentation jar, fit an air-lock and ferment out.

5 Rack into a clean jar, add one Campden tablet and when the wine is clear, rack again. Store for one year before bottling.

Note: This is another dry red table wine worth making in large quantities.

India Pale Ale

Malt extract	450 g	(1 lb)
Pale malt grains	450 g	(1 lb)
Crystal malt	100 g	($\frac{1}{4}$ lb)
Flaked wheat	100 g	($\frac{1}{4}$ lb)
Flaked rice	100 g	($\frac{1}{4}$ lb)
Invert sugar	225 g	($\frac{1}{2}$ lb)
Fuggle hops	25 g	(1 oz)
Golding hops	50 g	(2 oz)
Hardening salts	10 g	($\frac{1}{2}$ oz)
Water	9 litres	(2 gallons)

Beer yeast and nutrient

1 Place all the ingredients in a bin except the hops and yeast. Pour on $1\frac{1}{2}$ gallons of hot water, stir well, then mash at 66°C (150°F) for three hours.

2 Strain off the liquor, wash the grains, add the Fuggle hops, three quarters of the Goldings and boil for 30 minutes. Add the remaining hops and boil for a further 15 minutes. Leave to cool.

3 Strain into a fermentation bin, wash the hops, top up with cold water, adjust the S.G. to 1.050, pitch an active yeast and ferment to dryness at 15°C (60°F).

Skim and rouse as usual and at the end of fermentation, fine, bottle, prime, re-ferment and store for six weeks.

Rhubarb, Redcurrant and Raisin rosé

Fresh rhubarb	900 g	(2 lb)
Redcurrant cordial	48 cls	(17 fl oz)
Chopped raisins	225 g	(8 oz)
Sugar	900 g	(2 lb)
Water	$3\frac{1}{2}$ litres	(6 pints)

Pectic enzyme and Campden tablets
Bordeaux yeast and nutrient

1 Trim, wipe and dice the rhubarb, place it in a bin with the chopped raisins, pour hot water on to it and leave it to cool. Add the pectic enzyme and one Campden tablet, cover and leave for 24 hours.

2 Add the redcurrant cordial and an activated Bordeaux yeast and nutrient. Ferment for five days, pressing down the fruit cap daily.

3 Strain out and press the fruit, stir in the sugar, pour the must into a demijohn, fit an air-lock and ferment down to S.G. 1.004.

4 Rack into a clean jar, add two crushed Campden tablets, replace the air-lock and leave until the wine is clear.

5 Rack again, mature for six months, then bottle.

Lemon and Rosehip apéritif

Bottled pure lemon juice (PLJ)	34 cls	(12 oz)
Rosehip syrup	34 cls	(12 oz)
Concentrated white grape juice	500 g	(18 oz)
Sugar	900 g	(2 lb)
Water	3 litres	(5 pints)

Sherry yeast and nutrient

1 Mix together all the ingredients except the sugar and pour them into a fermentation jar, fit an air-lock and leave for seven days.

2 Stir in the sugar in four equal quantities and, when fermentation finishes, rack the clearing wine into a clean jar. Add one Campden tablet and, when the wine is bright, rack again.

3 Mature for one year and serve cold. Sweeten to taste if required.

June

FLAT pea pods before the peas begin to swell remind one of the good vegetable wines that can be made. The fragrance of elderflower sets one itching to capture the scent of flowers in wine. The bursting forth of shoots and leaves call to mind the wine called 'folly'. But fruits are few in June.

Now is the time, however, to take stock of wines made and containers in use. The next four months offer an abundance of not-to-be-missed ingredients. Make sure that as much wine is bottled as can be, and that there will be sufficient mashing and fermentation vessels available for the harvest to come. Check your stock of acid, tannin, nutrient, yeast and sugar. Anticipate your need for sultanas, raisins and concentrated grape juice. Many items can be bought more cheaply in bulk than in small packets. Fresh fruits demand immediate attention if you want to make quality wines.

RECOMMENDED RECIPES

Bramble wine
Tender blackberry shoots and leaves

	2¾ kg (5 lb)
Grape juice concentrate	250 g (9 oz)
Sugar	800 g (1¾ lb)
Citric acid	2 tsp
Grape tannin	½ tsp
Water	3½ litres (6 pints)

All-purpose wine yeast and nutrient

1 Wash the shoots and leaves in cold water, chop them up and boil them for half an hour.
2 When cool, strain the liquor on to all the other ingredients, stir well, pour into a fermentation jar and top up. Fit an air-lock and ferment out.
3 Rack into a clean jar, add one Campden tablet and store till bright, then bottle and keep the wine for three or four months at least.

Folly

Tender vine shoots and thinnings	2¼ kg (5 lb)
Grape juice concentrate (Hock style)	500 g (18 oz)
Sugar	800 g (1¾ lb)
Citric acid	2 tsp
Water	3½ litres (6 pints)

Hock yeast and nutrient

1 Make in exactly the same way as Bramble wine. The name of this wine comes from the French word *feuille* meaning leaf. It is a surprisingly delightful wine, especially when served chilled on a warm, sunny day.

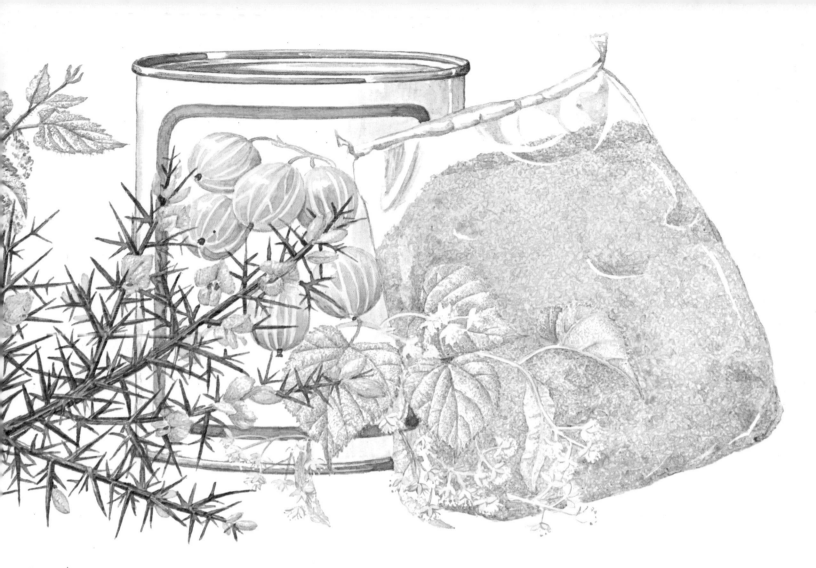

Walnut Leaf wine

Young walnut leaves	½ litre	(1 pint)
Grape juice concentrate	500 g	(18 oz)
Sugar	800 g	(1¾ lb)
Citric acid	2 tsp	
Water	3½ litres	(6 pints)
Hock yeast and nutrient		

1 Make in exactly the same way as Bramble wine. Walnut leaves are highly flavoured and the quantity mentioned should not be exceeded.

Lime Blossom wine

Bracts and flowers	2 litres	(2 quarts)
Cracked barley	250 g	(9 oz)
Chopped sultanas	450 g	(1 lb)
Sugar	800 g	(1¾ lb)
Citric acid	2 tsp	
Grape tannin	½ tsp	
Lactose	100 g	(3½ oz)
Water	4 litres	(7 pints)
Sauternes yeast and nutrient		

1 Chop up the flowers and bracts, crush the barley, chop the sultanas, place in a bin and pour boiling water over them. Macerate with the back of a wooden spoon for a few minutes.

2 When cool, add the acid, tannin, nutrient and active yeast. Ferment on the pulp for four days, pressing down the cap twice daily.

3 Strain and press, stir in the sugar, pour the must into a fermentation jar, top up, fit an air-lock and ferment in a warm place.

4 When fermentation is finished, rack into a clean jar, stir in the lactose, add one Campden tablet and store for six months. Then bottle and serve cold while young and fresh.

Elderflower sparkling wine

Freshly picked florets	1 litre	(1 quart)
White grape juice concentrate	1 kg	(1 can)
Water	3½ litres	(6 pints)
Champagne yeast and nutrient		

1 Dissolve the white grape juice concentrate in the water, add the active yeast and nutrient, cover and when fermenting well, stir in the elder florets.

2 Press the flowers down twice daily, so that the water and alcohol can leach out the bouquet and flavour.

3 After four days, strain out the flowers, pour the must into a fermentation jar, top up, fit an air-lock and ferment out. DO NOT add any sugar.

4 When fermentation is finished, rack into a clean

jar, add wine finings and leave in the cool to clear.

5 When the wine is bright rack again and store until it is six months old.

6 Add 70 grams (2½ oz) caster sugar and an active Champagne yeast, fit an air-lock and as soon as the wine is fermenting, pour it into champagne bottles.

7 Fit hollow-domed, plastic stoppers and wire them on to the bottle. Store the bottles on their sides, first in a warm place for seven days and then in a cool place for six months.

Sparkling Mead

Light flavoured honey such as lime or clover	1¼ kg (2¾ lb)
Fresh lemon	1
Tartaric acid	1 tsp
Grape tannin	½ tsp
Water	3½ litres (6 pints)
Champagne yeast and nutrient	

1 Thinly pare the lemon and gently boil the peel in half the water for 30 minutes.

2 Strain out the peel, stir in the honey, lemon juice, acid, and tannin and add the rest of the water, cold.

3 When the temperature is 20°C (68°F) add the yeast and nutrient, pour the must into a fermentation jar, fit an air-lock and ferment out.

4 Continue as from 4 in the previous recipe.

Pea pod

Fresh tender pods after shelling	2 kg (4½ lb)
White grape juice concentrate	250 g (9 oz)
White sugar	900 g (2 lb)
Citric acid	2 tsp
Grape tannin	½ tsp
Water	4 litres (7 pints)
Hock yeast and nutrient	

1 Chop up and boil the pea pods for half an hour and leave to cool.

2 Strain out the pods, stir in the grape juice, sugar, acid, tannin, yeast and nutrient. Pour into a fermentation jar, fit an air-lock and ferment out.

3 Rack into a clean jar, add one Campden tablet, store it till bright, then rack again.

4 Keep for at least nine months before bottling. Serve cold as an excellent light white wine.

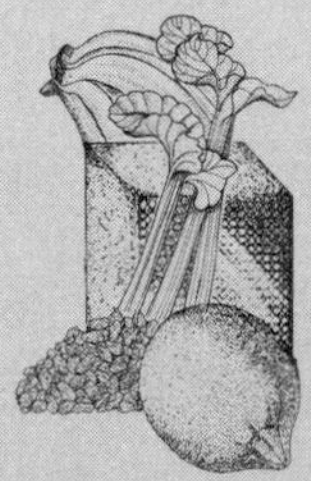

Mock 'Hock'

Rhubarb stalks	2 kg (4½ lb)
Chopped sultanas	450 g (1 lb)
Grape juice concentrate (Hock style)	250 g (9 oz)
Ripe bananas	2
Fresh lemon	1
Clover honey	450 g (1 lb)

White sugar	225 g (½ lb)
Grape tannin	1 tsp
Water	3½ litres (6 pints)
Pectic enzyme and Campden tablets	
Hock yeast and nutrient	

1 Wipe the rhubarb stalks and chop them into small pieces. Place in a mashing bin with the chopped sultanas, peeled and mashed bananas and thinly pared and chopped lemon rind.

2 Pour boiling water over them and when cool, stir in the lemon juice, pectic enzyme and Campden tablet.

3 Next day stir in the grape juice concentrate, honey, tannin, nutrient and active yeast.

4 Ferment on the pulp for six days, pressing down the fruit cap twice daily.

5 Strain out the fruit and press it dry. Stir in the sugar, pour the must into a fermentation jar, top up, fit an air-lock and ferment out.

6 Rack into a clean jar, add one Campden tablet and when the wine is clear, rack again.

7 Store for nine months before bottling.

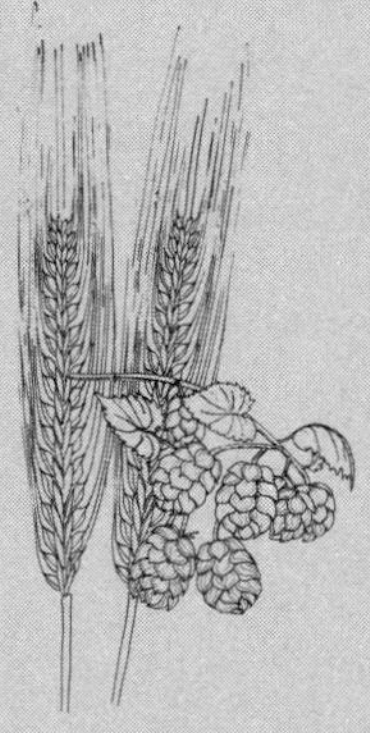

Pale Ale

Forest Maltings Supermalt 12	1.5 kg (3lb 5 oz)
Crushed crystal malt	112 g (4 oz)
White sugar	1 kg (2¼ lb)
Golding hops	56 g (2 oz)
Citric acid	5 g (1 tsp)
Table salt	3 g (½ tsp)
Water	22½ litres (5 gallons)
Lager yeast and nutrient	

1 Boil the sugar and acid in 1 litre (1 quart) water for 20 minutes and dilute with cold water to 1 gallon.

2 Heat the Supermalt, crystal malt and salt in 1½ gallons of water to 65°C (150°F) and maintain this temperature for 45 minutes.

3 Add the hops and boil steadily for a further 30 minutes.

4 Strain into a fermentation vessel, add the sugar syrup, top up with cold water and pitch an active yeast and nutrient.

5 Ferment in a warm place, skimming and rousing on the second and third days.

6 When fermentation is finished, rack the beer into a clean vessel, stir in 200 grams (7 oz) caster sugar and siphon into bottles.

7 Stopper or crown cap the bottles and mature the beer for three weeks before serving it well chilled.

Milk Stout

Pale malt	1 kg (2¼ lb)
Crystal malt	225 g (½ lb)
Black malt	100 g (¼ lb)

Brown sugar	225 g	(½ lb)
Lactose	225 g	(½ lb)
Fuggles hops	40 g	(1½ oz)
Table salt*	5g	(1 tsp)
Water	to 9 litres	(2 gallons)

Stout yeast and nutrient
*Omit salt if soft water is used.

1 Crack the grains and mash at 60°C (140°F) for up to four hours in soft water. When conversion is complete, strain off the liquor and wash the grains.
2 Add the hops, boil for 30 minutes, then leave to cool as quickly as possible.
3 Strain through the hops and stir in the brown sugar. Top up with cold water and check that the S.G. is about 1.036.
4 Stir in the lactose and an active yeast and ferment out at 15°C (60°F), skimming and rousing as usual.
5 Fine, rack, bottle, prime, re-ferment and store for six weeks.

Note: Do not add the lactose before checking the specific gravity. The lactose will not be fermented but would affect the reading. So check the S.G. *before* adding the lactose. This fine beer tastes slightly sweet and milky because of the lactose.

Nettle Beer

Malt extract	450 g	(1 lb)
Young nettle tops	900 g	(2 lb)
Water	4 litres	(7½ pints)

Ale yeast and nutrient

1 Boil the nettles in half the water for 20 minutes. Dissolve the malt in the other half of the water.
2 Strain out the nettle tops and pour the hot liquor on to the wort. When cool, stir in an activated yeast and nutrient.
3 Cover with a cloth, place in the warm and after two days skim off the dirty froth.
4 After five days move the beer to the cool for the sediment to settle, then siphon into eight one-pint beer bottles.
5 Prime each bottle with half-a-teaspoonful of white sugar and stopper tightly.
6 Return the bottles to the warm for two days and then store in the cool for ten days when the beer should be ready to serve. This is pleasant and an extremely ancient drink of our forefathers.

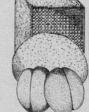

Mint Julep

1 sprig fresh garden mint
2 large tablespoonsful of honey
1 bottle chilled sherry-style wine
6 crushed ice cubes

1 Pour the wine into a large jug, add the crushed ice and stir in the honey.
2 Rinse the mint, shake off the loose water, remove the leaves, chop them finely and add to the wine. Serve at once

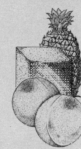

Prune Dessert

Fill a small jar with large prunes and cover them with sweet white wine. Fit an airtight lid and leave in a cupboard for three months. Serve the prunes on cocktail sticks with an apéritif. Drink the liquor yourself — it is near to nectar. Apricots and figs are almost as good!

Peach and Pineapple dessert wine

Canned pineapple juice	1.3 litres	(43 fl oz)
Canned sliced peaches	1 kg	(2 lb approx)
Concentrated white grape juice	1 kg	(1 can)
Blended white honey	450 g	(1 lb)
White sugar	1½ kg	(3¼ lb)
Citric acid	20 g	(2 tsp)
Water	approx 5½ litres	(5 quarts)

Tokay yeast and nutrient

1 Dissolve the honey in warm water, add the pineapple juice, the concentrated grape juice, the peach syrup, the mashed sliced peaches, the citric acid, the Tokay yeast and nutrient. Top up to the 14½ pints level, cover and leave for seven days, stirring twice daily.
2 Strain out the peach pulp, stir in 1 lb sugar, pour the must into a 2-gallon fermentation jar, fit an air-lock and leave for five days.
3 Stir in another 1 lb sugar and five days later, another 1 lb. When fermentation slows down in a week's time, add the last of the sugar.
4 Check the S.G. and at 1.020 rack into a clean jar and add two crushed Campden tablets to terminate fermentation. Replace the air-lock and when the wine is bright, rack again.
5 Store for six months longer, then bottle.

Apricot and Grapefruit apéritif

Canned grapefruit juice	1.3 litres	(43 fl oz)
Canned apricot halves	1 kg	(2 lb approx)
Concentrated white grape juice	1 kg	(1 can)
Blended white honey	450 g	(1 lb)
White sugar	1½ kg	(3¼ lb)
Citric acid	20 g	(¾ oz)
Water	approx 5½ litres	(5 quarts)

Madeira yeast, nutrient and vitamin B tablet

Make this wine in exactly the same way as the last recipe, but ferment it right out. When fully mature this is a very strong, piquant apéritif.

Both recipes make 12 full bottles or 24 halves.

July

Wines made last Autumn and Winter should be racked and bottled before starting on the July wines. Gooseberries make some of the very best wines this month, both still and sparkling. Use only the best fruit – 'Careless' for the sparkling and hock types, 'Leveller' for the sauternes style. Very ripe fruit and dessert varieties are less suitable. Elderflowers and rose petals are abundant, pea pods and broad beans too. The harvesting often overlaps the calendar months, so make the wines when you can.

The soft fruit season extends over a number of weeks. Save the daily collection of raspberries, strawberries, black and red currants etc. in the freezer compartment of the refrigerator until you have sufficient for wine.

With school holidays imminent start off with something for the children that has been very popular for generations.

RECOMMENDED RECIPES

Ginger beer

White sugar	450 g (1 lb)
Root ginger	25 g (1 oz)
Cream of tartar	7 g ($\frac{1}{4}$ oz)
Water	4 litres (7 pints)
Large lemons	2
Ale yeast and nutrient	

1 Stir the sugar, cream of tartar, thinly pared rinds of the lemons and the well-crushed ginger root into boiling water and leave to cool.
2 Add the expressed lemon juice and an active ale yeast and nutrient.
3 Cover and ferment in a warm place for three days, skimming the froth daily.
4 Strain into eight one-pint beer bottles, sweeten each one slightly with saccharin, stopper tightly and keep for four days.

Chill the ginger beer before serving this most refreshing drink which may safely be given to children since it is only slightly alcoholic.

Honey beer

Dark honey	450 g (1 lb)
Brown sugar	340 g ($\frac{3}{4}$ lb)
Hops	20 g ($\frac{3}{4}$ oz)
Water	4 litres (7 pints)
Large lemons	2
Ale yeast and nutrient	

1 Bring the water to the boil and then stir in the honey and sugar until both are dissolved.
2 Add the thinly pared and chopped lemon rinds with the hops, and boil rapidly for 20 minutes, making sure that the hops are kept as well-submerged as

possible. A weighted muslin bag is not recommended as it inhibits the distribution of the hop essences. A wooden spoon is more effective.

3 Leave to cool, then strain out the hops, add the lemon juice and the activated ale yeast and nutrient.

4 Ferment in an open vessel covered with a cloth so that the froth can be skimmed off on the second and third days.

5 After five days, move the beer into a cool place for two days while the sediment settles.

6 Siphon into eight one-pint beer bottles, prime each one with half a teaspoonful of white sugar then stopper tightly.

7 Return the bottles to a warm place for two days while the priming sugar ferments, then store in the cool for ten days.

This is a very ancient drink that was once very popular and only lost favour when malt extract became readily available.

1 Place the chopped sultanas in a bin with the thinly pared rind of the lemon. Express the juice and add to the bin. Discard the hulks.

2 Pour on cold water, the nutrient and active yeast, cover and ferment in a warm place for one week pressing down the sultanas daily.

3 Add the freshly-picked elderflowers, free from every trace of stem and leaf. Press them down to get them thoroughly wet.

4 Continue fermentation for another four days, pressing down the fruit and flowers daily.

5 Strain out and press the solids, stir in the sugar, pour the must into a fermentation jar, fit an air-lock and ferment down to S.G. 1.016.

6 Siphon the wine into a sterile storage jar, add two Campden tablets to terminate fermentation and store in the cool till the wine is bright.

7 Rack into another jar and keep the wine for nine months before bottling. Serve cold.

Elderflower and Sultana wine

Freshly picked elder florets	1 litre (1 quart)
Chopped sultanas	1 kg (2¼ lb)
White sugar	700 g (1½ lb)
Fresh lemon	1
Water	4 litres (7 pints)
Sauternes yeast and nutrient	

Rose Petal wine

Scented red rose petals	2 litres (2 quarts)
Concentrated rosé grape juice	250 g (9 oz)
White sugar	800 g (1¾ lb)
Citric acid	15 g (½ oz)
Grape tannin	3 g (½ tsp)
Water	3½ litres (6½ pints)
Bordeaux yeast and nutrient	

1 Place the rose petals in a bowl, pour boiling water over them and macerate them with the back of a wooden spoon.
2 When cool add the citric acid and one Campden tablet, cover and leave to infuse for three days, macerating the petals daily.
3 Strain out and press the petals, stir in the grape juice, tannin, sugar, nutrient and yeast, pour the must into a fermentation jar, fit an air-lock and ferment to S.G. 1.006.
4 Rack into a clean jar, add two crushed Campden tablets to terminate fermentation and as soon as the wine is bright rack again.
5 Keep for six months before bottling and sweeten to taste with lactose or saccharin.

Raspberry wine

Freshly picked raspberries	1½ kg (3½ lb)
Concentrated rosé grape juice	250 g (9 oz)
White sugar	1 kg (2¼ lb)
Water	3 litres (5 pints)

Pectic enzyme and Campden tablets
Bordeaux yeast and nutrient

1 Remove any stalks and leaves, mash the raspberries, pour cold water over them, add the pectic enzyme and one Campden tablet. Cover and leave for 24 hours.
2 Stir in the grape juice, nutrient and yeast and ferment on the pulp for four days, pressing down the fruit cap twice daily.
3 Strain out and press the fruit, stir in the sugar, pour the must into a fermentation jar, fit an air-lock and ferment to S.G. 1.010.
4 Rack into a clean jar, add two crushed Campden tablets to terminate fermentation and when the wine is bright rack again.
5 Store for nine months before bottling.

Broad Bean wine

Shelled broad beans, too old for normal use	2 kg (4½ lb)
Chopped sultanas	250 g (9 oz)
Fresh lemon	1
White sugar	1 kg (2¼ lb)
Water	4 litres (7 pints)

Cereal yeast and nutrient

1 Boil the beans and the thinly pared lemon rind in all the water for one hour, then leave to cool.
2 Strain the liquor on to the chopped sultanas, add the lemon juice, nutrient and active yeast.
3 Ferment for five days pressing down the fruit daily.
4 Strain out and press the sultanas, stir in the sugar, pour the must into a fermentation jar, fit an air-lock and ferment out.
5 Rack into a clean jar, add one crushed Campden

tablet and when clear rack again.
6 Mature this wine for nine months before bottling and serve it cool and dry.

Cherry wine: sweet

Mixed red and white cooking cherries	2 kg (4½ lb)
Morello cherries	225 g (½ lb)
Concentrated grape juice	250 g (9 oz)
Sugar	1¼ kg (2¾ lb)
Citric acid	5 g (1 tsp)
Grape tannin	3 g (½ tsp)
Water	3 litres (5 pints)

Pectic enzyme and Campden tablets
Port yeast and nutrient

1 Wash and stalk the cherries, pour boiling water over them and when cool, remove the stones. Add the acid, pectic enzyme and one Campden tablet, cover and leave for 24 hours.
2 Stir in the grape juice and one third of the sugar, the tannin, nutrient and active yeast. Ferment on the pulp for five days, pressing down the fruit cap twice daily.
3 Strain out and press the fruit, stir in half the remaining sugar, pour into a fermentation jar, fit an air-lock and continue fermentation.
4 Seven days later remove some wine from the jar, dissolve the last of the sugar in it and return it to the jar slowly to avoid frothing. Replace the air-lock and continue fermentation.
5 When fermentation is finished, rack the wine into a clean jar, add one Campden tablet, store the wine until it is bright, then rack it again.
6 Store this strong wine for one year before bottling and if necessary sweeten to taste – about S.G. 1.020.

Cherry wine: dry

Mixed cooking cherries	2 kg (4½ lb)
Concentrated white grape juice	250 g (9 oz)
White sugar	900 g (2 lb)
Citric acid	5 g (1 tsp)
Grape tannin	3 g (½ tsp)
Water	3½ litres (6 pints)

Pectic enzyme and Campden tablets
Graves yeast and nutrient

1 Make in the same way as just described, but add the second and third doses of sugar together when the fruit is strained out.

Cherry Plum wine

Ripe cherry plums	2 kg (4½ lb)
Concentrated rosé grape juice	250 g (9 oz)
White sugar	1 kg (2¼ lb)
Citric acid	5 g (1 tsp)

Grape tannin   3 g (½ tsp)
Water   3 litres (5 pints)
Pectic enzyme and Campden tablets
Bordeaux yeast and nutrient.

1 Make in the same way as the last recipe but terminate fermentation by racking at S.G. 1.006 and adding two crushed Campden tablets.

Gooseberry 'Hock'

Hard green gooseberries,   1.5 kg (3¼ lb)
   'Careless' if possible
Concentrated grape juice   250 g (9 oz)
   (Hock style)
Sugar   700 g (25 oz)
Citric acid   5 g (1 tsp)
Water   3½ litres (6 pints)
Pectic enzyme and Campden tablets
Hock yeast and nutrient

1 Wash, top and tail the gooseberries, pour boiling water over them and when cool squash the berries with your fingers.
2 Add the acid, pectic enzyme and one Campden tablet, cover and leave for 24 hours.
3 Stir in the grape juice, yeast and nutrient and ferment on the pulp for four days, pressing down the fruit cap twice daily.
4 Strain out and press the fruit, stir in the sugar, pour the must into a fermentation jar, top up, fit an air-lock and ferment out.
5 Rack into a clean jar, add one crushed Campden tablet and when the wine is bright rack again.
6 Store for one year before bottling.

Serve this delicious wine cold as a light, dry white table wine, as an aperitif or as a social wine on a warm evening.

Sparkling Gooseberry wine

1 Use similar ingredients and methods as just described but substitute a champagne yeast for the hock.
2 When the wine is six months old and star-bright, innoculate it with 70 g (2½ oz) caster sugar and an active champagne yeast. Fit an air-lock and as soon as the wine starts fermenting pour it into six heavy champagne bottles. Fit hollow-domed plastic stoppers, wire them down, store for two weeks at room temperature 20°C (68°F) and then in the cool for a further six months, at least, preferably for a year. The longer the better.

Note: This is one of the finest wines that can be made in the home and surpasses many champagnes. Once tried this wine will become an annual 'must'. It is worth making at least twelve bottles.

Gooseberry Wine: Chablis style

'Leveller' gooseberries   1800 g (4 lb)
Concentrated white grape juice 500 g (18 oz)
   (Chablis style)
White sugar   700 g (25 oz)
Water   3 litres (5 pints)
Pectic enzyme and Campden tablets
Chablis yeast and nutrient

1 Prepare in the same way as for Gooseberry 'Hock'.

This wine has more flavour, body and alcohol, however, and is a superb table wine.

Note: Because of their acidity and flavour, gooseberries make better dry wines than sweet.

Summer Rosé

Selection from:
Raspberries   up to 200 g (7 oz)
Strawberries   up to 200 g (7 oz)
Blackcurrants   up to 125 g (4½ oz)
Redcurrants   up to 250 g (9 oz)
White currants   up to 250 g (9 oz)
Gooseberries   up to 250 g (9 oz)
Cherries   up to 250 g (9 oz)
Golden Plums   up to 250 g (9 oz)
Early apples   up to 1 kg (2¼ lb)
White grapes   up to 1 kg (2¼ lb)
Total soft fruit and stone fruit about
                       1.5 kg (3¼ lb)
plus apples and/or grapes   about 1 kg (2¼ lb)
Sugar   up to S.G. 1.090
Water   up to 4½ litres (1 gallon)
Pectic enzyme and Campden tablets
Bordeaux yeast and nutrient

1 Wash and prepare the fruit, top and tail, stalk, stone etc. Mash or chop finely, cover with cold water (about 2¼ litres – 2 quarts) add the pectic enzyme and one Campden tablet, cover and leave overnight.
2 Pour off some juice, measure the specific gravity and calculate the amount of sugar required – from 700 to 900 g (1½ to 2 lb) depending on the quality of the fruit.
3 Return the juice to the bin and stir in an active yeast and nutrient. Ferment on the pulp for five days, pressing down the fruit cap daily.
4 Strain out and press the fruit, stir in the sugar, pour the must into a fermentation jar, top up with cold water, fit an air-lock and ferment down to 1.006.
5 Rack into a clean jar, add two crushed Campden tablets to terminate fermentation and when the wine is clear, rack again.
6 Store for one year before bottling.

Serve this wine cold and medium dry/sweet at any time. It is among the very best that can be made.

August

AFTER the hectic making of wine in July there is often something of a gap in August, possibly because of school holidays – and sometimes poorer weather. For those at home with time and containers to spare there is, however, a good selection of wines to make. Towards the end of the month some wild blackberries may be available in warmer parts of the country and the cultivated variety is usually at its peak.

At fruit markets it is sometimes possible to purchase in bulk at reduced prices, but beware of buying poor quality fruit, because it is cheap. It is sometimes already infected or oxidised. Only buy the best if you want good wine. Look out for peaches and pineapples in particular. Morello cherries are sometimes hard to find so do not miss any opportunity to buy some.

One's stock of beer always needs replenishing, so try some draught for quickness.

RECOMMENDED RECIPES

Draught Mild Ale

Malt extract	1.5 kg (3 lb)
Flaked barley	70 g (2½ oz)
Invert sugar	1 kg (2½ lb)
Golding hops	15 g (½ oz)
Fuggle hops	100 g (3½ oz)
Caramel	2 level 5 ml spoonsful
Citric acid	1 level 5 ml spoonful
Table salt	2 level 5 ml spoonsful
Water	23 litres (5 gallons)

Ale yeast and nutrient

1 Place the malt extract, citric acid, salt and sugar in a bin, pour on some warm water and stir until all is dissolved.

2 Boil the Fuggle hops and caramel vigorously for 40 minutes, then add the Goldings and boil for a further five minutes. Leave to cool, then strain the liquor on to the wort.

3 Boil the flaked barley in a quart of water for ten minutes, strain off through a sieve into the wort and repeat the process.

4 Adjust the liquor quantity to five gallons and S.G. to 1.034.

5 Pitch an active yeast and ferment at 15°C (60°F), skimming as necessary with particular attention to the liquor line.

6 When fermentation is finished, stir in some finings and leave for 48 hours for the beer to clear.

7 Rack into a pressurized plastic cask and prime with 5 oz of sugar dissolved in some of the beer. Mature for 2 to 3 weeks, or longer if possible.

Blackberry wine

Cultivated blackberries	2 kg	(4½ lb)
Ripe bananas	2 only	
Red grape juice concentrate	250 g	(9 oz)
Sugar	900 g	(2 lb)
Citric acid	10 g	(2 tsp)
Grape tannin	3 g	(½ tsp)
Water	3 litres	(5 pints)

Pectic enzyme and Campden tablets
Burgundy 'Super' wine yeast and nutrient

1 Wash and drain the blackberries, peel the bananas; liquidise them or mash everything with the back of a wooden spoon; pour cold water over them, add the acid, pectic enzyme and one Campden tablet. Cover and leave for 24 hours.
2 Stir in the grape juice, yeast and nutrient and ferment on the pulp for five days, pressing down the fruit cap daily.
3 Strain out the pulp, stir in the sugar, pour the must into a fermentation jar, top up with cold water, fit an air-lock and ferment out.
4 Rack into a clean jar, add one crushed Campden tablet and when the wine is bright rack again and store for one year before bottling. Keep for a further six months or so, then serve free from chill with cheese or roast meats.

Loganberry wine

Freshly picked loganberries	1,360 g	(3 lb)
Sultanas	450 g	(1 lb)
Ripe bananas	450 g	(1 lb)
Sugar	900 g	(2 lb)
Water	3½ litres	(6 pints)

Pectic enzyme and Campden tablets
Burgundy yeast and nutrient

1 Stalk, rinse and crush the loganberries, peel and mash the bananas, wash and chop the sultanas and place all the fruit in a mashing bin.
2 Pour boiling water on to the pulp and when cool add the pectic enzyme and one Campden tablet. Cover the bin and leave for 24 hours.
3 Stir in the active yeast and nutrient and ferment on the pulp for five days, pressing down the fruit cap daily.
4 Strain out the solids, stir in the sugar, pour the must into a fermentation jar, top up, fit an air-lock and ferment out.
5 Rack into a clean jar, add one crushed Campden tablet and when the wine is bright, rack it again.
6 Store for one year before bottling.

Note: Because of their strong flavour the quantity of loganberries should not be exceeded.

Pink 'Champagne'

Freshly picked red currants	1,360 g (3 lb)
Chopped sultanas	250 g (9 oz)
Sugar	700 g (1½ lb)
Water	4 litres (7 pints)

Pectic enzyme and Campden tablets
Champagne yeast and nutrient

1 Wash and strig the currants but small stalks may be left to provide a little tannin. Crush the fruit, add the chopped or liquidised sultanas. Pour cold water over them, then add the pectic enzyme and one crushed Campden tablet.
Cover and leave for 24 hours.
2 Stir in an active yeast and nutrient and ferment on the pulp for four days, pressing down the fruit cap twice daily.
3 Strain out and press the fruit, stir in the sugar, pour the must into a fermentation jar, top up, fit an air-lock and ferment right out to dryness.
4 Rack into a sterile jar and rack again when the wine is bright, then store for six months.
5 Prime the wine with 70 g (2½ oz) sugar and an active champagne yeast then fit an air-lock and move the jar to a warm place.
6 As soon as fermentation starts, pour the wine into six sterile champagne bottles, fit hollow-domed plastic stoppers and wire them down.
7 Leave the bottles on their sides in a warm room for one week and then in a cool store for at least six months, preferably much longer.

White Currant wine

A splendid sparkling white wine may be made by using white currants instead of red. The quantities of ingredients, and the methods just given should be used.

Black Currant dessert wine

Freshly picked black currants	900 g (2 lb)
Ripe bananas	450 g (1 lb)
Chopped raisins	450 g (1 lb)
Dried apricots	225 g (½ lb)
Sugar	1,250 g (2¾ lb)
Tartaric acid	10 g (2 tsp)
Grape tannin	3 g (½ tsp)
Water	3½ litres (6 pints)

Pectic enzyme and Campden tablets
Port yeast and nutrient

1 Wash the black currants, remove the main strigs and squash the fruit, peel and mash the bananas, wash and chop the dried apricots and raisins. Place them all in a mashing bin and pour water over them. When cool, add the acid, tannin, pectic enzyme and one Campden tablet. Cover the bin and leave it for 24 hours.

2 Stir in the active yeast and nutrient and ferment on the pulp for seven days, pressing down the fruit cap twice daily.
3 Strain out and gently press the fruit, stir in a quarter of the sugar, pour the must into a fermentation jar, fit an air-lock and place the jar in a warm position.
4 Every five days stir in another quarter of the sugar until all is used.
5 When fermentation appears to be finished, give the wine a stir and check the specific gravity. If necessary add sufficient sugar to increase the reading to 1.020.
6 Rack into a sterile jar and when the wine is bright, rack it again. Store it for at least one year before bottling and if possible for two years.

Morello Cherry dessert wine

Ripe morello cherries	2 kg (4½ lb)
Ripe bananas	250 g (9 oz)
Chopped raisins	250 g (9 oz)
Sugar	1,250 g (2¾ lb)
Tartaric acid	5 g (1 tsp)
Grape tannin	3 g (½ tsp)
Water	3½ litres (6 pints)

Pectic enzyme and Campden tablets
Port yeast and nutrient

1 Wash, stalk, stone and mash the cherries. Treat the other ingredients as just described for the black currant dessert wine. Follow the same method to produce a superb dessert wine.

Greengage wine

Fresh greengages	2 kg (4½ lb)
Chopped sultanas	450 g (1 lb)
Sugar	900 g (2 lb)
Citric acid	5 g (1 tsp)
Grape tannin	3 g (½ tsp)
Water	4 litres (7 pints)

Pectic enzyme and Campden tablets
Chablis yeast and nutrient

1 Wash, stalk, stone and mash the greengages, place them in a bin, add the chopped sultanas and pour boiling water over them. When cool, add the acid, tannin, pectic enzyme and one Campden tablet. Cover and leave for 24 hours.
2 Stir in the active yeast and nutrient, and ferment for five days, pressing down the fruit cap twice daily.
3 Strain out and press the fruit, stir in the sugar, pour the must into a fermentation jar, fit an air-lock and ferment to dryness.
4 Rack into a sterile storage jar, add one crushed Campden tablet and when the wine is bright rack again.
5 Store for nine months before bottling.

Apricot wine

Fresh apricots	2 kg (4½ lb)

Other ingredients and methods as just described for greengage wine.

These are two excellent table wines that are well worth making.

Pineapple Aperitif

Fresh pineapples of medium size	4
White grape juice concentrate	500 g (18 oz)
Sugar	900 g (2 lb)
Tartaric acid	5 g (1 tsp)
Grape tannin	3 g (½ tsp)
Water	3½ litres (6 pints)

Pectic enzyme and Campden tablets
Tokay yeast and nutrient

1 Top and tail the pineapples but do not peel them. Chop up into dice-sized pieces, mash or liquidise them, place in a mashing bin and pour boiling water over them. When cool add the acid, tannin, pectic enzyme and one Campden tablet. Cover and leave for 24 hours.
2 Stir in the grape juice, nutrient and yeast and ferment on the pulp for five days, pressing down the fruit cap twice daily.
3 Strain out the fruit, roll it around a nylon sieve and then discard it. Stir in the sugar, pour the must into a fermentation jar, fit an air-lock and ferment to dryness.
4 Rack into a clean jar, add one Campden tablet and when the wine is bright, rack again. Store for nine months before bottling.

This is a strong, dry, white aperitif that should be served very cold.

Peach 'Sauternes'

Fresh ripe peaches	2 kg (4½ lb)
Fresh ripe bananas	450 g (1 lb)
White grape juice concentrate (Sauternes style)	500 g (18 oz)
Scented yellow rose petals	50 g (2 oz)
Sugar	900 g (2 lb)
Glucose	50 g (2 oz)
Tartaric acid	15 g (½ oz)
Grape tannin	3 g (½ tsp)
Water	3 litres (5 pints)

Pectic enzyme and Campden tablets
Sauternes yeast and nutrient

1 Halve or mash the peaches, discard the stones, peel and mash the bananas, place them in a mashing bin, add the rose petals and pour boiling water over them. Cover and leave to cool.
2 Add the acid, tannin, pectic enzyme and one

Campden tablet, cover and leave for 24 hours.
3 Stir in the grape juice concentrate, nutrient and active yeast and ferment on the pulp for five days, pressing down the fruit cap twice daily.
4 Strain out and roll the fruit pulp round a nylon sieve, then stir in the sugar and glucose, pour the must into a fermentation jar, top up with cold water, fit an air-lock and ferment to S.G. 1.016.
5 Rack into a clean jar, add two crushed Campden tablets to terminate fermentation and rack again when the wine is bright.
6 Store for nine months before bottling.

Serve the wine cold with the sweet course of a meal, as the basis for liqueurs or in summer wine cups.

Melon wine

Large yellow water melon	2½–3 kg (5½–6½ lb)
White grape juice concentrate	500 g (18 oz)
White sugar	900 g (2 lb)
Citric acid	15 g (½ oz)
Grape tannin	3 g (½ tsp)
Water	3 litres (5 pints)

Pectic enzyme and Campden tablets
All-purpose wine yeast and nutrient

1 Wipe over the melon and cut it into small pieces. Place all the fruit, skin and seeds in a bin, add the acid, tannin, pectic enzyme, one crushed Campden tablet and pour on cold water. Cover and leave for 24 hours.
2 Stir in the grape juice, nutrient and active yeast and ferment on the pulp for five days, pressing down the fruit cap twice daily.
3 Strain out the solids, stir in the sugar, pour the must into a fermentation jar, top up, fit an air-lock and ferment down to S.G. 1.012.
4 Siphon the wine into a clean jar, add two crushed Campden tablets to terminate fermentation, and when bright rack again.
5 Store for nine months then bottle.

A Summer wine cup

Rosé wine	2 bottles
Strawberries	160 g (6 oz)
Caster sugar	100 g (3½ oz)
Large ice cubes	12
Fizzy lemonade	50 cls (18 oz)

1 Wash, stalk and cut the strawberries into pea-sized pieces, sprinkle sugar over them and leave for a few minutes.
2 Add the rosé wine, previously chilled, the ice cubes and the fizzy lemonade.
3 Serve at once with some strawberries and ice in each glass. This is enough for twelve persons.

September

THERE are so many wines to make this month that it is difficult to know which to tackle first. All of the fruits available make excellent wines on their own, and blend happily with other fruits to make even better wines. An especial advantage of this factor is that wine can still be made even if the quantities available of any one ingredient are too small to make wine on its own.

Wild blackberry wine should certainly be made if it is possible to get out into the country to gather the berries. They have a stronger flavour than the cultivated varieties and are ideal for dessert wines, being high in alcohol.

Victoria plums too, make a superb wine, especially of the dry sherry style.

Windfall apples are often available for the taking — or very cheaply — at least to those who live in the country or on the edge of towns. Such apples produce a white table wine that will splendidly accompany fish, pork, poultry and cheese, as well as being a wine for drinking, German fashion, unaccompanied by food, on a warm summer evening.

Mulberry wine that has been fermented with a Madeira yeast makes a superb dessert wine after adequate maturation. Bilberry wine is one of our very best red table wines, fruity and well-balanced. Many gardeners now grow a bush or two along with the currants and gooseberries. Blackcurrant is an old favourite, long recognised for its beneficial qualities to health. Black plums make an everyday table wine, the more acceptable because it can be drunk on so many occasions.

The vegetables make good support wines, well worth making if they are in surplus. Runner bean wine blends well with elderberry wine, giving it body and diluting its sometimes overpowering flavour.

Since so many fermentation bins and jars will be needed this month, wines made earlier this year may have to be bottled first.

RECOMMENDED RECIPES

Blackberry dessert wine I

Wild blackberries	2 kg (4½ lb)
Chopped raisins	500 g (18 oz)
Sugar	1250 g (2¾ lb)
Water	4 litres (7 pints)

Pectic enzyme and Campden tablet
Port yeast and nutrient

1 Pick only the largest and ripest blackberries on a dry day. Remove all the stalks and rinse the berries in cold running water to remove hairs, dust and insects.
2 Place the berries in a bin and mash them with the back of a wooden spoon or the like.
3 Wash and chop the raisins and add to the blackberries.
4 Pour cold water on to the fruit, add the pectic enzyme, and a crushed Campden tablet, cover and leave for 24 hours.
5 Add an activated yeast and nutrient, and ferment on the pulp for 5–7 days, pressing down the fruit cap twice daily.
6 Strain out and gently press the fruit, stir in half the sugar, pour into a dark fermentation jar, leaving space for the remaining sugar, fit an air-lock and continue fermentation.

7 After 8 days add half the remaining sugar and 8 days later add the rest.

8 When fermentation finishes, move the wine to a cooler position and 4 days later siphon it into a sterilised storage jar. Add 1 Campden tablet and store the wine for 2 months.

9 Again rack the wine and then store for at least 10 months before bottling, and follow with another 6 months storage.

10 Always keep blackberry wine in dark glass or opaque containers so that the colour does not fade in the light.

Blackberry dessert wine II

Blackberries	2 kg	($4\frac{1}{2}$ lb)
Blackcurrants	250 g	(9 oz)
Elderberries	250 g	(9 oz)
Grape juice concentrate	500 g	(18 oz)
Bananas — very ripe	250 g	(9 oz)
Sugar	1250 g	($2\frac{3}{4}$ lb)
Water	4 litres	(7 pints)

Pectic enzyme and nutrient

1 Selecting the best quality fruit, remove all the stalks and rinse under cold running water.

2 Simmer the elderberries and peeled bananas in 1 litre of water for 20 minutes and then pour them into a bin containing the crushed blackberries and blackcurrants.

3 Add the rest of the water, pectic enzyme and Campden tablet. Cover and leave for 24 hours.

4 Stir in the grape juice concentrate — port type — together with an active yeast and nutrient. Ferment

on the pulp for 5–7 days, pressing down the fruit cap twice daily.

5 Continue as described above.

Apple wine

Assorted windfall apples	5 kg	(11 lb)

    [Mostly cooking (70%), include a few eating (20%) and some crab apples (10%)]

Sugar	1 kg per $4\frac{1}{2}$ litres of must	($2\frac{1}{4}$ lb per gallon)

Water to cover the apples approx 2 litres ($3\frac{1}{2}$ pints)
Pectic enzyme and Campden tablets
Champagne yeast and nutrient

1 Do not use fewer apples than mentioned. Cut out bruised portions and maggot caves. Slice or crush the apples and drop them into a bin containing the water, pectic enzyme and a Campden tablet. Cover and leave for 24 hours.

2 Stir in the active yeast and ferment on the pulp for 7–8 days, stirring thoroughly twice daily.

3 Strain out and press the apples dry, then measure the liquor, stir in 1 kg sugar to every $4\frac{1}{2}$ litres of must and continue fermentation under an air-lock.

4 When fermentation is finished, rack into sterilised storage jars, add 1 Campden tablet per gallon and keep for 2 months.

5 Rack again and if necessary add wine finings.

6 As soon as the wine is bright, rack again and store until it is 6 months old, then bottle.

Note: 'All-purpose' or Sauternes yeasts may also be used. 250 grams white grape juice concentrate can also be added per $4\frac{1}{2}$ litres of must, and improves the wine substantially. Reduce the sugar by 200 g.

Apple and Blackberry table wine

Apples, assorted	3 kg	(6¾ lb)
Blackberries	1 kg	(2¼ lb)
Sultanas	250 g	(9 oz)
Sugar	1 kg	(2¼ lb)
Water	3 litres	(5½ pints)

Pectic enzyme and Campden tablets
Pommard or Burgundy yeast and nutrient

1 Stalk, wash and crush the blackberries. Place them in a mashing tin with the pectic enzyme, 1 crushed Campden tablet and 3 litres of cold water.
2 Wash and crush the apples (or cut them into small pieces) and drop them at once into the bin.
3 Wash and chop the sultanas and add them to the apples, then cover the bin and leave it for 24 hours.
4 Stir in the sugar, yeast and nutrient and ferment on pulp for 7 days, pressing down the fruit cap twice daily, keeping the bin covered meanwhile.
5 Strain out and press the fruit, pour the must into a fermentation jar, fit an air-lock and ferment out.
6 Siphon into a sterilised jar, add 1 Campden tablet and some wine finings, then store for 4 weeks.
7 Rack again and store for 4 months, then bottle and keep for a further 2 months.

Note: This is a rosé-to-light-red dry table wine; serve fairly young and cool (15°C).

Apple and Plum table wine

Assorted apples	3 kg	(6¾ lb)
Assorted plums	1 kg	(2¼ lb)
Sugar	1 kg	(2¼ lb)
Water	2½ litres	(4 pints)

Pectic enzyme and Campden tablet
Pommard or Burgundy yeast and nutrient

1 Wash the ripe plums in very hot water, then remove the stones and drop them into a bin containing cold water, pectic enzyme and a Campden tablet.
2 Wash and crush the apples and drop them into the bin as soon as they are crushed.
3 Cover and leave for 24 hours.
4 Stir in the sugar and active yeast and ferment on the pulp for 7–10 days, stirring twice daily.
5 Strain out and press the fruit, pour the must into a fermentation jar, fit an air-lock and ferment to dryness.
6 Siphon into a sterilised storage jar and continue as for apple and blackberry.

Mulberry 'Madeira' wine

Ripe mulberries	2 kg	(4½ lb)
Raisins	500 g	(18 oz)
Bananas	250 g	(9 oz)
Rosehip syrup	170 g	(6 oz)
Brown sugar	1250 g	(2¾ lb)
Grape tannin	½ tsp	
Tartaric acid	1 tsp	
Water	3 litres	(5½ pints)

Pectic enzyme and Campden tablets
Madeira yeast and nutrient

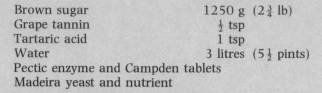

1 Select the largest mulberries, rinse them quickly in cold water, mash them with the back of a wooden spoon and place them in a mashing bin containing the water, pectic enzyme, tartaric acid, tannin and Campden tablet.
2 Wash and chop the raisins and add them to the bin, with the peeled, very ripe, mashed bananas.
3 Cover the vessel and leave for 24 hours.
4 Stir in the active yeast and nutrient and ferment on the pulp for 5–7 days, stirring twice daily.
5 Strain out and gently press the fruit, or roll it round a nylon sieve.
6 Stir in the rosehip syrup and half the brown sugar and continue fermentation for 8 days.
7 Stir in half the remaining sugar and 8 days later add the rest.
8 When fermentation is finished, rack the wine into a sterilised jar, add 1 Campden tablet and store the wine in as warm a place as possible.
9 Rack again after 2 months and return to the warm. Store for 1 year before bottling. Sweeten to taste.

Blackcurrant table wine

Blackcurrant	1350 g	(3 lb)
Sugar	1350 g	(3 lb)
Water	4 litres	(7 pints)

Pectic enzyme and Campden tablet
Burgundy yeast and nutrient

1 Stalk and wash the blackcurrants, mash and place in a bin containing the water, pectic enzyme and one Campden tablet. Cover and leave for 24 hours.
2 Stir in an active yeast and ferment on the pulp for five days stirring twice daily.
3 Strain out and press the fruit, stir in the sugar, pour into a fermentation jar, fit an air-lock and ferment out.
4 Rack into a sterilised jar, add 1 Campden tablet and store for 2 months, then rack again and store for 6 months before bottling.

Bilberry table wine

Bilberries – garden fresh	1350 g	(3 lb)
Sugar	1250 g	(2¾ lb)
Water	4 litres	(7 pints)

Pectic enzyme and Campden tablets
Bordeaux yeast and nutrient

1 Stalk and mash the bilberries and make the wine in exactly the same way as for blackcurrants.

Black Plum table wine

Ripe plums	3 kg (6¾ lb)
Sugar	1250 g (2¾ lb)
Water	4 litres (7 pints)

Pectic enzyme and Campden tablet
Burgundy yeast and nutrient

1 Stalk the plums and wash them in very hot water containing a handful of washing soda to remove the waxy bloom which causes an irremovable haze in the wine. Rinse in cold water and then remove the stones.
2 Place the plum pieces in a mashing bin containing the water, pectic enzyme and Campden tablet. Cover and leave for 24 hours.
3 Stir in the sugar, activated yeast and nutrient and ferment on the pulp for 5–7 days.
4 Press down the fruit cap twice daily and keep the bin well covered meanwhile.
5 Strain out and press the fruit gently, pour the must into a fermentation jar and ferment to dryness.
6 Rack into a sterilised jar, add 1 Campden tablet and store for 4 months before bottling.

Note: This is another excellent everyday red table wine worth making in good quantities.

Victoria Plum Sherry

Victoria plums	4 kg (9 lb)
Peaches	1 kg (2¼ lb)
Grape juice concentrate (Dry sherry type)	1 kg (2¼ lb)
Sugar	1500 g (3½ lb)
Calcium sulphate (gypsum)	50 g (2 oz)
Cream of tartar	25 g (1 oz)
Water	6 litres (11 pints)

Pectic enzyme and Campden tablets
Sherry yeast and nutrient

1 Stalk the Victoria plums and wash them in very hot water, remove the stones and drop the plums into hot water containing the cream of tartar and gypsum.
2 Peel the peaches, remove the stones, cut the halves into pieces and add them to the bin.
3 When cool add the pectic enzyme and 1 Campden tablet. Cover and leave for 24 hours.
4 Stir in the grape juice concentrate, an activated sherry yeast and nutrient.
5 Ferment on the pulp for 4 days, then strain out the fruit and roll it round a nylon sieve rather than pressing it.
6 Leave the must in a bin, stir in half the sugar, cover with a lid and ferment in a warm place.
7 After 8 days stir in half the remaining sugar and 8 days later add the rest and make the total quantity up to 9½ litres (17 pints) with cold water. This will produce 12 full bottles of wine.
8 As soon as fermentation is finished move the bin to a cool place for a few days to encourage the sediment to settle.
9 Siphon the clearing wine into a storage jar or jars until they are about three-quarters full. Plug the necks of the jars with unmedicated cotton wool — NOT a cork or rubber bung. Place them in a temperate store at about 15°C (59°F), and leave them undisturbed for at least 1 year and preferably longer.
10 During this time a flor may appear on the surface of the wine like a creamy, crinkled skin. This is advantageous in the making of a dry sherry.
11 The wine, being very strong in alcohol, will keep well without the aid of a Campden tablet. The oxidation that occurs is an essential part of the flavour.
12 For winemakers using an hydrometer a total specific gravity of 1.120 should be obtained and fermented right out.

Runner Bean Social wine

Runner beans	2 kg (4½ lb)
Grape juice concentrate (white or red)	500 g (18 oz)
Sugar	1 kg (2¼ lb)
Tartaric acid	2 tsp
Water	3½ litres (6 pints)

Campden tablets
All-purpose wine yeast and nutrient

1 Wash the runner beans, cut them into slices, boil them till tender, then leave them to cool.
2 Pour the liquor into a fermentation jar, stir in the grape juice, sugar, acid, yeast and nutrient. Leave a little air space in case of frothing. Excess must may first be placed in a bottle beside the jar and then used to top up.
3 Fit an air-lock and ferment to S.G. 1.005.
4 Rack and add 2 Campden tablets.
5 Rack again as soon as the wine is clear and store for 4 months before bottling.

Marrow and Ginger Social wine

Marrow	2 kg (4½ lb)
Root ginger	50 g (2 oz)
Grape juice concentrate (white or red)	500 g (18 oz)
Sugar	1 kg (2¼ lb)
Tartaric acid	2 tsp
Water	3½ litres (6 pints)

Campden tablets
All-purpose wine yeast and nutrient

1 Wipe the marrow clean from soil, then cut it into small pieces. Skin, pip and pulp, then boil till tender.
2 Continue as for runner bean wine.
Do not try to stuff the marrow with sugar. It does not work!

October

ANOTHER busy month, especially for the making of red wines. England's grape – the elderberry – hangs full and black on stalks turned red with ripeness. Grapes themselves now ripen in many gardens, whilst sloes, bilberries, damsons and late black plums all contribute to the red wine harvest. Crab apples and quince enrich the scene visually and improve the flavour of white wines made from apples and pears; but store them for a few weeks to mellow.

All too often it is not possible to obtain enough ingredients to make sufficient red wines to meet the needs of the family. In such circumstances try 'stretching' the red wines with apples, or use red grape juice concentrate with windfall apples, or fresh, frozen or canned blackcurrants with apples. Instead of making small quantities of separate wines, blend the ingredients at the outset to make a much larger quantity of, say, a light red table wine. Because the elderberry flavour and colour is so strong you may, if necessary, reduce the quantity in any recipe and replace it with another fruit. Boiling elderberries is the most efficient method of extracting the colour and flavour and even then they may still be used for a second 'run', at least to provide colour in a rosé. Any excess of fruit may be frozen for later use, so gather as many elderberries as you can find.

Wines made previously in the year may have to be bottled somewhat earlier than recommended, to release jars for the fermentation of new wines. Label and store the bottles until the wine is really mature, but taste a few to encourage you to make more.

Check up on your stock of yeasts, nutrient, acids, sugar and, of course, sulphite. Watch out for birds; they love the ripe berries and will quickly clear the crop unless prevented.

RECOMMENDED RECIPES

Red table wine
Fresh black grapes
Sugar
Campden tablets
Burgundy yeast

1 Remove the main stalks, crush the grapes, but not the pips, run off some juice and check the specific gravity. If needs be, stir in sufficient sugar to increase the reading to 1.086 or thereabouts.
2 Add one crushed Campden tablet per gallon ($4\frac{1}{2}$ litres) of must, cover and leave for 24 hours.
3 Add an activated Burgundy yeast and ferment the wine on the pulp of skin and pips for 12–14 days, keeping the floating cap submerged in the juice with a weighted plate – but ensure that no metallic object is used. Cover the bin effectively at all times.
4 Strain out and press the pulp dry, pour the wine into a fermentation jar, fit an air-lock and continue fermentation to dryness.
5 Rack into a clean jar, add one crushed Campden tablet per gallon and when the wine is bright, rack again.
6 Mature for at least one year before bottling and preferably longer.

White table wine
Fresh white grapes
Sugar
Campden tablets
Hock yeast

1 Make in the same way as just described, but adjust the specific gravity to 1.076 or so and remove

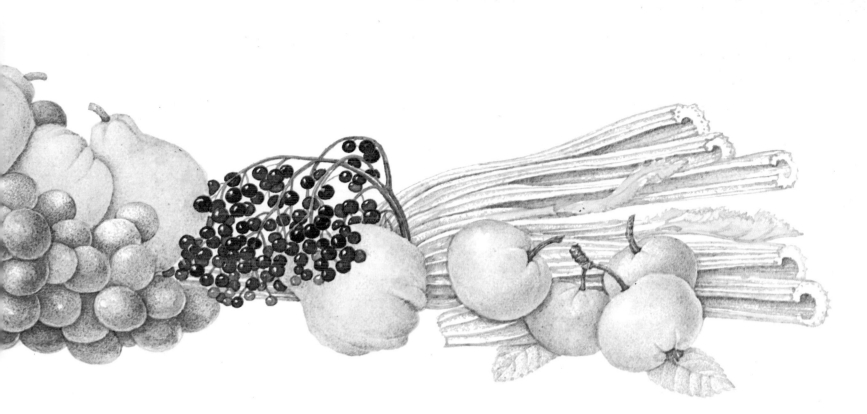

the pulp on the second day after fermentation has started.

2 Keep for 8–9 months before bottling.

Rosé table wine

Black grapes or a mixture of both black and white
    grapes
Sugar
Campden tablets
Bordeaux yeast

1 Make in the same way as described but adjust the specific gravity to 1.080 and remove the pulp as soon as the must has turned a 'pretty pink'.

2 When the must has fermented down to 1.004, rack into a clean jar and add two crushed Campden tablets to terminate fermentation.

3 Store the wine for 8–9 months before bottling.

Elderberry table wine

Fresh picked elderberries	900 g	(2 lb)
Ripe bananas	250 g	(9 oz)
Red grape juice concentrate	250 g	(9 oz)
Sugar	900 g	(2 lb)
Tartaric acid	10 g	(2 tsp)
Water	4 litres	(7 pints)

Pectic enzyme and Campden tablets
Bordeaux yeast and nutrient

1 Wash the elderberries and remove them from their stalks. Peel and slice the bananas. Boil these together for 15 minutes, then empty them into a mashing bin.

2 When cool add the pectic enzyme and one Campden tablet, cover and leave for 24 hours.

3 Stir in the grape juice, yeast and nutrient and ferment on the pulp for 4 days, pressing down the fruit cap daily.

4 Strain out the fruit, stir in the sugar, pour the must into a fermentation jar, fit an air-lock and ferment out.

5 Rack into a clean jar, add one crushed Campden tablet and when the wine is bright rack again. Mature this wine for at least one year and serve it free from chill.

Elderberry dessert wine

Freshly picked elderberries	900 g	(2 lb)
Chopped raisins	450 g	(1 lb)
Ripe bananas	250 g	(9 oz)
Dried apricots	125 g	(4½ oz)
Grape juice concentrate (port style)	250 g	(9 oz)
Sugar	700 g	(1½ lb)
Tartaric acid	15 g	(½ oz)
Water	4 litres	(7 pints)

Pectic enzyme and Campden tablets
Port yeast and nutrient

1 Wash the elderberries and remove them from their stalks. Peel and slice the bananas. Wash and chop the apricots. Boil them all together for 15 minutes then empty into a mashing bin containing the chopped raisins.

2 Continue as described in 2 and 3 above but ferment for 7 days.

3 Strain out the fruit, stir in half the sugar, pour the must into a fermentation jar, fit an air-lock and continue fermentation for another 7 days.

4 Remove some of the wine, stir in half the remaining sugar and return the wine to the jar. Re-fit the air-lock and resume the fermentation.

5 Repeat this process seven days later.

6 When fermentation is finished, stir the wine and leave in the cool for four days. Siphon it into a clean jar, add one crushed Campden tablet and when the wine is bright, rack it again.

7 Mature this wine for 18 months, then sweeten to taste, bottle and keep for a further six months.

This is a strong dessert wine to serve after any meal.

Elderberry and Damson dessert wine

Freshly picked elderberries	900 g (2 lb)
Freshly picked damsons	900 g (2 lb)
Ripe bananas	250 g (9 oz)
Dried apricots	125 g (4½ oz)
Grape juice concentrate	250 g (9 oz)
Sugar	700 g (1½ lb)
Tartaric acid	10 g (2 tsp)
Water	4 litres (7 pints)

Pectic enzyme and Campden tablets
Port yeast and nutrient

1 Follow the same methods as just described.

Autumn Harvest

Freshly picked elderberries	450 g (1 lb)
Freshly picked blackberries	450 g (1 lb)
Freshly picked black plums or damsons	
	450 g (1 lb)
Blackcurrants	225 g (½ lb)
Mixed cooking apples	1 kg (2½ lb)
Grape juice concentrate	250 g (9 oz)
Sugar	900 g (2 lb)
Tartaric acid	5 g (1 tsp)
Water	3½ litres (6 pints)

Pectic enzyme and Campden tablets
Burgundy yeast and nutrient

1 Wash, stalk and mash all the fruit, place in a bin and pour hot water over it. When cool, stir in the acid, pectic enzyme and one Campden tablet, cover and leave for 24 hours.

2 Continue as described for Elderberry table wine.

Damson table wine

Freshly picked damsons	2 kg (4½ lb)
Grape juice concentrate	250 g (9 oz)
Sugar	900 g (2 lb)
Tartaric acid	5 g (1 tsp)
Water	4 litres (7 pints)

Pectic enzyme and Campden tablets
Burgundy yeast and nutrient

1 Quickly wash the damsons in very hot water to remove the bloom. Squash them and extract the stones. Pour cold water over them and add the acid, pectic enzyme and one crushed Campden tablet.

Cover and leave for 24 hours.

2 Continue as described for Elderberry table wine.

Sloe Gin

Fresh sloes	450 g (1 lb)
Sugar	125 g (4½ oz)
Gin	1 litre (35 fl oz)

1 Stalk, wash and drain the fruit, prick it all over with a bodkin or carpet needle and place it in a suitably sized Kilner or similar wide-necked jar.

2 Dissolve the sugar in the gin and pour this over the sloes.

3 Fit the lid and place the jar in a dark cupboard for three months, giving it a gentle shake every week to distribute the colour and flavour.

4 Strain off into small sterile bottles, cork tightly, label and store for a few more months while the sloe gin matures.

Crab Apple wine I

John Downie Crab Apples	2½ kg (5½ lbs)
(cream and red, the size of a small egg)	
White grape juice concentrate	250 g (9 oz)
Sugar	700 g (1½ lb)
Citric acid	5 g (1 tsp)
Water	3 litres (5 pints)

Pectic enzyme and Campden tablets
Champagne yeast and nutrient

1 Wash, stalk and crush the crab apples and drop them at once into a bin containing cold water, the citric acid, pectic enzyme and one crushed Campden tablet. Cover and leave for 24 hours.

2 Stir in the grape juice, nutrient and activated yeast and ferment on the pulp for seven days, keeping the fruit submerged the whole time.

3 Strain out and press the pulp dry, stir in the sugar and pour the must into a fermentation jar. Top up, fit an air-lock and ferment out.

4 Rack into a clean storage jar, add one Campden tablet and when the wine is bright rack again. Store for 9 months before bottling and sweeten to taste.

Crab Apple wine II

Siberian crab apples — the red spherical variety about the size of a golf ball — also make a good wine. Because the fruit contains more acid, the wine needs longer storage. Make it in the same way as just described but omit the citric acid, use a sauternes yeast and add one tablespoonful of glycerine with the sugar. If needs be the wine may be sweetened to taste but it makes an excellent dry white table wine.

These crab apples also make an excellent base for other fruit, especially elderberries, raisins, dates, sultanas and plums.

Celery wine

Celery stalks	2 kg (4½ lb)
White grape juice concentrate	250 g (9 oz)
Sugar	900 g (2 lb)
Citric acid	15 g (½ oz)
Grape tannin	3 g (½ tsp)
Water	4 litres (7 pints)
Hock yeast and nutrient	

1 Remove all the leaves and stump. Wash the stalks quite clean, chop them into small pieces and boil them for half an hour.

2 Strain when cool and stir in all the other ingredients, pour the must into a fermentation jar and continue as described for elderberry wine.

Russian stout

Pale malt	1.35 kg (3 lb)
Crystal malt	113 g (4 oz)
Black malt	113 g (4 oz)
Wheat malt	113 g (4 oz)
Brown sugar	113 g (4 oz)
Fuggle hops	50 g (2 oz)
Table salt	3 g (½ tsp)
Citric acid	3 g (½ tsp)
Water	to 9 litres (2 gals)
Beer yeast and nutrient	

1 Crack the grains and mash at 65°C (149°F) for up to 4 hours.

2 When end point has passed, draw off the liquor and wash the grains, then add the hops and boil vigorously for 30 minutes.

3 When cool stir in the sugar and top up with cold water. The S.G. should be about 1.054 and if it is not quite high enough stir in a little more sugar.

4 Add the salt, acid and an active yeast and ferment at 15°C (59°F) until the end in about 10 days. Skim and rouse as usual.

5 Fine, rack, bottle prime and store for 10 weeks.

This is a very fine strong beer, best served by the half rather than the pint.

Bitter beer

Pale malt	1.35 kg (3 lb)
Crystal malt	450 g (1 lb)
Diastatic malt extract	450 g (1 lb)
Flaked barley	225 g (½ lb)
Invert sugar	1 kg (2¼ lb)
Fuggle hops	100 g (3½ oz)
Golding hops	25 g (1 oz)
Hardening salts	25 g (1 oz)
Water	to 23 litres (5 gals)
Beer yeast and nutrient	

Brew as just described. Adjust the S.G. to 1.040 and mash at 66°C (150°F) to obtain a good dextrin extraction.

These are two excellent but different beers, worth making for comparison.

Mock Pommard table wine

Mixed cooking apples	2½ kg (5½ lb)
Mature beetroot	450 g (1 lb)
Chopped raisins	225 g (½ lb)
Ripe bananas	450 g (1 lb)
Sugar	1 kg (2¼ lb)
Citric acid	2 level tsp
Grape tannin	1 level tsp
Water	3½ litres (6 pints)
Pectic enzyme and Campden tablets	
Pommard wine yeast and nutrient.	

1 Top, tail, scrub, dice and boil the beetroot until tender, together with the peeled and sliced bananas. Pour into a bin, leave to cool, then add the acid, pectic enzyme and one crushed Campden tablet.

2 Wash and crush the apples, then drop them at once into the bin. Wash and chop the raisins and add them to the bin. Cover and leave in a warm place for 24 hours.

3 Add the wine yeast, nutrient and tannin and ferment on the pulp for six days keeping the floating cap submerged with a weighted plate.

4 Strain out and press the solids, stir in the sugar, pour the must into a fermentation jar, fit an airlock and ferment out.

5 Rack into a sterile storage jar, add one crushed Campden tablet and store till the wine is bright, then rack again.

6 Store for one year, bottle and keep for six months.

Bullace wine

Ripe Bullaces	2 kg (4½ lb)
Chopped raisins	250 g (9 oz)
Sugar	900 g (2 lb)
Water	4 litres (7 pints)
Pectic enzyme and Campden tablets.	
Bordeaux yeast and nutrient	

1 Stalk, wash and crush the bullaces and place them in a bin with the chopped raisins. Pour boiling water over them and when cool remove the stones. Add the pectic enzyme and one crushed Campden tablet, then cover and leave for 24 hours.

2 Add the yeast and ferment on the pulp for four days, stirring daily. Strain out the fruit, stir in the sugar, pour into a jar, fit an air-lock and ferment.

3 Rack into a clean jar, add one Campden tablet and mature for nine months before bottling. Serve as a red table wine.

November

THE wines to be made in the first half of November may well be a carry-over from October. Alas! there is sometimes a limit to how much wine can be made at a time. The September wines can now be racked and stored, thus releasing the fermentation jars. Apple wine should be made, and if at all possible include some quince and crab apples and a few pears. Make as much as you can, using a large polythene bag as a mashing and fermentation bin. Set some of it aside for a sparkling wine.

Main crop vegetables are now ready, sloes are at their peak, rosehips are ripe, the tasks seem endless but always worthwhile.

RECOMMENDED RECIPES

Sparkling white wine

Bramley cooking apples	2 kg	(4½ lb)
Hard Conference pears	1 kg	(2¼ lb)
Cydonia japonica quince	250 g	(9 oz)
White grape juice concentrate	250 g	(9 oz)
Sugar	700 g	(1½ lb)
Water	3½ litres	(6 pints)

Pectic enzyme and Campden tablets
Champagne yeast and nutrient

1 Wash and mash the fruit and drop it into a bin containing the pectic enzyme and one Campden tablet dissolved in the water. Cover and leave for 24 hours.
2 Stir in the grape juice, one third of the sugar, the yeast and nutrient and ferment on the pulp for seven days, always keeping the must submerged.

3 Strain out and press the fruit, stir in the rest of the sugar, pour the must into a fermentation jar, fit an air-lock and ferment to dryness.
4 Rack into a clean jar, add one crushed Campden tablet and when the wine is bright, rack it again and store for 6 months.
5 Stir in 70 grams (2½ oz) caster sugar and an active champagne yeast, fit an air-lock and stand the jar in a warm place for a few hours.
6 Sterilize the champagne bottles and hollow-domed plastic stoppers with suitable cages.
7 As soon as the wine is fermenting, pour it into the bottles, fit the stoppers and wire down the cages.
8 Leave the bottles in a warm room for one week then store in the cool for a further six months.

Apple wine

Mixed apples	4–5 kg	(9–11 lb)
White grape juice concentrate	250 g	(9 oz)
Sugar	800 g	(1¾ lb)
Water	3 litres	(5 pints)

Pectic enzyme and Campden tablets
Sauternes yeast and nutrient

1 Follow the same method as just described but store for one year before bottling and do not re-ferment.

Apple and Elderberry I

Mixed apples	4 kg	(9 lb)
Freshly picked elderberries	450 g	(1 lb)
Sultanas	225 g	(½ lb)

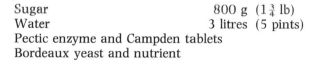

Sugar	800 g (1¾ lb)
Water	3 litres (5 pints)

Pectic enzyme and Campden tablets
Bordeaux yeast and nutrient

1 Wash the elderberries, remove them from their stalks and boil them for 15 minutes. Pour them into a mashing bin containing the chopped sultanas.
2 Wash and crush the apples and drop them into the bin. When the must is cool, add the pectic enzyme and one crushed Campden tablet. Cover and leave for 24 hours.
3 Stir in the yeast and nutrient, and ferment on the pulp for 7 days, keeping the fruit well submerged.
4 Strain out and press the fruit, stir in the sugar, pour the must into a fermentation jar, fit an air-lock and ferment to dryness.
5 Rack into a clean jar, add one Campden tablet and when the wine is bright, rack it again.
6 Store for one year.

Apple and Elderberry II

A 'second run rosé' may be made by using the fruit pulp left over from either of the apple recipes mixed with the pulp left over from an elderberry wine. Pour on only half as much water as previously used and add 250 grams (9 oz) grape juice concentrate. There will be sufficient yeast to restart the fermentation which should be continued for only five days.

Strain and press the fruit and stir in 1 kg (2¼ lb) sugar per 4½ litres (1 gallon). Pour into a fermentation jar, fit an air-lock and ferment to dryness.

This is a remarkably attractive rosé wine, best served very slightly sweet.

Peach 'Sauternes'

Fresh peaches	2 kg (4½ lb)
Ripe bananas	1 kg (2¼ lb)
Ripe rosehips	170 g (6 oz)
White grape juice concentrate	500 g (18 oz)
Sugar	700 g (1½ lb)
Acid blend	20 g (¾ oz)
Water	3½ litres (5 pints)

Pectic enzyme and Campden tablets
Sauternes yeast and nutrient

1 Halve the peaches and discard the stones. Cut the halves into small pieces and place them in a mashing bin containing 2 litres (3½ pints) of water, the acid, pectic enzyme and one Campden tablet.
2 Peel and slice the bananas, wash and crush the rosehips and boil these together for 30 minutes. Leave to cool, then add them to the peaches. Cover and leave for 24 hours.
3 Stir in the grape juice concentrate, the nutrient and yeast and ferment on the pulp for five days, pressing down the fruit cap daily.
4 Strain out but do not press the fruit, stir in the sugar, pour the must into a fermentation jar, fit an air-lock and ferment in a warm place.
5 When the specific gravity has fallen to 1.016 rack the wine into a clean jar, add two crushed Campden tablets to terminate fermentation and store till bright.
6 Rack again and keep for one year before bottling.

Note: Over-ripe peaches may be used, provided the bruised parts are cut away, but it is better to buy a tray or box of perfect fruit.

113

'Sauternes' II

Freshly dug parsnips	2 kg	(4½ lb)
Ripe bananas	1 kg	(2¼ lb)
Ripe rosehips	170 g	(6 oz)
White grape juice concentrate	500 g	(18 oz)
Sugar	700 g	(1½ lb)
Acid blend	20 g	(¾ oz)
Glycerine	2 tbs	
Water	3½ litres	(6 pints)

Pectic enzyme and Campden tablets
Sauternes yeast and nutrient

1 Wash the parsnips thoroughly, remove the top close to the crown, chop up the parsnips and boil them with the peeled and sliced bananas and the washed and crushed rosehips for half an hour. Leave them to cool.
2 Strain the liquor into a fermentation jar, add the pectic enzyme, acid and one crushed Campden tablet. Stopper and leave for 24 hours.
3 Stir in the grape juice, nutrient and yeast, fit an air-lock and ferment in a warm place.
4 After 5 days, remove some wine, stir in the sugar and return the wine to the jar. Add the glycerine and if needs be, top up with cold water. Refit the air-lock and re-commence fermentation down to S.G. 1.016.
5 Rack into a clean jar, add two crushed Campden tablets to terminate fermentation and when the wine is bright, rack it again. Store for 12 months before bottling.

Sloe table wine

Fresh sloes	1 kg	(2¼ lb)
Ripe bananas	450 g	(1 lb)
Chopped raisins	250 g	(9 oz)
Red grape juice concentrate	250 g	(9 oz)
Brown sugar	700 g	(1½ lb)
Citric acid	15 g	(½ oz)
Water	4 litres	(7 pints)

Pectic enzyme and Campden tablets
Chianti wine yeast and nutrient

1 Wash and stalk the sloes, place them in a pan with the peeled and sliced bananas, add the water and boil the fruit for 30 minutes.
2 Strain the juice on to the chopped raisins and leave it to cool. Add the pectic enzyme, acid and one Campden tablet, cover and leave for 24 hours.
3 Stir in the red grape juice, nutrient and yeast and ferment on the pulp for seven days, pressing down the raisins twice daily.
4 Strain out and press the fruit, stir in the sugar, pour the must into a fermentation jar, fit an air-lock and ferment to dryness.
5 Siphon into a clean jar, add one Campden tablet and when the wine is bright, rack it again, then store for 9 months before bottling.

Carrot 'Sherry'

Freshly dug carrots	1 kg	(2¼ lb)
Cooking apples	1 kg	(2¼ lb)
Chopped sultanas	450 g	(1 lb)
Grape juice concentrate (sherry style)	500 g	(18 oz)
Sugar	700 g	(1½ lb)
Tartaric acid	10 g	(2 tsp)
Water	3½ litres	(6 pints)

Pectic enzyme and Campden tablets
Sherry yeast, nutrient and Vitamin B tablet

1 Top, tail, scrub, dice and boil the carrots for 30 minutes.
2 Wash and crush the apples and drop them into a bin containing enough water to cover them, the acid, pectic enzyme and one crushed Campden tablet. Cover and leave for 24 hours.
3 Add the chopped sultanas and, when cool, the carrot liquor. Cover and leave for 24 hours.
4 Stir in the grape juice concentrate, nutrient and active yeast and ferment on the pulp for seven days, pressing down the fruit cap twice daily.
5 Strain out and press the fruit, stir in the sugar, pour the must into a fermentation jar, fit an air-lock and ferment to dryness if possible.
6 Siphon the clearing wine into a clean jar, not quite full, plug the neck with cotton wool and store till bright, then rack again and store for one year.

Beetroot 'Madeira'

Freshly dug beetroot	2 kg	(4½ lb)
Chopped raisins	450 g	(1 lb)
Ripe bananas	250 g	(9 oz)
Grape juice concentrate (Madeira style)	500 g	(18 oz)
Brown sugar	450 g	(1 lb)
Tartaric acid	15 g	(½ oz)
Water	3½ litres	(6 pints)

Pectic enzyme and Campden tablets
Madeira yeast and nutrient

1 Top, tail, scrub, dice and boil the beetroot together with the peeled and sliced bananas for one hour.
2 Strain the hot liquor on to the chopped raisins, and when cool add the acid, pectic enzyme and one crushed Campden tablet. Cover and leave for 24 hours.
3 Stir in the yeast and nutrient and ferment for 7 days, pressing down the floating raisins twice daily.
4 Strain out and press the fruit, stir in the grape juice concentrate, pour the must into a fermentation jar, fit an air-lock and ferment in a warm place for 7 days.
5 Remove some of the wine, dissolve the sugar in it and return it to the jar. Replace the air-lock and continue fermentation as long as possible.

6 When fermentation has finished, siphon the wine into a clean jar, add one Campden tablet and store till bright.

7 Rack again and store in a very warm place for about 4 months and then in a cool place for a further 8 months. Sweeten to taste before bottling.

Rosehip wine

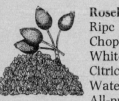

Ripe fresh rosehips	2 kg (4½ lb)
Chopped sultanas	225 g (½ lb)
White sugar	1¼ kg (2¾ lb)
Citric acid	10 g (2 tsp)
Water	4 litres (7 pints)

All-purpose wine yeast and nutrient

1 Wash the rosehips, cut in half, crush or coarsely mince them. Place in a bin with the chopped sultanas, half the sugar and the acid, and pour boiling water over them.

2 When cool stir in the nutrient and active yeast, cover and ferment in a warm place for 10 days, pressing down the fruit cap twice daily.

3 Strain out and press the fruit, stir in the rest of the sugar, pour the must into a fermentation jar, fit an air-lock and ferment out.

4 Rack into a clean jar, add one crushed Campden tablet and when the wine is bright rack it again and store for 9 months.

Quince wine

Fresh large quince	2 kg (4½ lb)
Fresh large lemons	2 only
White grape juice concentrate	250 g (9 oz)
Sugar	1 kg (2¼ lb)
Water	3½ litres (6 pints)

Pectic enzyme and Campden tablets
All-purpose wine yeast and nutrient

1 Wash the quince and grate them close to the core or cut them into small pieces.

2 Thinly pare and chop the rinds of the 2 lemons.

3 Place the quince and lemon rinds into a bin and pour boiling water over them. When cool add the pectic enzyme and one crushed Campden tablet. Cover and leave for 24 hours.

4 Stir in the grape juice and half the sugar, the nutrient and yeast. Ferment on the pulp for 10 days, pressing down the fruit cap twice daily.

5 Strain out and press the fruit, stir in the rest of the sugar, pour the must into a fermentation jar, fit an air-lock and ferment out.

6 Rack into a clean jar, add one Campden tablet, store until the wine is bright, then rack again and store for 9 months. Sweeten to taste if necessary before bottling. This wine has a strong and delicious bouquet and flavour. It sometimes ferments slowly, but do not be anxious.

Export ale

Malt extract	2¼ kg (5 lb)
Crystal malt	450 g (1 lb)
Invert sugar	700 g (1½ lb)
Fuggle hops	50 g (1½ oz)
Golding hops	75 g (3 oz)
Hardening salts	20 g (¾ oz)
Water to	18 litres (4 gallons)

Beer yeast and nutrient

1 Dissolve the malt extract, sugar and salts in one quarter of the water, suitably warmed.

2 Crack the crystal malt grains and boil them with all the Fuggle hops and two-thirds of the Golding hops in another quarter of the water for 30 minutes, then add the remaining hops and continue the boil for a further 15 minutes. Leave to cool.

3 Strain through the hops on to the wort, top up with cold water and adjust the S.G. to 1.050 or a little lower.

4 Pitch an active yeast and ferment at 20°C (68°F) for 7 days, skimming and rousing as usual.

5 Fine, rack into bottles, prime and store for at least 4 weeks.

London Porter

Malt extract	450 g (1 lb)
Black malt grains	50 g (2 oz)
Flaked barley	50 g (2 oz)
Brown sugar	140 g (5 oz)
Hops	20 g (¾ oz)
Table salt	1 saltspoonful
Water	4 litres (7 pints)

Beer yeast and nutrient.

1 Dissolve the malt and sugar in the warm water, add the salt, malt grains, and barley. Finally add the hops squeezing them in the liquor with your hand to make them thoroughly wet.

2 Boil in a large covered vessel for one hour, then remove from the heat and leave to cool.

3 Strain into a fermentation vessel, top up to 5 litres (8½ pints) with cold water, add an activated yeast, cover and leave in a warm place.

4 Remove the frothy scum on the second and fourth days and when fermentation finishes move the beer to a cool place for two days to encourage the sediment to settle.

5 Siphon into eight one-pint beer bottles, add one level teaspoonful sugar to each, stopper tightly and leave in a warm room for one week.

6 Mature for two months before serving.

Note: The flaked barley adds crispness to the beer, the black malt grains provide colour and flavour. This is a strong beer with a good body and head retention. It was once the popular drink of London porters who originally mixed stout with mild ale.

December

THE hectic part of the season is now over. The colder weather helps wines to clear, so racking and bottling is the important task. Sparkling gooseberry wine should be re-fermented and bottled. Wines and beers made earlier in the year with the Christmas festivities in mind should be looked out and checked over. Put aside the bottoms of racked wines into a single bottle and leave it to clear. This makes excellent cooking wine when racked from its deposit.

When racking your stock, earmark some bottles of red wines for making into mulled wines. They need not be your best.

RECOMMENDED RECIPES

Christmas Punch

Red wine such as elderberry	1 bottle
Fresh lemon	1 only
Sugar	100 g (3½ oz)
Honey	1 tbs
Cloves	10 only
Root ginger	1 large piece

1 Pour the wine into a saucepan, add the thinly pared rind of the lemon (well-chopped), the honey, cloves and root ginger (well bruised), and sugar.
2 Place on the heat and slowly raise the temperature to 60°C (140°F). Hold it there for a few minutes,

add the lemon juice, strain, serve in heated glasses.

Wassail Bowl

Apple wine	1 bottle
Small cooking apples	3 only
Powdered ginger	1 level tsp
Grated nutmeg	to taste
White sugar	85 g (3 oz)

1 Wash, core and bake the apples until they are soft enough to mash.
2 Remove the skins, mash the pulp and mix in the ginger, sugar and a grating of nutmeg.
3 Heat the wine slowly to 60°C (140°F) and then pour it over the apple pulp and gently stir it all up. Serve quickly in heated glasses.

Note: The name wassail comes from the old English *waes hael* which meant 'be of good health'. It used to be served in a wooden mazer and was handed around like a loving cup.

Bishop

Large sweet orange	1 only
Whole cloves	12
Red table wine	1 bottle
Sugar	to taste

116

1 Wipe the orange and stick the cloves in it. Place it in a small casserole, put on the lid and roast it slowly in a low oven for 10–15 minutes until it is golden brown.

2 Remove the orange and cut it into six or eight pieces. Place in a saucepan, pour the wine over and heat slowly to 60°C (140°F).

3 Hold it there for a minute or two, then strain into a heated jug. Sweeten to taste and serve at once.

Negus

Large fresh lemon	1 only
Whole cloves	6
Small stick of cinnamon	1
Blade of mace	1
Sweet red wine	1 bottle
Sugar	85 g (3 oz)

1 Prepare the lemon in the same way as the orange in the last recipe. When roasted, cut it up and place the pieces in the wine that has been previously slowly heated, together with the spices and sugar, to 60°C (140°F).

2 Leave the negus in a warm place for ten minutes then strain and serve.

There are many variations on the last two drinks depending on the wine and spices used.

Caudle

Stale white bread	2 thick slices
Fresh egg	1
Sweet white wine	1 bottle
Caster sugar	85 g (3 oz)
Table salt	1 saltspoonful
Ground mixed spice	1 saltspoonful

1 Cut the crusts off the bread, dice the slices, place in a bowl, sprinkle them with the salt and the spice.

2 Pour in just enough wine to soften the bread, then beat in the white and yolk of the egg until a good mash has been made.

3 Warm the rest of the wine to 60°C (140°F), pour it on to the mashed bread and egg and stir well. Serve at once in heated glasses.

Liqueurs

Vodka 65.5° Proof	1 litre (35½ fl oz)
Caster sugar	700 g (1½ lb)
Strong sweet wine	2½ bottles
Assorted liqueur essences	4

1 Dissolve the sugar in the vodka and pour equal quantities into four sterilised wine bottles.

2 Add two-thirds of a bottle of a different Noirot liqueur essence to each bottle and top up with strong sweet wine.

117

3 Taste each bottle and if necessary adjust with a few drops more of essence or a little more sugar. Never add all the essence at first, nor more than the recommended amount of sugar. The essences vary somewhat and additions can easily be made but dilution is never successful.

Note: Use a sweet red wine, when imitating Cherry Brandy, Kirsch or Cassis.

Orange gin
Large Seville orange	1
Large lemon	1
Sugar syrup	6 tbs
Gin	1 bottle

1 Very thinly pare the orange and lemon, ensuring that no white pith is removed. Chop it finely and add it to the gin and sugar syrup in a litre size bottle.
2 Stopper, shake well and keep for one week, shaking the bottle gently for a few moments each day to distribute the flavour.
3 Remove the peel and the liqueur is ready for serving with crushed ice.

Methyglin
Blended brown honey	1 kg (3¼ lb)
Large lemon	1 only
Demerara sugar	200 g (7 oz)
Tartaric acid	20 g (¾ oz)
Water	3½ litres (6 pints)

Sauternes yeast and nutrient
Either a bouquet garni of mixed herbs such as: mint, rosemary, sorrell, mace, balm etc.
or a sachet of mixed spices including bruised root ginger, cloves, cinnamon and nutmeg.
(Some Home Brew shops sell prepared sachets of both herbs and spices.)

1 Dissolve the honey and sugar in warm water and pour into a fermentation jar. Add the thinly-pared and chopped lemon rind, the expressed lemon juice and tartaric acid, the bouquet garni or sachet of spices and finally the nutrient and active yeast.
2 Fit an air-lock and ferment in a warm place for seven days, then remove the solids, top up and continue fermentation to S.G. 1.020.
3 Rack into a clean jar and terminate fermentation with two crushed Campden tablets. As soon as the methyglin is bright, rack again and store for one year before bottling.
4 It is essential to serve methyglin fairly sweet and cool rather than cold.
This is a very ancient drink that has long been connected with the Celts and Wales. The very name has both a witchy and a Welsh sound. Make it at least once if you are Welsh!

'Liebfraumilch'
Cooking apples	2 kg (4½ lb)
Dessert apples	1 kg (1¼ lb)
Chopped raisins,	450 g (1 lb)
Ripe rosehips	450 g (1 lb)
White sugar	550 g (1¼ lb)
Citric acid	10 g (2 tsp)
Grape tannin	3 g (½ tsp)
Water	3½ litre (6 pints)

Pectic enzyme and Campden tablets
Hock wine yeast and nutrient

1 Crush the rosehips and apples and drop them into cold water containing the acid, pectic enzyme and one crushed Campden tablet. Cover and leave for 24 hours in a warm place.
2 Add the chopped raisins, tannin, wine yeast and nutrient and ferment on the pulp for seven days. Keep the fruit submerged the whole time, by the aid of a weighted plate or similar non-metallic device.
3 Strain out and press the fruit, stir in the sugar, pour the must into a fermentation jar, top up if necessary, fit an air-lock and ferment the wine to dryness.
4 Siphon into a clean jar, add one Campden tablet and when the wine is bright rack again, then store for six months before bottling.

Parsnip 'Tokay'
Freshly dug young parsnips	2 kg (4½ lb)
Ripe rosehips	450 g (1 lb)
Ripe bananas	450 g (1 lb)
Grape juice concentrate	500 g (18 oz)
Sugar	900 g (2 lb)
Glycerine	40 g (1½ tbs)
Acid blend	28 g (1 oz)
Water	3½ litres (6 pints)

Pectic enzyme and Campden tablets
Tokay yeast, nutrient and vitamin B tablet

1 Top, tail, scrub and dice the parsnips. Wash and crush the rosehips. Peel and slice the bananas. Boil them together in two-thirds of the water for half-an-hour, then leave them to cool.
2 Pour the liquor into a fermentation jar, add two-thirds of the acid blend, pectic enzyme and one Campden tablet and leave for 24 hours.
3 Dissolve the grape juice concentrate in half the remaining water, add it to the jar together with yeast, nutrient and one 3 mg Vitamin B tablet. Fit an air-lock and ferment for one week.
4 Boil the sugar in the remaining water and acid for a quarter of an hour and when cool, add half of it to the jar. Replace the air-lock and continue fermentation. Store the sugar syrup well-corked.
5 One week later add the remaining syrup and the glycerine, replace the air-lock and continue fermentation for as long as possible.

6 When fermentation has quite finished, rack the wine into a clean jar, add one Campden tablet and when the wine is bright, rack again and store for one year at least.

7 Taste the wine and if necessary, sweeten slightly before bottling.

Cock ale

Pale malt flour	450 g (1 lb)
Flaked maize	56 g (2 oz)
Flaked rice	56 g (2 oz)
Invert sugar	113 g (4 oz)
Brown sugar	113 g (4 oz)
Golding hops	28 g (1 oz)
Water	4¼ litres (7½ pints)
Dry white wine	30 cl (10 fl oz)

Bones, wings, skin, neck, tail and trimmings of a plainly cooked chicken
Ale yeast and nutrient

1 Dissolve the malt flour and sugar in one third of the water, suitably warm.

2 Boil the maize, rice and hops for 30 minutes in the remaining water and leave it to cool.

3 Strain on to the wort and pitch an activated yeast.

4 Break up the chicken bones, cut up the pieces and steep them in the wine for 48 hours. It is best to use a jar with a lid and to place it in the refrigerator.

5 After two days skim the froth off the beer, pour the wine into the beer through a strainer, place the chicken into a nylon bag and suspend this in the beer until fermentation is finished.

6 Remove the bag of chicken and discard it, then move the beer to a cool place for the sediment to settle or add some finings.

7 After four days siphon the beer into eight one-pint beer bottles, prime each one with half a teaspoonful of white sugar, stopper tightly and mature the beer for at least six weeks.

This is an extremely smooth and tasty, liqueur-like beer, the like of which has been made for a thousand years or more. It is extremely satisfying and deserves to be more widely made.

Treacle ale

Black treacle	450 g (1 lb)
Brown sugar	225 g (½ lb)
Water	4 litres (7½ pints)
Large lemons	2

Ale yeast and nutrient

1 Dissolve the treacle and sugar in hot water. When cool add the thinly-pared and chopped rinds of the two lemons and their expressed juice, followed by the activated ale yeast and nutrient.

2 Cover and leave the jar in a warm place, but skim off the dirty froth on the second day.

3 After four days move the jar to a cool place for one day, for some of the sediment to settle.

4 Siphon into eight one-pint beer bottles and stopper tightly. Priming is not necessary since fermentation is not complete.

5 Mature for eight days or more if possible.

This is a very old recipe, once very popular in Scotland. Treacle ale has a somewhat bitter flavour and no hops are necessary.

Lemon and Ginger ale

Fresh lemons	2
Root ginger	50 g (2 oz)
Malt extract	450 g (1 lb)
Water	to 4½ litres (1 gallon)

Ale yeast

1 Thinly pare the lemons, bruise the ginger and boil in one quart of water for 20 minutes. Dissolve the malt extract in one quart of warm water and strain the lemon and ginger liquor on to the malt wort. Top up with cold water.

2 When cool, add the lemon juice and ale yeast, cover and ferment for a full four days, skimming on the and third days as usual.

3 Pour into eight one-pint beer bottles, stopper tightly and keep for two weeks.

Country ale

Bouquet of botanic herbs	1 packet
Malt extract	450 g (1 lb)
Water	to 4½ litres (1 gallon)

Ale yeast, nutrient and juice of one lemon

Dissolve the malt extract in tepid water, add the yeast, suspend the herbs in the wort, cover, skim, rack, prime and bottle as usual.

Herb beers

These are made like nettle beer (see June recipes). Any of the herbs mentioned in the section on herb wines may be used. These beers were once widely made in the country, mainly for variety. They are somewhat of an acquired taste for our more sophisticated palates.

Fruit beers

Made like wines but with malt instead of sugar and with starting gravities nearer 50 than 90. These beers were also once very popular in the cottages of country people. Equal quantities of mashed fruit and malt extract should be used. No hops are used. Ferment on the pulp. Prime as usual.

Brewing Beer: A Short History

THE secret of how to make a fermented drink from barley may well be 5,000 years old. We know that the cereal has certainly been cultivated for that long since pieces of pottery imprinted with barleycorn have been dated at around 3,000 BC. We also have evidence that at the time of the great Egyptian civilisation an ale was made and given to the workers who built the Pyramids. We know that ale was made from a malted barley and flavoured with herbs when the Romans came to Britain. In the first century AD a British coin was struck at Colchester and on one side an ear of cultivated barley was shown. Pliny the Elder (AD 23–79), a Roman historian, mentions a drink called *cerevisia* which we now know to be an old Gaulish word for beer. It is now the name applied to the yeast used in brewing.

We know that so much ale, mead and cider were drunk in Ancient Britain, that as early as the 6th century St. David had to decree laws to control drunkenness. In the 7th century Theodore, seventh Archbishop of Canterbury, imposed 15 days penance for drunkenness. The ale of the time was of course, made in the home and nettles and other herbs were used for flavouring. Beer – which was ale flavoured with hops – was not popular. The Romans imported hops from Holland and used them to flavour their own beer, but 1,000 years were to pass before hops became widely accepted.

It is always a surprise to discover how advanced our forebears were in some respects. For example, in the 10th century. King Edgar (959–975) closed many of the vast number of ale houses which had sprung up all over the country. Under his decree each village was permitted only one! Furthermore, mugs and tankards had to conform to a standard size, to ensure that customers received the correct quantity. The quality of the ale was such that a shipment made to France in 1158 was described as 'most wholesome, clear of all dregs, equalling wine in colour and surpassing it in flavour.' At the end of the 12th century the first tax was charged on ale – and it has been increasing ever since!

Ale-making has given many new words to our vocabulary: ale-wife – a woman who brewed ale; ale-conner – an inspector of ale quality; ale-stakes – a branch, bush or stick placed outside a house to show that ale had been freshly brewed there. There were also church-ales or fairs, where ale was brewed by priests or monks and sold to raise money for charity or for repairing the church. Bridge-ales were for the building of bridges and so on. Money for public works of all kinds was raised by selling beer or ale.

Gradually small breweries were set up and replaced the ale-wife who was the traditional brewer of beer both for use in the home and for sale. In the 16th century brewers began to export beer in substantial quantities to Scandinavia, Europe, Africa, America, the West Indies and so on. The quality of

the water used in brewing was recognised as being significant and Burton-on-Trent became famous for bitter beers because of the mineral salts in its Springs. Today we can analyse and adjust water to our needs and location is therefore no longer of such importance. In the 18th century were founded the big breweries that have since developed into the famous names of today. Home brewing began to decline and eventually died out until after the Second World War.

In the last 30 years or so the quality of brewery beer has varied considerably. Because of high taxation, high cost of ingredients and high cost of overheads, the quality has tended to fall steadily. As a result, an increasing number of people have

Left: *Egyptians brewing nearly 4,000 years ago*

Above: *British brewhouse some 200 years ago*

returned to the homecraft of their forebears and are brewing a wide variety of good beer styles. A great fillip has been given by the companies producing malt extract and this can now be bought already adjusted with hops and adjuncts to produce a given beer style. All that is necessary is to add some water and yeast, and occasionally some sugar. Within a few weeks you can actually be drinking your own very good beer, at but a fraction of the cost of commercial beer. A little 'shopping around' amongst the various packs available will enable you to determine the one you like best.

In spite of the great popularity of these packs, many people prefer to brew their own beer in the traditional way from grains and hops. There is no doubt that such beers are truly superb. The flavour, value and satisfaction are far greater than from beers one can buy 'ready-made'. They have to be brewed with care and attention to detail, then matured for quite a while longer than other beers, but the result is undoubtedly worth the effort. Well-made, primed and securely stoppered, these beers will keep and improve for one year or more.

Brewing your own beer is a creative and satisfying hobby for men and women of all ages. It requires very little in the way of equipment, is inexpensive, and good results can be obtained from the very first brew. In brewing for your household you will be carrying on the traditions that began almost with the beginning of civilisation.

Basic Beer Styles

Mild and Bitter

TRADITIONALLY the British working man has always enjoyed a pint of mild. This is a low alcohol beer, slightly hopped, slightly sweet and full bodied. Sometimes it has been varied by mixing half of mild with half of bitter, hence the name mild and bitter. It was customary for the more skilled craftsman to drink all bitter or else a brown ale.

Bitter is, as its name suggests, a beer containing more hops to the gallon than mild beer. It is also drier, crisper and slightly more alcoholic. Different barley, hops and water are used. There are many variations of bitter, from a pale ale to an export ale, depending on the hopping rate and the initial

Export ale

At one time this beer was better known as India Pale Ale because it used to be exported from Britain to the troops stationed there. This single piece of information is sufficient to describe the beer in some detail. To travel so far in differing temperatures and humidity, and to withstand the buffeting of the journey, the beer would need to be fairly high in alcohol and hops. When it reached the troops it would need to be full-bodied and tangy to slake the thirst, and clean the palate of the soldiers. A high mashing temperature would be required to ensure a dextrinous wort and a blend of hops to ensure a clean fresh flavour. Hard water would give it that

gravity. Both mild and bitter may be bottled or casked, although the mild seems more suitable for drinking as a draught beer.

Brown ale

Halfway in colour between a pale ale and a stout, brown ale is available in different styles in different places. There is no one standard style. So called Southern brown ales are darker in colour and sweeter in taste than the Northern brown ales, which are amber coloured and almost dry. Both have a light alcohol content, however, around 3.5%. A good oatmeal coloured head is characteristic of this beer. A soft water is preferred when making it.

final crispness. There is no doubt that this beer was appreciated by the troops and when they returned home they created a demand for it in the United Kingdom. It has remained a real beer in spite of the ever-deteriorating qualities of other beers. The style is now widely known and enjoyed, although sometimes by other names.

Stout

There is an amusing story told about the person who invented stout, although it has never been verified. In the days when well-to-do people in Ireland still had their beers made on their estate, there was a young man who had the misfortune to over-roast the barley grains for his master's beer.

Not wishing to get into trouble, he mixed the almost black grains with some newly malted barley and brewed a beer from the concoction and offered it as something very special. The master of the house agreed that it WAS very special, commended the young man and commanded that in future it should be made regularly for the household.

After a while the young man, supported by the compliments of all those who had tasted this new beer, decided to start up in business on his own, making his special beer for sale. The young man was, of course, Arthur Guinness and the beer was his now famous Irish stout, a beer enjoyed by millions of people, men and women alike. It has been

Happily, brewing at home is nothing like this nowadays

described as 'a domino black beverage, with a glorious head, creamy oatmeal in colour'. Stout is a dry beer with a somewhat hard after-taste. It is full-bodied and full-flavoured, a beer to be enjoyed with a certain respect.

There are now a number of variations on this basic beer, like milk stout, oatmeal stout, Russian stout and so on. These are superb beers if you like them, but they must be carefully made and matured. When well brewed at home they are often superior to those that can be bought, and should be served with care. A pint or two would be more than enough for most people. They are all nourishing, and Russian stout is quite strong too, so serve them in half-pint glasses.

Barley wine

This is neither wine nor beer in either of the accepted senses, but a hybrid, a beer brewed so strong that in many ways it resembles a wine. The high alcohol content will inhibit head retention but the bead of condition should be apparent and lively. Barley wine is dark brown in appearance, with a pronounced bouquet. The taste should be smooth and round, yet quite malty. It must be matured for as long as a wine – at least one year. Like wine it should be drunk in small quantities and is not a beer to be quaffed. For this reason it is usually marketed in bottles containing only 5 fl oz (14 cl). It is normally served at 20°C (68°F) with snacks or biscuits and cheese. It is not really suitable for serving with a meal.

Lager

Although this beer is becoming increasingly popular, it is not an easy beer to brew in the home. Most of the adjusted malt extract packs make a beer more like a light ale than a lager. Lager should have a subtle and pleasing aroma, a full round flavour and an attractive cleanliness on the palate. The colour should be a star-bright pale amber, gold-like may be a better description. The bead should be vigorous and continuous. Even professional brewers have difficulty in making this beer and that is why so much is imported.

Fundamentally the Continental system of brewing is different from others and the ingredients of lager are different, too. Lager malt is roasted even less than pale malt. The hops are seedless as opposed to the seeded varieties used in other beers. When buying hops for lager, ask for Hallertau, Styrean or Brewers' Gold. Make sure that you use the lager yeast, *saccharomyces carlsbergensis*. This is a bottom fermenting yeast and creates almost no scum to skim off. The water should be soft, rather than the hard water used for brewing pale ales and bitter beers.

The system of brewing other beers is called 'infusion', because the malt is mashed at one even temperature until the end point is reached. The lager system is called 'decoction' since varying temperatures are used during the mashing. Finally the lager wort is fermented at a lower temperature and therefore much more slowly than other beers.

Lager comes from the old Boer word meaning 'store'. It needs to be matured for three months if it is to reach the degree of perfection that you will certainly seek. If you are really fond of lager, then you will want to brew in as large a quantity as you can. The recipe that follows on page 135 is therefore for 1 gallon ($4\frac{1}{2}$ litres) so that you can easily multiply the ingredients by the number of gallons you wish to make. A recipe is also given in the Calendar for January so that the lager can be well-matured by the following Christmas.

Beer from Kits

It is only natural that the beginner brewer should want his task made as simple as possible. Also, many would-be brewers live in flats or homes where the kitchen is so small that there just is not room to brew beer the real way. Suppliers of malt extract soon appreciated the size of this potential market and at the time of writing you can buy a great variety of cans of malt extract that include hop oils and resins and the other ingredients necessary to produce a beer similar to well-known styles. All that the home brewer usually has to provide is some sugar and water. Frequently the manufacturers include a sachet of yeast and nutrient salts, as well as finings. Some also include attractive labels and even a large polythene bag in which to brew the beer. It could hardly be made more simple.

The method is equally easy, and detailed step-by-step instructions are provided with each can. Briefly, the can is warmed to soften the malt, opened and the contents poured into a pan of hot water, stirred and dissolved. Sugar is then stirred in and the liquor is brought to the boil and simmered for a few minutes. It is then poured into a fermentation bin, topped up to the required amount with cold water and as soon as the temperature has fallen to 20°C (68°F) an activated yeast is added. The bin is loosely covered and left in the warm for five days. On the second day dirty froth is skimmed off and the beer is stirred up. On the third day more froth is removed. On the fifth day finings are stirred in and the bin moved to a cool place for two days while the beer clears.

Meanwhile bottles are prepared, together with stoppers or caps. The beer is then poured — or preferably siphoned – into the bottles which are then primed with a level teaspoonful of sugar per pint (just over $\frac{1}{2}$ litre). The bottles are then tightly stoppered or crown capped, labelled, given a shake to dissolve the sugar and stood in a warm place for two days while the sugar is fermented. The bottles should now be stored in the cool for at least one week before the beer is served. These beers improve considerably if kept for three or four weeks.

Instead of bottling, the beer may be racked into a pressure cask, and primed at the rate of $1\frac{1}{2}$ oz of sugar per gallon (42 g per 5 litres), then stored for a week or two while the beer develops condition. Careful racking is necessary since a substantial yeast paste is formed during fermentation and deposited on the bottom of the bin. It is not required and may be discarded.

The variety of beer kits at present available in shops includes: mild, bitter, pale ale, export ale, lager, brown ale, Northern brown, stout, Irish stout, shandy and barley wine. The cans may be bought in sizes to produce 16, 24 or 40 Imperial pints. Pressure casks are available in similar sizes.

As with all merchandise, some concentrated worts seem to be better than others, and it is worth while trying as many different brands as possible to find the one that suits your palate best. The beer drinker with a sophisticated palate may find some of the beers produced from these kits to be a little on the thin side. The amount of sugar required in proportion to the amount of malt provided is sometimes relatively high. Some also tend to be rather bitter due to the presence of an excess of hop resins used as a preservative. As a result, it is not possible to improve the body by reducing the amount of water, since this increases the bitterness. A more satisfactory alternative is to add some additional plain malt extract in place of some of the sugar. Malt flour from barley or maize is also a useful additive.

Experience over 30 years of home brewing has shown that 680 grams ($1\frac{1}{2}$ lb) of malt flour or 900 grams (2 lb) of malt extract are the minimum required to make 16 pints (9 litres) of a satisfying beer. Sugar produces alcohol, but alcohol without flavour is of no interest to the home brewer. The quantity of sugar to use should never exceed the quantity of malt used, and for really fine beers the proportion should be 3 malt to 1 sugar. A proportion of 2 malt to 1 sugar produces a very good beer, but as the proportion reduces, the flavour and body diminishes.

A few cans of concentrate are available which require no sugar, some require less sugar than others and, alas, some require more. The choice is yours. Having chosen a suitable kit, these cans of malt extract are an ideal way for beginners to learn something of the craft of brewing, and are well worth the making.

Some firms market a dry pack consisting of malted barley grains, malt flour, hops, nutrient salts and yeast, together with some finings. Again, all that is required is sugar and water. The malt flour and sugar has to be dissolved in tepid water, whilst the grains and hops are simmered in boiling water for one hour. This liquor is then poured on to the syrup and the total quantity of liquid made up with more cold water. The yeast and nutrient are then added, and fermentation is conducted as usual. At S.G. 1.005 the beer is racked, bottled, primed and stored.

The quantity of malt in these packs is rather on the low side compared with the amount of sugar recommended. A minimum of $\frac{3}{4}$ oz (21 g) hops is required to flavour and keep 8 pints of beer ($4\frac{1}{2}$ litres). 2 oz (56 g) is therefore on the low side for 40 pints ($22\frac{1}{2}$ litres), whilst 4 lb (1,800g) of sugar seems very high. The flavour and quality of this particular brew can be improved by omitting 1 gallon ($4\frac{1}{2}$ litres) of water and 1 lb (450 g) of sugar. But this is all a matter of choice depending on your palate. The manufacturer knows the quality of his ingredients and prepares his instructions accordingly. You may, or may not, think highly of the result. Nevertheless, it is well worthwhile making up at least one of these packs if only to gain some additional experience from using different ingredients.

Essential Ingredients

Malt

THE main cereals grown in the world are wheat, oats, barley, maize, rice and rye. Generally, wheat is used for making bread, oats for feeding to animals, maize and rice are cooked and eaten as food, rye is used for whisky, and barley is used for brewing beer. However, all the grains are to some extent interchangeable and are used for different purposes from time to time.

Before barley, or any other cereal, can be used for brewing it must first be malted. Briefly, this is done by soaking the grains in water and then leaving them in a warm atmosphere for a few days so that they can germinate. During this time the enzymes in the grain first break down the cell walls containing the starch and then convert the starch into maltose. When the shoot appears this process is completed and the grain is then kiln-dried to stop it from growing. To produce the depth of flavour required – from a pale malt to a black malt – the grains are roasted.

The process of malting is complex and the amount of water used, the time allowed for germination and the heat used in roasting are all critical. Good barley can be damaged in many ways by poor malting. The grains may grow too little or too much and so diminish the yield of malt, or be imperfectly roasted and so change the required flavour.

150 kg (336 lb) grain, known as a 'quarter' should yield about 45 kg (100 lb) of malt. When 1 lb (450 g) of malt is dissolved in a gallon ($4\frac{1}{2}$ litres) of water it produces a specific gravity of about 1.030 the making of a pleasant beer. It is most unlikely that you will be able to malt your own barley efficiently, and you are recommended only to buy and use barley grains that have already been malted. Always buy pale malt since this will give you the highest quantity of malt extract. Colour and flavour may be added by the use of coloured malts, whether amber, crystal, brown, chocolate or black.

When a pale malt is cracked between the teeth, a powdery sweetish content is revealed. Sometimes this is milled and sold as malt flour. It can be used in the making of malt bread as well as beer. Brown and chocolate malts, as their name implies, are heavily roasted after being kiln-dried. As a result the yield of malt extract is reduced and the flavour is increased with the degree of roasting.

Crystal and amber malts are less heavily roasted and are, therefore, lighter in colour. The content is more brittle than powdery. These malts add a smoothness and fullness to a beer as well as a little colour and a good flavour.

Black malt is roasted until the malt is caramelised but the process is stopped before it is carbonised. It is used in the brewing of stout and imparts that special flavour so much enjoyed by so many.

Maltose is the sugar that gives malt its name. It is converted from the starch in the grain by the presence of an enzyme called amylase. The starch is first converted to dextrin and then to maltose.

During the mashing process of brewing beer, the dextrin and maltose are extracted and then they become available for subsequent conversion into carbon dioxide and alcohol by the enzymes secreted by the yeast. The dextrin is more difficult to convert into alcohol and the unconverted dextrin remains in solution to give body and sweetness to a beer.

Malt is available in a variety of forms. The best known being the toffee-like malt extract, widely available for other purposes as well as for brewing. Malt flour (already mentioned) can be obtained from firms baking their own breads or from home-brew shops and departments. Sometimes it is available in prepared packs with hops and yeast, ready for use.

Malted barley grains are also widely available now, especially from home-brew shops and departments of some stores, as well as from mail order houses such as Loftus. It is cheaper to buy a large quantity at a time – say 25 kg (56 lb) and to store it in an absolutely air tight and moisture proof container. Once the malt begins to pick up moisture it begins to deteriorate. A thick paper sack inside a heavy gauge polythene bag tightly fastened at the neck is recommended.

Before use the malt has to be cracked so that the maltose can be extracted in solution. Some home brewers use a rolling-pin on a formica surface, others a coarse mincer. In either instance the process is expedited by soaking the grains for an hour or so in tepid water to soften them. If the grains are broken up too much, difficulty will be experienced in the mashing stage, since the wort becomes porridge-like and unworkable. The mere cracking of the grains is sufficient. Indeed it is best to buy grains already 'crushed' if you can.

As in all other ingredients there are various qualities of malt, whether it be in the form of extract, flour or grains. The quality depends partly on the original barley, but the variety of seed used, the soil, the season, the harvesting and the storage all play their part. The skill of the maltster is the next variable and after that the skill of the manufacturer in extracting and packing the malt. Experience has shown that it always pays to buy the best quality available. Relative to the total cost a few pennies either way is not going to make that much difference, but it could affect the quality of the finished beer considerably. Always buy the best malt you can and store it efficiently.

Malt flour solidifies if it becomes the least bit damp, and is then more difficult to dissolve. It is best bought as required and all used or else stored absolutely dry, in an absolutely moisture proof box or bag. Similarly with malt extract. Left in a half empty can or container, it can oxidise and deteriorate to the point of not being worth using.

Hops

Anyone familiar with Britain's East Kent, Hereford-shire or Worcestershire, or who has toured through these areas in August or early September, will have seen a hop garden. These counties have been famous for their hops since the 16th century. The hop is essentially a flower which grows in clusters on a bine which climbs up strings to a height of 8 to 10 feet (3 m). The flower consists of many layers of small, leaf-like, green petals. When it is picked at the end of August and in September, the bunches of flowers are dried in a kiln and then packed tightly into a large sack for storage until required.

The two most popular varieties are Fuggles which are used mainly in the brewing of mild ales, brown ales and stouts, and Goldings which have a more delicate aroma and are used in the brewing of light ales and bitter beers. There are also crossed varieties of these two as well as the American hop, Bullion. Like Northern Brewer, this is an extremely bitter hop normally used in conjunction with other varieties. There are many others, more of interest to the grower than to the amateur brewer, because of their resistance to mildew and cropping character-istics. Hallertau, the hop most commonly used in the brewing of lager, is seedless, very delicate in bouquet and imported from the Continent of Europe. It is essential to the brewing of this delicious beer.

The purpose of adding hops to the malt solution is not only to give flavour and bite to the beer, but also to preserve it from infection and assist in clearing the beer to brilliance.

Because some oils which provide aroma are evaporated during the boiling, the addition of some dry hops during fermentation is recommended by some brewers. Others advise that a quarter of the total hops be added for the last 10 or 15 minutes of the boil. Either method produces good results, but the former makes skimming impossible unless the hops are added after skimming has been completed.

Hops may be purchased from the same sources as malt. When buying hops, smell them to ensure that they are free from any cheesy or dirty odour, and possess a clean and fragrant bouquet. Look for a pale green in Fuggles and a golden colour in Goldings. Decline any hops that have brownish leaves, since this indicates excessive age and oxidation. Their flavour will be poor and their preservation qualities diminished. Rub a flower between the palms of your hands, which should then feel sticky and be coated with a golden powder. If not then the hops are stale and should not be purchased.

First you will want to experiment with different varieties but when you have found the hops you like best, purchase six to nine months' supply of the new crop and store them in a cool dry place. Humidity and warmth will cause deterioration. Properly packed, they can be successfully kept in a

Hop-picking in Kent 100 years ago. Like grape-gathering, the work is extremely arduous

freezer although this is not strictly necessary. Purchasing small quantities at a time will inevitably mean variations in quality and flavour, and therefore, some disappointments. Hop oil is sometimes offered. It is very highly concentrated and is not recommended as a substitute for fresh hops.

Adjuncts

The cost of malting barley grain is quite high and most brewers seek other and cheaper ingredients to mix in with the barley for reasons of economy. These ingredients are called adjuncts. Oats have been tried but the results were below the standard expected. Flaked rice and flaked maize are fairly commonly used together with some unmalted barley. The reasons for using adjuncts are not wholly economic, however; in fact, they help to clear the beer and make it look more attractive. Furthermore, a little flaked maize added to a pale ale mash produces a drier, crisper finish than the same beer without maize. Flaked oatmeal added to a stout mash produces a distinctive flavour that many people find most attractive.

Like malted barley, stocks of adjuncts must be stored absolutely dry until required. When preparing a recipe or formulation of your own including adjuncts, ensure that of the total weight of grain used not more than 10% is in the form of adjuncts.

Adjunct grains consist of starch which is unfermentable as such. The flaking process opens up the grains and removes the fibrous materials. The malted barley contains an enzyme called diastase which is usually present in sufficient quantities to convert the starch into fermentable sugar and so increase the specific gravity of the mash. The serious home-brewer will undoubtedly experiment with adjuncts and some recipes are included using them.

Sugar

To the average home brewer sugar means granulated white sugar and this is generally quite adequate. It is pure and although now much dearer than once it was, is still good value for money in brewing terms. Furthermore, it is easy to store, easy to measure, quick to dissolve and readily convertible into alcohol. Rarely should it be necessary to use more than 250 grams per 5 litres (8 oz per gallon). Sugar is used solely as a less expensive way of producing alcohol. It has no other merits in brewing. If too much is used the flavour and quality of the beer suffers.

The enthusiastic brewer, however, will wish to use invert sugar. Ordinary household sugar, technically called sucrose, is composed of two single sugars, fructose and glucose, combined in such a way that they have to be separated before the real process of fermentation can begin. This separation is normally made by the enzyme invertase which is secreted by the yeast, but it can be made artificially and the separate sugars are then called invert sugar.

Commercial invert sugar looks rather like white coconut icing and is usually bought in blocks. It contains 25% water and so 4 measures of invert sugar are only equal to 3 measures of granulated sugar. It has a tendency to absorb water and to become sticky and runny. Because of the process involved, it is more expensive than ordinary sugar. It can be made quite easily in the home, however, by gently boiling for 20 minutes 2 lb (900 g) white sugar with 1 teaspoonful of citric acid in one pint ($\frac{1}{2}$ litre) of water. The result is a quantity of invert sugar syrup sufficient to use in the brewing of 32 Imperial pints (18 litres) of beer.

A great many home winemakers and brewers use sugar in this form. It is easier to dissolve than the crystals and more readily fermentable. It is particularly useful as a priming syrup and should be used at the rate of 10 fl oz per 5 gallons. In metric terms this is equivalent to 30 cl per 25 litres. In the USA the rate is 10 fl oz per $6\frac{1}{4}$ gallons.

Glucose by itself is sometimes used, because it is immediately fermentable. It is sometimes referred to as dextrose. It is obtained from starch in grain by the presence of the enzyme complex diastase which consists of at least two enzymes known as alpha amylase and beta amylase. The former converts the starch to dextrins and the latter converts some of the dextrins to maltose which is then converted by the enzyme maltase into glucose. It is sometimes possible to buy maltose dextrin which gives alcohol, sweetness and body to a beer as well as assisting with head retention.

Brown and demerara sugar may be used in the brewing of brown ales and stouts. The caramel in the sugar adds a little colour and flavour, but the impurities slightly diminish the conversion rate to alcohol. Sometimes caramel is added direct to a brown ale or stout beer specifically for flavour and darkening. Caramel is, of course, burnt sugar, and it has a very bitter flavour. It should be used with the greatest moderation, adding a few drops at a time.

Stout with a slightly milky flavour has long been popular although it is no longer permissible to describe such a beer as milk stout. The sweetness and flavour comes from a sugar called lactose found in small quantities in milk. It is quite unfermentable by beer yeast or wine yeast, although it can be fermented by a yeast named *saccharomyces fragilis* indigenous to Mongolia where it is used to ferment asses milk into a drink called *koumiss*.

Treacle may be used in place of some sugar when making stout, but its flavour is too strong for most other beers. Golden syrup, which is a mixture of sucrose, invert sugar and flavourings, may be used when brewing strong flavoured bitters. The flavour of molasses is too strong to be used in brewing.

Yeast

The story of how man first came to know and use yeast in making bread and brewing beer is a fascinating one. We know that at first the name 'balm' was used for both. In biblical days the word was leaven, not very different from the French word for yeast – levure. Nowadays baker's yeast is kept separate from brewer's yeast. The former has developed a doughy taste and the latter a beery taste which makes them no longer interchangeable. They are nevertheless the same strain of yeast, the botanical name for which is *saccharomyces cerevisiae*.

This particular variety has the ability to ferment very rapidly, forming large clouds of carbon dioxide in the process. In bread-making this rapidly raises the dough and makes it palatable when cooked. In brewing, the foam – now called a yeast head – protects the beer from contamination. *Saccharomyces cerevisiae* is a surface fermenting yeast and halfway through fermentation some of this yeast has to be skimmed off, otherwise there will be too much yeast in the beer and it will develop a yeasty flavour.

Beer yeast, which looks like a putty-coloured cream when used by the brewers, can be bought in liquid or granule form. Before use it should be activated in a starter bottle with a little malt dissolved in water. Not until it is fermenting vigorously should it be pitched into the wort (as a solution of hop-flavoured-malt is called). Fermentation of the whole then starts without delay and off flavours due to infection are avoided.

This yeast prefers a coolish temperature of around 15°C in which to ferment, but no lower. Too slow a fermentation causes a somewhat bitter taste in the beer and is called 'yeast bite'. There is a similar effect if fermentation is conducted at too high a temperature.

If you live near a brewery, you can probably obtain yeast from that source. Do not be greedy, however, for it will not keep long before going stale and spoiling your beer when you do use it. Buy only sufficient for your immediate needs. Up to one week in the coldest part of the refrigerator is about long enough to keep it without risk. You can however, freeze yeast without killing it. Make sure that it is well packaged and frozen very rapidly so that only small ice crystals are formed which do not damage the cell walls. Make it up into separate small packets for each brew so as not to disturb the bulk by having to break bits off. In these conditions it will keep for over a year. It may be used half an hour after taking it from the freezer, but activate it before use. Like wine yeast, brewers' yeast needs a nutrient and an acid base in which to ferment, but this is available in the malt which makes an excellent food.

As already indicated, lager requires a different yeast to give it the special flavour of this splendid beverage. Its botanical name is *saccharomyces carlsbergensis*, named after Herr Carlsberg who invented lager. The main difference between beer yeast and lager yeast is the fermenting position. Ordinary beer yeast is a top fermenting yeast while lager yeast is a bottom fermenting yeast. Lager yeast also performs best at a lower temperature than beer yeast. Between 7 and 10°C seems ideal. Both wine and bread yeast detract from the beery flavour.

Some bottled beer is sold with a yeast sediment still in it. This may be used in the home by adding it to a yeast starter bottle and developing a sufficient quantity of an actively fermenting yeast. It makes a very good clean brew. You can continue to use your own yeast if you brew beer regularly. Avoid and discard the first skimming and use instead the yeast thrown up in the second stage of fermentation. Alternatively you can use the sediment from your bottle fermentation, thus helping to ensure a continuity of flavour.

Although malt contains adequate nourishment for the yeast colony required for fermentation, the packs of malt extract which require a substantial quantity of sugar to be added may be deficient in nutrient. To ensure that a large enough colony is quickly established to conclude fermentation in five days, it is always as well to add some nutrient salts.

Water

It has long been known that the quality of certain beers depends to some extent on the water from which they are brewed. The hard water of the Burton-on-Trent area, for example, produced the best light ales and bitter beers in Britain. Conversely the somewhat softer water in the London area produced better stout-type beers and mild ales.

Analysis has shown that it is the presence or absence of mineral salts that causes this variation of quality. Bitter beers need a higher proportion of calcium sulphate and a lower proportion of calcium chloride. Mild beers need a low proportion of sulphate and a higher proportion of chloride. The quantities are minute and yet of very considerable importance to the quality. A balanced mixture of different salts can now be obtained for different beers. The contents usually include calcium sulphate (gypsum), magnesium sulphate (Epsom salts), calcium chloride, and sodium chloride (table salt), together with calcium carbonate (common chalk).

The quantities required vary according to the beer style as indicated in the following table. They assume a neutral water.

Salt	Pale ale	Export ale	Mild ale	Stout
Calcium sulphate	15–25	40–50	10–15	–
Magnesium sulphate	4–6	4–6	2–4	2
Calcium chloride	2–4	4–6	6–8	5–10
Sodium chloride	4–6	4–6	8–10	15–20
Calcium carbonate	2	2	2	8–12

The figures are in grains per gallon at the rate of 437½ grains per oz. 15.4 grains = 1 gram.

Brewing from Malt Extracts

A simple way of brewing your own style of beer at home is to use a straight extract of malt and to add hops and adjuncts to your own liking. In this way, the more difficult part of extracting the malt from the barley is done for you, whilst the more interesting part of designing and brewing the beer is left for you to carry through.

The following most simple, yet most satisfying, basic recipe has been brewed with much success on countless occasions. It can be varied in dozens of ways. It takes little time and less trouble and the beer matures in 10 days or so.

Extract of malt	450 g (1 lb)
or Malt flour	340 g (¾ lb)
White or brown sugar	225 g (½ lb)
Hops	28 g (1 oz)
Water	4¼ litres (7½ pints)
Granulated beer yeast and nutrient	1 sachet

Method: Dissolve the malt extract and sugar in one third of the water, warmed to blood heat.

Boil the hops in half the water for 45 minutes.

Pour the hop liquor on to the wort and top up with cold water to 1 Imperial gallon (4½ litres).

When cool enough, sprinkle on the yeast and its nutrient, cover and leave for five days, skimming on the second and third days.

When fermentation is finished, move the beer to a cool place for two days, then rack into eight one-pint bottles.

Prime each bottle with a level teaspoonful of sugar.

Stopper or cap the bottles, shake them to dissolve the sugar and leave them standing in the warm for two days.

Store the beer for eight days at least, before serving.

This bright, well-flavoured beer should be served cool and poured carefully to avoid disturbing the sediment.

From this basic recipe all types of beer – mild, bitter, brown and stout – can be brewed easily and quickly, simply by varying the contents slightly:

Mild ale Ingredients as above, but omit sugar and use only 21 g (¾ oz) hops. This beer has a full malt flavour but is less alcoholic and not so bitter as the first recipe.

Old ale Ingredients as above but use 450 g (1 lb) of brown sugar and 42 g (1½ oz) hops. This beer is much stronger in alcohol and contains more hop flavour to balance it. The beer needs at least one month in which to mature. It is a well-flavoured 'real' beer. Excellent at Christmas for adding to the pudding or for mulling with a hot poker.

Brown ale Ingredients as above but use brown sugar and include 56 g (2 oz) 'chocolate' malt grains when boiling the hops. This is a nutty flavoured brown beer that needs keeping for a week or two.

Stout Ingredients as for basic recipe but use 340 g (12 oz) brown sugar, 112 g (4 oz) black malt grains, 42 g (1½ oz) hops and a level 5 ml spoonful of table salt. Strong and bitter like an Irish stout, this beer will keep for a year or more and needs at least a month to mature.

Milk stout Ingredients as for stout but use only 28 g (1 oz) hops and include 112 g (4 oz) of lactose milk sugar. This beer is not so bitter as the stout and has a smooth velvet texture that is most enjoyable. No milk as such is included, only unfermentable milk sugar.

Bitter

Malt extract	450 g (1 lb)
Demerara coffee sugar	675 g (1½ lb)
Golden syrup	450 g (1 lb)
Hops	56 g (2 oz)
Water	8½ litres (15 pints)
Beer yeast and nutrient	1 sachet

Method: Mix all the ingredients together except the yeast, and boil for 30 minutes. If a large enough pan is not available, use only half the water and add the remainder in the form of cold water after boiling has taken place.

When the temperature of the wort has fallen to 20°C (68°F) sprinkle on the yeast and ferment as usual.

This is a crisp, tangy beer, so good that the recipe is for 16 bottles. It is less malty in flavour but does not taste thin. Hard water should be used for preference. If it is not available naturally, add a sachet of hardening salts.

Brewing from Grains

Preparing the mash

WHILST the vast majority of home brewers will always use malt extracts for brewing their own beers, there is a substantial minority who enjoy the challenge of brewing their beer from grains in the traditional manner. They can produce a cleaner beer with a better body, full of fresh flavour, a good head and great satisfaction. Such brewers believe that in the concentration of the malt extract, there is inevitably a loss of flavour to say the least.

Since each palate is different and one person appreciates one style of beer more than another person, the only way to find out whether you prefer a grain beer to an extract beer is to brew some from grains and some from malt extract and to compare the results.

It is strongly recommended that if you have never made beer before, you first brew up a few gallons of already adjusted malt extract kits. Then brew a few gallons of plain malt extract that you adjust yourself with grain adjuncts and hops. Finally brew some beer from dry packs. After this small amount of experience you will feel more confident in brewing from grains and you will undoubtedly make a better job of it.

Barley, like everything else, comes from different varieties of seed and it is worth enquiring around for a good quality malted barley. Decide on the type of beer that you want to make and ask for a grain suitable for that type of beer. Brewers don't just use barley, they use selected barley that has been kept in good, dry conditions — barley that they specifically select for a type of beer, whether it be a bitter, a brown, a stout or a lager.

Before the malted grains can be used they have to be crushed (or rather cracked), and this is usually done between steel rollers, so arranged as to crack, rather than crush, the grains. If you can buy your grains prepared in this way, so much the better. If you can't, then soak them for an hour in warm water to soften them. Drain off the loose water, spread them thinly on a hard surface and roll them with a length of heavy pipe or a rolling-pin.

Place the cracked grains in a boiler for preference — Burco market one for this purpose — or in a fish-kettle, or a preserving pan, or a large stewpan. Add any other grains that may be needed, the required quantity of water adjusted as may be necessary with gypsum and Epsom salts for light beers, or a softening agent such as salt for stout. It is important to add such salts at this stage because the gypsum, for example, separates out nitrogenous matter during the boiling process which are then removed with the hops. Recipes indicate how long to maintain a precise and even temperature. This is most important to ensure extraction of all the maltose and its conversion into fermentable sugar. The required amount of dextrin is also extracted to give the beer body, residual sweetness and a good head.

Maintaining this temperature is fairly easy with a boiler since a thermostat can be fitted which switches the heat on and off as necessary. High density polythene mashing bins fitted with a thermostat and an immersion heater are equally suitable if you wrap some insulating material around the bin to prevent heat loss.

If such sophisticated equipment is not available to you, then heavily insulate your fish-kettle or stewpan with glass fibre or blankets and obtain very good results. Every 20 minutes or so check the temperature and adjust if necessary. A table 'keep-warm' is also very effective in maintaining a given temperature.

For commercial brewers it is very important to extract every possible molecule of fermentable mal-

Perfect ingredients make the best beer

tose, so they mash for four hours. Their equipment enables them to draw off some of the wort after two hours and to continue mashing by washing the grains with a fine spray of hot water for another two hours, a process called sparging. At home the sticky malt sugar can be washed from the grains simply by pouring hot water through them after mashing is complete.

The moment when mashing is complete can be identified very simply. On to a clean white saucer place a teaspoonful of wort, and on to that drop a small quantity of iodine. If the wort remains yellow, mashing is complete. If it turns dark or blue, then there is still some starch in the wort not yet converted into glucose. Mashing should be continued and tested again in half an hour. There is no point in testing the wort before the grains have been mashed for at least two hours, but there is no reason why testing should not begin then. How soon the end point is reached depends on many factors and varies from mash to mash. All that can be said in general terms is that it is somewhere between two and four hours.

When the grains have been mashed and washed they can be discarded to the compost heap in the garden, assuming you have no chickens.

The hops are then added to the wort and boiled for the extraction of their essential oils and resins. A rolling boil is always recommended rather than a simmer. The vigorous action is more effective than the gentle in coagulating the complex protein substances. Many brewers use two different varieties of hops, adding the second one of them for only the last 15 minutes of the boil. This adds a freshness to the hop flavour in the beer and enables one hop to be used for one purpose and the second for another.

When the boiling is complete the wort must be cooled as rapidly as possible, but leave the hops in until they settle. Chemical activity is going on all the time and the 'hop break' (as the settling is called) is an integral part of the brewing process. If possible, draw off the wort through the hops as a kind of filter, then wash them with a little tepid water to remove any glucose that may be stuck to them.

When the temperature of the wort reaches 15°C (59°F) adjust both the specific gravity and the quantity of liquor. Invert sugar syrup is recommended if you propose to brew as near to the professional as possible. It should be well stirred in for easy assimilation. In the absence of invert sugar, ordinary white or brown sugar may be used, depending on the style of beer being brewed. First boil the sugar with a teaspoonful of citric acid for some 20 minutes. Allow this syrup to cool before adding it to the wort. Always make enough wort to fill the required number of bottles or cask after racking when the sediment has been left behind. For example, if you wish to fill eight one-pint bottles then adjust the quantity to say, $8\frac{1}{4}$ pints. Similarly eight half-litre bottles requires 4.2 litres. The excess becomes the discarded lees.

The yeast is next pitched. Whether you use fresh yeast from a brewery, yeast granules or liquid beer yeast, always activate it first in a starter bottle. Some of the wort cooled after mashing will do and the activation can go on whilst the wort and hops are boiling and then cooling. Use about $\frac{1}{3}$ litre ($\frac{1}{2}$ pint) to the 9 litres (2 Imperial gallons – $2\frac{1}{2}$ USA gallons). One sachet of yeast is enough for this quantity or from bulk use one 5 ml spoonful. When the yeast is pitched, give the wort a good stir and cover the bin with a lid or cloth to keep out dust and infection. Stand the bin in such a position that it cannot be knocked over and is not in the way, whilst readily 'get-atable' for skimming.

Fermentation

Half-an-inch of fresh brewer's yeast at the bottom of a cream tub is likely to contain 250,000 million yeast cells! Within three hours of pitching this into a suitable wort, the number will have doubled and in a further three hours there will be a million million yeast cells busily at work converting the maltose, fructose and glucose into ethyl alcohol and carbon dioxide gas. The latter will be rushing to the surface and some will be bursting with a faint hissing sound. The hop resins will be holding some of them together and this number will steadily increase until the whole surface of the wort is covered in a creamy froth. In among the froth will be minute particles of hops, albuminous matter and concentrated starch. The appearance will deteriorate to look like a dirty scum. Follow your inclinations to skim this off and throw it away. A second head will appear and grow into 'rocky' clumps or develop a cauliflower-like appearance. This too should be skimmed off and the beer given a thorough rousing. A third head or seal will now appear and this should be left until fermentation is finished and the bubbles in the froth burst and the froth itself slowly disappears.

A splendid example of a 'rocky' head

Beer is normally fermented in open vats both commercially and at home. No air-lock is needed, but it is desirable to keep the fermenting beer sufficiently covered to keep out dust and insects.

All temperatures are important in brewing, including the fermentation temperature. Lager should be fermented at 10°C (50°F), grain mashed beers at 15°C (59°F), and malt extract beers at 20°C (68°F). Try to create conditions so that the temperature can remain even and free from fluctuations. In hot weather it may be necessary to ferment in a relatively cool place to avoid spoilage by fermenting at too high a temperature.

After about five days the gravity has usually been attenuated to about S.G.1.008 or below, especially in malt extract and light ale types. Heavy gravity beers of 1.055 may take up to another week. Fermentation will normally stop in beers containing a high proportion of dextrin, because the yeast has converted all the readily available sugar that it can. Dextrin is not fermentable but is valuable for its other virtues.

Remember to keep the liquor line free from residual and coagulated yeast cells and discarded particles of hop resin. This avoids an acrid bitterness in the finished beer.

As soon as attenuation is complete and the specific gravity remains constant, move the bin to as cool a place as possible – around 10°C is best.

If the final S.G. is higher than 1.008, beware! Give the beer a good stir and wait for a day or two.

The process described may seem a little involved but in practice works out quite easily, especially after the first few brews. The results certainly make the effort well worth while.

Basic Recipes

It will be appreciated that there is nothing critical about the quantities given in the following recipes; slightly more or less of any ingredient may be used to suit your palate. Although these recipes have been made up into excellent beers time and time again, variations on them are frequently made and produce equally excellent beers. The metric/imperial conversions are not precise but have been balanced to produce an equivalent beer.

Draught mild ale

Pale malt	1 kg	(2½ lb)
Crystal malt	100 g	(¼ lb)
Wheat syrup	200 g	(½ lb)
Invert sugar	250 g	(½ lb)
Golding hops	15 g	(½ oz)
Fuggle hops	25 g	(1 oz)
Water	to 9 litres	(2 gallons)
Beer yeast and nutrient		

Method: Crack the malt grains, pour hot water on to them (70°C, 158°F), stir in the wheat syrup and mash at 60°C (140°F) for two hours or until the conversion end point is reached.

Draw off the wort, wash the grains with hot water, add the hops and boil vigorously for half an hour. Leave to cool.

Strain out the hops, wash them, stir in the sugar and adjust the quantity of liquor to an S.G. 1.030.

Pitch an active beer yeast and ferment at 15°C (60°F).

When fermentation is finished, stir in some finings and leave in a cool place for 48 hours to clear.

Rack into a pressurized keg and prime with 50 g (2 oz) of sugar. Mature for three to four weeks.

Pale ale

Pale malt	1.5 kg	(3½ lb)
Crystal malt	350 g	(¾ lb)
Flaked barley	200 g	(7 oz)
Diastatic malt extract	50 g	(2 oz)
Invert sugar	1.35 kg	(3 lb)
Fuggle hops	100 g	(4 oz)
Golding hops	25 g	(1 oz)

Hardening salts	2 level 5 ml spoonsful	
Water	to 23 litres	(5 gallons)
Beer yeast and nutrient		

Method: Boil the flaked barley as described in the previous recipe.

Crack the malt grains and place them in a mashing bin, together with the diastatic malt extract, the barley liquor and hardening salts.

Mash at 63°C (140°F) to end point. Draw off the wort and wash the grain.

Boil the wort with the Fuggle hops for 40 minutes, then add the Goldings and boil for a further 10 minutes. Leave to cool.

Strain through the hops and adjust the quantity of liquor and the S.G. to 1.046.

Pitch an active yeast and ferment at 15°C (60°F), skimming on the second and third days.

When fermentation has finished, stir in some finings and move the beer to a cool place to clear for 48 hours.

Rack into a pressure keg or, better still, into bottles.

Dissolve 200 g (7 oz) sugar in warm water and prime. Mature for six weeks.

Brown ale

For a basic recipe:

Pale malt	450 g	1 lb
Crystal malt	100 g	(¼ lb)
Amber malt	100 g	(¼ lb)
Brown sugar	100 g	(¼ lb)
Fuggle hops	15 g	(½ oz)
Table salt	2 g	(⅓ tsp)
Water	4½ litres	(1 gallon)
Beer yeast and nutrient		

Method: Crack the malt grains and mash them at 60°C (140°F) to end point. Draw off the wort and wash the grains, then boil with the hops and salt for 45 minutes and leave to cool.

Strain through the hops, adjust the quantity to 5 litres (8¼ pints) and the S.G. to 1.030.

Pitch an active beer yeast and ferment at 15°C (60°F) to end.

It is the hop that gives beer its bitter flavour. Always use the best

Taste the beer and if it is not sweet enough for you, add a little lactose or saccharin.

Fine, bottle, prime and store as usual.

Mature this pleasant beer for three weeks.

Irish stout

Pale malt	1.35 kg (3 lb)
Black malt	225 g ($\frac{1}{2}$ lb)
Burnt raw barley	100 g ($\frac{1}{4}$ lb)
Brown sugar	350 g ($\frac{3}{4}$ lb)
Fuggle hops	40 g ($1\frac{1}{2}$ oz)
Water	to 9 litres (2 gallons)
Beer yeast and nutrient	

Method: Crack the grains, pour on some hot water and mash at 66°C (150°F).

When conversion is complete, strain off the liquor and wash the grains, stir in the sugar and hops, boil for 30 minutes then leave to cool.

Strain off the hops, adjust the quantity and the specific gravity — S.G. 1.040 is adequate.

Pitch an active yeast and ferment at 15°C (60°F), skimming and rousing as usual.

When fermentation is finished, fine, rack, prime and bottle, then mature for 6–8 weeks.

This is a crisp, full-bodied, well-flavoured dry stout, typical of its style.

Export ale

Pale malt	3.5 kg ($7\frac{1}{2}$ lb)
Crystal malt	140 g (5 oz)
Malt flour	140 g (5 oz)
Diastatic malt extract	275 g (10 oz)
Demerara sugar	275 g (10 oz)
Invert sugar	275 g (10 oz)
Fuggle hops	50 g (2 oz)
Golding hops	125 g (4 oz)
Northern Brewer hops	15 g ($\frac{1}{2}$ oz)
Hardening salts	25 g (1 oz)
Water	to 23 litres (5 gallons)
Beer yeast and nutrient	

Method: Heat half the water and unless it is very hard already, add the hardening salts. Crack the grains and add them to the liquor together with the malt flour and diastatic malt extract.

Mash at 66°C (150°F) for three hours or until end point, then draw off the wort and wash the grains.

Stir in the two sugars, all the Fuggle and Northern Brewer hops and three-quarters of the Golding hops.

Boil steadily with a rolling boil for 30 minutes, then add the remaining hops and boil for a further 15 minutes.

Leave the liquor to cool, then strain it off through the hops and wash them with some tepid water.

Adjust the liquor to 23 litres (5 gallons) and the S.G. to 1.055, adding a little more invert sugar if necessary.

Pitch an active yeast and ferment at 15°C (60°F) to the end.

Skim and rouse thoroughly on the second and third days and when fermentation is finished, rack into a clean bin. Stir in some finings and move the bin to a cool place for the beer to clear, then rack into bottles, prime with 20 cl (7½ fl oz) strong sugar syrup between the bottles, stopper tightly, re-ferment at 20°C (68°F) for four days, then store for six weeks to mature.

Lager

Lager malt	680 g (1½ lb)
Hallertau hops	25 g (1 oz)
Flaked maize	100 g (4 oz)
Invert sugar	100 g (4 oz)
Soft water	4½ litres (1 gallon)
Carlsbergensis yeast	

Method: Crack the malt grains and place them in a mashing bin with the flaked maize. Pour on the cold water and leave for one hour.

Heat the water to 38°C (100°F) and maintain this temperature for half an hour.

Draw off 3 pints of wort, boil this separately for 20 minutes.

Return this to the mash, thus increasing the temperature to 49°C (120°F). Maintain this for 15 minutes and then repeat the process.

The temperature should then be about 65°C (149°F) which should be maintained for a further 15 minutes before repeating the process for a third and last time.

The temperature will by now have reached about 71°C (160°F) and should be allowed to cool to 60°C (140°F). Then slowly increase the heat until the temperature reaches 63°C (145°F) by which time the end point of conversion should have been reached.

Check with iodine in a saucer and if the liquor turns blue, reheat to 71°C (160°F) for 10 minutes before checking again.

When the iodine remains yellow and the end point is passed, draw off the liquor and wash the grains with hot water.

Add the hops and boil vigorously for 45 minutes then cool as quickly as possible and check the specific gravity. Adjust the quantity to one gallon and the S.G. to 1.040.

Pitch an active yeast and ferment in the coolest place possible – about 7° 10°C (45°–50°F).

When fermentation is finished, bottle, prime in the usual way and mature for at least two months and preferably longer.

A lot of trouble but well worth the effort.

Barley wine

Pale malt	700 g (1½ lb)
Crystal malt	150 g (6 oz)
Black malt	25 g (1 oz)
Wheat syrup	25 g (1 oz)
Diastatic malt extract	25 g (1 oz)
Brown sugar	As required
Golding hops	25 g (1 oz)
Citric acid	5 g (1 tsp)
Nutrient	3 g (½ tsp)
Water	4½ litres (1 gallon)
Champagne yeast	1 sachet

Method: Crack all the malt grains and mash in 3½ litres (6 pints) of water together with the diastatic malt extract and wheat syrup at a temperature of 67°C (154°F) for at least two hours until the end point of the maltose conversion is reached.

Draw off the wort and wash the grains with ½ litre (1 pint) of warm water. Make up to 4½ litres (1 gallon) and boil with the hops for 40 minutes. Then leave to cool.

Strain and adjust the quantity of liquor to 5 litres (8¼ Imperial pints) and the S.G. to 1.084, by stirring in sufficient brown sugar and cold boiled water.

Stir in the acid, nutrient and an active yeast. The champagne wine yeast recommended has an adequate alcohol tolerance, can withstand the pressure of the carbon dioxide and settles firmly.

Ferment the wort in a warm place at 20°C (68°F) until the specific gravity falls to 1.008, then stir in some wine finings and move the barley wine to a cool place for two days while the solids settle and the wine begins to clear.

Siphon into small bottles without priming sugar, stopper tightly and store for twelve months.

Wine bottles and corks are quite unsuitable and small beer bottles properly stoppered or crown capped should be used. The barley wine will continue to ferment in bottle and throw a further sediment, so care will be needed not to disturb this when serving or it will make the drink cloudy.

Old ale

Pale malt flour	450 g (1 lb)
Crystal malt grains	225 g (½ lb)
Brown sugar	225 g (½ lb)
Fuggle hops	35 g (1¼ oz)
Table salt	2 g (1 salt-spoonful)
Water	4½ litres (1 gallon)
Ale yeast and nutrient	

Dissolve the malt flour and sugar in warm water, then boil with the hops, salt and crushed grains for one hour. Strain into a bin and wash the hops. When cool, add an active yeast, then skim, rack, bottle, prime, cap and store for four months.

Equipment & Additives

Mashing

WHETHER you mash your own grains or use only malt extract, a bin in which to ferment your beer is essential. There are a number of natural polythene bins available in assorted sizes, with grommets in their lids for an immersion heater which can be coupled with a thermostat to maintain a predetermined temperature. These bins can be insulated with a blanket or the like and used for mashing grains. Stainless steel boilers are also available complete with a temperature control and a draw-off tap, for both mashing and boiling.

White polypropylene paddles with very long handles for rousing and stirring the wort are quite inexpensive, but an ordinary wooden spoon will do.

A Beerometer serves the same purpose as an hydrometer but has a narrower scale. It is a most valuable piece of equipment and is essential in the production of quality beers. A long thermometer in a polythene case is also very useful.

Bottling

Orthodox beer bottles are essential. Non-returnable beer bottles are too thin for use at home and are dangerous. New ones are mainly available in the one pint size (20 fl oz) but half-size bottles can sometimes be obtained from a public house or licensed restaurant or club and from the same source, quart bottles may be obtained. New rubber rings are available for screw stoppers. Crown caps and plastic re-seals are also in good supply. A simple capping tool and dead-head hammer may be bought for fastening crown caps. A more sophisticated two-handed lever capping machine is also available.

A wide variety of attractive and descriptive labels can be bought to give the bottles a professional finish.

For the draught beer enthusiast, there are some splendid 25 litre (5½ gallons) heavy duty plastic pressure kegs available complete with draw-off tap and a CO_2 injector. The CO_2 bulbs may be bought separately. Natural polythene funnels in assorted sizes and a suitable siphon as used by winemakers are essential pieces of equipment.

Malts

In addition to the wide range of hopped malt extracts and wort concentrates, the following malted grains are available: Pale malt, Black malt, Chocolate malt, Crystal malt, Lager malt, Wheat malt.
Dried malt extract, both light and dark, malt flour and Diastic malt extract complete the range.

Adjuncts

These include all carbohydrates other than malt. At present the following items are available:
Roasted unmalted barley for use when making stout. Barley grains, Flaked barley, Cracked maize, Flaked maize, Flaked rice, Wheat, Wheat flour, Porridge oats, Torrified barley.

White polypropylene paddle

Wooden spoon

English Golding hops developed by a Mr Golding from a fine hop bine found at Canterbury in Kent at the end of the 18th century

Hops

The varieties most widely stocked are:
English Fuggles, English Goldings, Northern Brewer and Hallertau. Occasionally one can find a stockist of Styrian Goldings and Saaz hops. The quality is often more important than the variety. Hop oil and hop extract are also available in small bottles.

Sugar

Brewing sugar in 14 lb (6.35 kg) tins is popular with the mashing enthusiast. Invert sugar, glucose chips and another brewing sugar known as glucose 'D' can be bought, along with lactose which is essential for making a milk stout. Ordinary white granulated

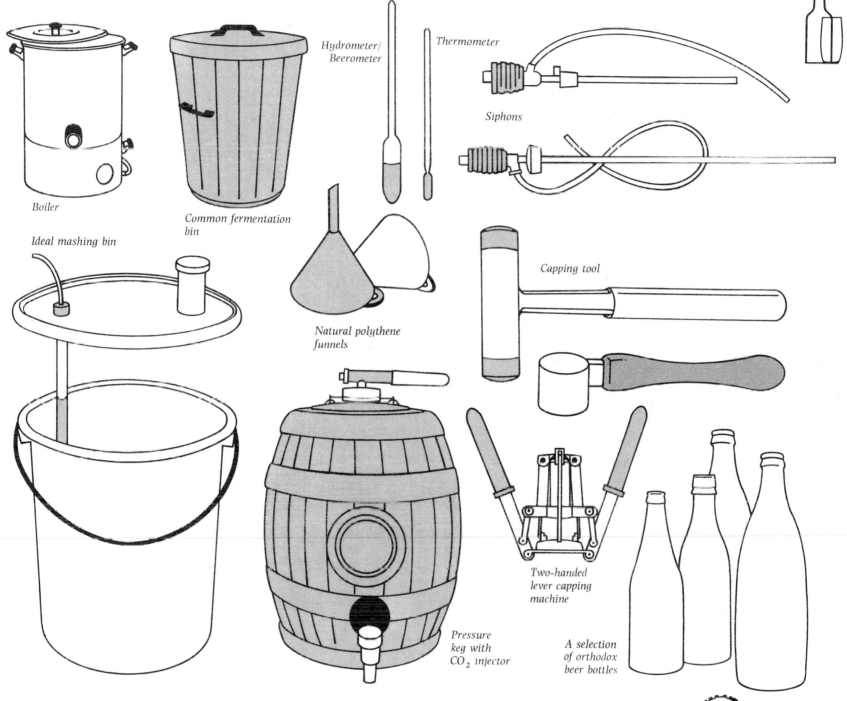

Boiler

Ideal mashing bin

Common fermentation bin

Hydrometer/ Beerometer

Thermometer

Siphons

Natural polythene funnels

Capping tool

Pressure keg with CO_2 injector

Two-handed lever capping machine

A selection of orthodox beer bottles

Crown caps, stopper and rubber rings

household sugar is perfectly suitable. Brown sugar may be used especially when some darkening is also required.

Yeast

Three pure yeast cultures have been marketed specifically for British ale, lager and stout. Dried beer yeast granules are also available in sachets sufficient for 40 pints ($22\frac{1}{2}$ litres) and in drums. Sometimes the yeast granules are supplied complete with nutrient salts but nutrient salts are also available separately. Lager yeast – *saccharomyces carlsbergensis* – is available both in granule and liquid culture form.

Other items

Hardening salts, gypsum and common salt will be required for water adjustment, and caramel for colouring. Heading liquid can be helpful, as well as finings. The most popular are: Isinglass, Irish Carragheen Moss, Gelatin and proprietary brands of liquid finings.

All ingredients are best used fresh but will keep for many months stored in airtight containers in a cool dark place. It is much more economic to buy the very best available and to buy them in bulk. Poor ingredients make poor beer.

Bottling & Storing Beer

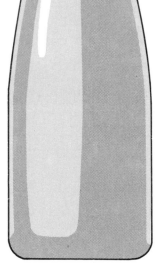

Finings

HAVING checked that fermentation has completely finished, finings may be added in accordance with the instructions given for the variety you are using. The procedure is usually to dissolve the finings in some of the beer, to mix this with the whole and to leave the beer in a cool place for the sediment to settle. It is normally ready for racking off the lees within 48 hours. Beer finings usually consist of isinglass mixed with a little tannin and some citric acid. However, gelatin may be used, or albumen in some form or other.

Priming draught beer

Draught beer has always been popular in the United Kingdom although not in America or Australia. In recent years high density polythene casks have been developed for the home brewer in which the beer can either be primed or carbonated or both. The casks withstand a high degree of pressure and the beer can be drawn off at the turn of a tap. Before racking off the beer, the cask or keg in which it is to be stored should be sterilised with plenty of hot water and drained dry. The young beer that you put into it should be fairly clear, but still with sufficient yeast in it to ferment the priming sugar which should now be added. Priming is done in the normal way by the addition of 40 g ($1\frac{1}{2}$ oz) of sugar per $4\frac{1}{2}$ litres (1 gallon).

Leave the cask in a warmish place for two or three days and then move it into a cool store for another five or six days at least. If a mild, low gravity beer, it will now be ready for drinking. All beers improve if kept somewhat longer, but cask beer will not keep in good condition as long as bottled beer.

In addition to priming the beer, you can attach a soda siphon type carbonator to fit the cask. In this method, as soon as the beer begins to lose condition and liveliness, a twist of the carbonator injects some CO_2 into the beer and it can be drawn off with renewed life and condition. Although it is more expensive to do so, a beer that you intend to carbonate may be cleared and filtered to brilliance before being poured into a cask. Carbonation then has to be used all the time. The only advantage is the brilliance of the beer. Casked beer that has been

This two-handed capping tool ensures a perfect gas-tight seal

primed is usually just the least bit hazy, though by no means unacceptably so. Discerning palates claim that the flavour of carbonated beer is not as good as that of primed beer that has a natural 'life'.

Priming bottled beer

If you chose to bottle your beer, first sterilise your bottles and stoppers or crown caps in a sulphite solution. Then fill the bottles only to within 4 cm ($1\frac{1}{2}$ in) of the top of the bottle. Add 5 g (1 level teaspoonful) of sugar to each bottle of the 1 pint (20 fl oz) size and *pro rata* for other sizes. In practice it is easier to dissolve the total amount of sugar to be used in a little of the beer and then to distribute this evenly between the bottles before filling them. Now screw down the stoppers really tight or crimp on the crown caps with equal efficiency. It is imperative that the bottles be absolutely gas tight under pressure, or else the beer will not remain in good condition when it is poured out.

Shake the bottles a few times to distribute the syrup, then place them in the warm for a few days for the priming sugar to ferment. Remove them to a cool store for a minimum of one week and preferably for a month. The better the beer, the longer storage it will require. A really good beer will keep for as long as a year or more. This applies especially to lagers and to export ales, although all grain mash and strong beers need several months to develop their best potential. In general terms the higher the starting specific gravity the longer the beer will take to mature. Lower starting gravity beers tend to mature more quickly. Before putting beers away into store, check that their seal is perfect and label the bottles with the type of beer and date it was brewed. Bottles may be stood in an upright position so that the sediment may settle firmly on the base of the bottle. Keep them in a cool dark place, free from vibration.

Caution

On no account should beer ever be stored other than in a properly-made bottle able to withstand the pressures caused by a secondary fermentation. Unsuitable bottles may burst and the flying glass may cause serious damage to persons nearby or to fittings and equipment.

Ailments & Hygiene

HOME brewed beer suffers from few ailments. If anything goes wrong, this will most likely be due to a lack of cleanliness, or insufficient care in the preparation, fermentation or cellarcraft. Malt extracts, such as those marketed by Boots, Edme, Geordie, Muntona, Tom Caxton and Unican, are prepared under the most hygienic conditions. There are constant laboratory checks to ensure that no micro-biological infection has occurred and that when the extract is sealed in the can it is absolutely pure. Stored unopened in a cool place it will keep in this condition for years. The can should be warmed for an hour or two before opening it to soften the malt.

When making beer from grains you could possibly have an occasional problem, such as:

Set mash: If the barley is crushed too hard its floury content coagulates into lumps and must be roused or stirred up to break them into separate pieces. The prevention is in the careful cracking of the grains.

Sluggish fermentation: Malt extracts are made for fast fermentation and some manufacturers recommend a temperature of $24°-26°C$ ($75°-80°F$). Grain-mashed worts should be fermented around $15°C$ ($59°F$) but if the temperature is too low or too widely variable, the fermentation may become slow. Weak or stale yeast may also cause slow fermentation; so, too, will a poorly balanced wort or one containing too much hop resin. Aeration of the wort in a warm place is the remedy. Attention to preparation and fermenting temperature is the prevention.

Yeast bite: When too much yeast has been used, or skimming has not been carried out effectively or even omitted, or if the beer has been left in contact with the yeast for too long, a bitterness develops in the beer which remains on the palate long after the beer has been swallowed. Yeast bite can also be caused by a too-low or a too-high fermentation temperature. There is no known remedy, but prevention is easy. Use only sufficient yeast, rouse the beer well in the first twelve hours after pitching the yeast, skim off the surplus yeast and impurities at least twice, paying special attention to the liquor line. Finally, ferment at the right temperature and keep it steady.

Lack of head retention: This is perhaps the most common fault. It is due to poor ingredients, poor fermentation and poor cellarcraft. Good malt grains and good malt extract should contain sufficient dextrin and other head retention ingredients to maintain a creamy head on the beer, at least for a short while. Hop resins help too. The dextrins are extracted from the malted grains by mashing them at a temperature of at least $66°C$ ($150°F$). During storage chemical reactions are going on in the beer which affect the head retention properties. There must be sufficient priming, an absolutely gas tight seal and adequate maturation, for a beer to develop and retain a good head. Certain firms market an additive which assists with head retention but nothing surpasses good ingredients and good techniques.

Yeast gush: This is almost the opposite effect. It is due to excessive priming and serving the beer too warm. If too much sugar is used in the priming, or if the beer has not completed fermentation when the priming sugar is added, the secondary fermentation will produce more carbon dioxide than the beer can hold. There will be an intense pressure of gas within the bottle and when the stopper is removed the gas will escape with such a rush that it lifts the yeast off the bottom of the bottle and stirs it up in the beer. Sometimes the whole bottle of beer will come off in foam impregnated with yeast.

The precise amount of sugar to use in priming depends on the specific gravity of the beer when it is bottled. The amount recommended is for a beer that has fermented right out. No beer should be bottled or casked if the S.G. is 1.008 or higher; fermentation should be continued for a few more days. Indeed it is always safer to wait until fermentation has completely finished before racking and priming.

Poor condition: The condition of a beer is its effervescence and liveliness after it has been poured into a glass.

The two most common causes of poor condition are:

1 Inadequate sealing due to imperfect crimping of crown caps, or using perished rubber on stoppers.

2 Pouring beer into glasses that have not been thoroughly rinsed and dried after being washed in a detergent solution.

Note: If priming and re-fermentation has been omitted, the beer will have no condition at all.

Serving Beer

It has been said that a good beer deserves a good thirst. Indeed on a warm day after a spell of digging in the garden, decorating the house, or a long walk in the sunshine, few beverages taste as good as a long cool drink of beer, with its palate-cleansing bitterness, its tangy flavour and its general thirst-quenching satisfaction. But this is only one aspect of beer — there are many more.

Beer should be sufficiently matured to be at its peak, that is, in prime condition. Pale ales and lager are best cooled to about 10°C (50°F) since at this temperature they taste more crisp and tangy. Mild ales, brown ales and stouts taste better some degrees warmer — around 15°C (60°F) — but above this they tend to go flabby and lose flavour.

Silver, pewter, ceramic or glass tankards may be used. Lids on tankards are no longer as popular as they once were in Britain (and still are in parts of Europe, such as Bavaria). The silver, pewter and ceramic tankards are thought to keep the temperature more steady than glass, are less likely to break and have a more personal identification. Unfortunately they suffer from the defect that you cannot enjoy the beer with your eyes before drinking it. To this end a well-shaped tulip glass with a short stem and base as wide as the bowl is ideal. A spotless and polished glass shows off the colour and clarity of the beer, as well as the lively conditions of the scurrying bubbles hurrying to the foamy, creamy head. These joys should not be overlooked when serving beer at home.

After use, tankards or glasses of whatever kind, should be washed in warm water containing a mild detergent to remove greasy fingerprints, and oiliness from the hops and dextrins. They should then be thoroughly rinsed in clean cold water to remove the last traces of detergent, before drying them and putting them away. Detergent has a deadening effect on the head of a beer and glasses washed in detergent should always be well-rinsed in clean cold water.

Inevitably bottled beers contain a small residue of yeast cells from the essential secondary fermentation in the bottle. This residue can be removed by chilling the beer hard to about 1°C (35°F) and gently pouring or siphoning it into a clean bottle, leaving the sediment behind. The beer is then recapped or stoppered and allowed to warm up to an appropriate temperature before serving. Very little life will have been lost and when served the beer will pour clean and lively.

Alternatively when the bottle is opened, the beer can first be poured into a jug or, with some care, directly into carefully positioned glasses. The bottle should be held very steady and the beer poured slowly down the side of a tilted glass in such a manner that large globules of air do not enter the bottle and stir up the sediment. When one glass is full the next is moved into position and pouring is continued without reverting the bottle to the upright. Once the bottle is returned to the upright, the sediment is thoroughly stirred up and the remaining beer is made cloudy. It is, of course, still wholesome to drink but contains such a quantity of yeast as to affect the flavour.

Many people enjoy a glass of beer of whatever type as an aperitif, although it tends to fill up the stomach and leave less room for food. Beer does have a tonic effect, however, and induces a feeling of well-being. It makes a splendid accompaniment to crusty bread and rolls, with butter and cheese. Highly-flavoured salads such as onion, shallot and radish accompany beer quite happily. Instead of a wine and cheese party, a beer and beef party makes a pleasant change.

A group of antique ale glasses nearly 8″ high engraved with ears of barley or hop bines. Probably used in high society for barley wines and strong ales

A plate of cold beef, some salads, crusty bread and a tankard of cool beer makes a very successful meal.

Generally speaking beer does not make a good companion to hot meals. Lagers seem to go very well with curries, however, and a dark beer drinks very well with fish and chips. Beer makes a useful ingredient in cooking. Sausages poached in beer are fairly well-known, but there are many other dishes in which beer can be used.

Try adding a $\frac{1}{4}$ pint (14 cl) of ale to soup. Light ales, milds and bitters are first choice. Two herrings poached in a $\frac{1}{4}$ pint of bitter beer with a teaspoonful of sugar, a tablespoonful of malt vinegar, a bay leaf, two cloves and four peppercorns make a wonderfully delicious meal for one person. Serve it with tomato, brown bread and butter and a glass of cool bitter or, if you prefer, a tankard of stout. Both do it justice. In all recipes for poached or baked fish, a $\frac{1}{4}$ pint of light ale may be included with advantage as part of the total liquid. It makes a most interesting change.

With meat be equally adventurous. A $\frac{1}{2}$ pint (28 cl) of brown ale in a beef casserole instead of water makes a richer meal. Try a $\frac{1}{4}$ pint of brown ale in a pot roast and a $\frac{1}{2}$ pint of pale ale when cooking brisket of beef. Similarly with boiled bacon. Use $\frac{1}{2}$ pint of light ale or bitter beer and $\frac{1}{2}$ pint water instead of all water. The flavour is greatly enhanced. The sauces and gravies from all these dishes are out of this world, too.

Exhibiting Beer

ALTHOUGH wine competitions have long been included in British horticultural shows, and have been held in their own right in more recent years, beer competitions are relatively new. They are increasing, however, and classes usually include lager, pale ale, brown ale and stout. Occasionally extra classes may be put in for Irish stout, export ale and barley wine. Normally the beer must be exhibited in a 1 pint bottle with a screw stopper, although crown caps and plastic re-seals are sometimes permitted.

The Amateur Winemakers' National Guild of Judges in Great Britain now includes a panel of specialists in adjudicating beer. They have a substantial and proven experience in brewing excellent beer themselves and have passed an examination in the theory of brewing, another in the theory of adjudicating and a third in the practical examination of adjudication of a number of different beers.

At a competition the judge examines each bottle for cleanliness both inside and out – and the cap or stopper, too. The rubber ring on a stopper must be new and the composition of the stopper free from stain of any kind. There must be no old labels or other markings on the bottle, which must be of an orthodox shape and brown in colour. The beer must fill the bottle to within 2 cm ($\frac{3}{4}$ in) of the bottom of the stopper.

When the beer is poured out the colour and clarity will be examined. It must be star-bright, and of a colour that is typical for its style. Next the beer is inspected for its condition – the speed and size of the rising bubbles – and for the size and consistency of the head as well as its retention qualities. The bottle will then be re-examined to see whether the sediment is light or heavy and whether it is firm on the bottom of the bottle or has risen and so clouded the remainder of the beer.

The bouquet is inhaled and evaluated before a good mouthful of the beer is taken, rolled around the mouth and ejected. The judge will be looking for a clean smell and taste, free from all off-flavours due to yeastiness or dirty equipment. The bitterness must be hoppy and not acrid. The judge will award marks for the cleanliness of the beer on the nose and palate, the hop flavour, the maltiness, smoothness due to maturity, tangy appeal and general satisfaction. In brief, a well-balanced beer. Marks will be deducted for yeast bite, acetic acid taint and any other off-flavours. He will appraise the texture and general impression related to the style of beer under examination. Marks are awarded as follows:

Presentation of the bottle: up to 2 points.
Colour, clarity and condition: up to 4 points.
Bouquet: up to 4 points.
Flavour, texture and appeal: up to 20 points.

The total of 30 marks are never awarded in full, since that would be the perfect beer upon which no one could ever improve. A prize-winning beer might get as many as 24 or 25 points and the average would be between 18 and 20.

There is often considerable confusion in the minds of exhibitors as to what constitutes a suitable beer for a class. Not infrequently a beer is entered in one class when it should have been in another. The following descriptions should help would-be exhibitors:

Pale ale: some brewers describe such a beer as a dinner ale, other as a light ale, other as a bitter beer. It should be clean and light on the palate, with only a mild hop flavour. The original gravity should have been about 1.030 and the beer should now be dry and free from residual sweetness. It should have been mashed at 65°C (149°F) so as not to include too much dextrin. The colour should be a pale gold.

Burton-type pale ale: is a stronger beer, crisp and firm on the palate from the hardening salts. The malt and hops are more pronounced and are balanced with a little more body. The original gravity should have been between 1.044 and 1.050. The mashing temperature a degree higher at 66°C (151°F).

Export ale: will be at the top of the gravity scale, with malt, hops and dextrins in balance.

Brown ale: this is a very dark beer but definitely brown and not black. It should be lightly hopped, light in alcohol, and faintly sweet rather than dry. This will be partly due to the softer water from which it will have been brewed and the higher temperature at which it will have been mashed, 67°C (154°F). The original gravity should have been between 1.030 and 1.034.

Irish stout: this is a full-bodied beer with a rich bouquet reminiscent of roasted barley. The taste should have an underlying bitterness and be quite dry to the palate, entirely free from sweetness. It should taste both smooth and rich. The head should be creamy and close-knit and very retentive. The original gravity should have been between 1.046 and 1.050 and soft water should be used.

Milk stout: although full-bodied this beer is less heavily hopped than Irish stout, but should possess the same creamy head and excellent condition. The flavour should be soft, round and smooth, with a sweet finish provided by lactose. The original gravity should have been about 1.036.

Lager: this is the class where most bottles are not really according to schedule. It is difficult to make a beer strong in alcohol but with a delicate colour, a light body and with only a subtle hop flavour. The condition should be vigorous and continuous, the head a very pale cream, almost white, but with superb retention. Pale ales are not good enough for this class. Compare the lager you propose to exhibit with a commercial lager first.

Before entering beers into a competition, obtain a copy of the schedule of classes and regulations. Check the details carefully. Select your beers, apply for exhibition labels and prepare your bottles. Fill them as indicated, stick on the labels precisely as instructed, wipe the bottles clean and keep the beers as cool as possible till they reach the show bench. Be rigorous with your selection and enter only outstanding beers. The average ones, consume with

your family and friends. Each beer entered should be a potential winner and your aim should be perfection.

If a bottle contains a heavy sediment or one that does not settle firmly, chill the bottle very hard to about 1°C (34°F) and siphon the clear beer into a clean and chilled bottle. Top up with beer from a second bottle. Better still, fill a one-pint bottle from a quart. Little gas will be lost because of the intense coldness of the beer, but the sediment will be eradicated.

In this way you can be sure that your beer will travel well and pour clear in all conditions. Balanced, well-brewed and bottled beers win prizes.

Elegant 19th and early 20th century beer and other bottles

Mead: Mankind's Oldest Drink

THERE is good reason to believe that *mead* was known to man some 12,000 years ago, although we do not know how the drink was discovered. It was certainly very popular in England in Anglo-Saxon times, and in 'polite society' right up to the end of the 17th century.

Mead is an alcoholic beverage obtained by fermenting a solution of honey and water with yeast. The difference in the quality and the flavour of the honey obtained from different flowers and blossoms is quite noticeable. Different kinds of honey, therefore, make up into quite differently flavoured meads and it is almost impossible to make two meads exactly alike.

Eucalyptus honey from Australia, for example, makes a mead with a most unpleasant flavour, although as a honey it is quite pleasant to eat on bread and butter. When the sweetness is removed the taste is quite different. Californian orange blossom honey, on the other hand, makes a delicious dry mead, in which the flavour of the oranges can be subtly detected. Canadian clover honey also makes a good mead, sweet or dry but with a little extra body. English honey, although expensive, is generally rated the best in the world and is worth using if you can get hold of enough. It may well be described as England's 'nectar of the gods'.

Everyone knows that honey is formed from the nectar collected from the flowers by the bees and taken to their hive for storage into winter food. Indeed, a bottle of mead is likely to consist of the nectar collected from as many as 30,000 flowers.

Honey consists of about 77% sugar (40–50% fructose, 32–37% glucose and 2% sucrose) and $17\frac{1}{2}$% water. The remaining $5\frac{1}{2}$% includes salts of iron, calcium, manganese, phosphorus, potassium, sodium and sulphur. There are slight traces of citric, formic, malic and succinic acids, together with some amino acids, albumen, dextrin, enzymes, fats, gums, oils, pollen, protein, vitamins and waxes. The specific gravity at 20°C varies between 1.452 and 1.486 depending on the liquidity of the honey.

In general honey is made into mead in much the same way as grape juice concentrate is made into wine. It must be remembered, however, that honey has insufficient acid, no tannin, and insufficient nutrient for an adequate fermentation by yeast. It is, therefore, ALWAYS necessary to ensure that these essential ingredients are added in sufficient quantities.

The honey must first be diluted to the required strength and for this, hot water is required — 50°C (122°F) is about right. Some mead makers recommend a gentle boil for about 15 minutes, both to pasteurise the honey solution and to coagulate the waxes, gums and ash into a scum which can be skimmed off and discarded. Unfortunately boiling diminishes the goodness of the honey. Acid, tannin and nutrient must then be added. At least 15 g ($\frac{1}{2}$ oz) of citric or tartaric acid is needed and twice the quantity of nutrient required for a fruit wine. The precise quantity depends on the manufacturer's recommendations for his product.

All kinds of fruits and juices, as well as herbs and spices, may be added to honey to vary the flavour of the mead. Similarly honey may be added to other wines in part place of sugar. Because of its water content 450 grams (1 lb) of honey replaces only 340 grams ($\frac{3}{4}$ lb) of sugar. White honey is best for making dry light meads, with subtle flavours.

A beautiful and rare glass about 5″ high, designed for mead about 1710

Use brown honey for strongly flavoured sweet meads. The heavier and stronger meads — and especially the spiced meads — are rather more of an acquired taste. After the straight table meads, both dry and sweet, cyser and pyment are likely to prove the most attractive to the majority of people. Once you get a liking for mead, however, the whole range is well worth making and will be found to justify the apparent high cost of the honey. Mead is a distinctive alternative to wine.

3 lb honey in one gallon of mead must has an average specific gravity of 1.090 — quite adequate for a dry table mead.

4 lb honey added TO one gallon of water is equal to 3 lb IN one gallon.

Cider & Perry

By definition, cider is the beverage resulting from the fermentation of apple juice. At first, cider apple trees grew wild. Their fruit was too sour and bitter to be eaten. One can imagine someone who knew something of the process of making wine from grapes finding a rotting pile of cider apples that were emitting a tangy, fruity smell and wondering whether he could use these countless apples to make a wine-like drink. The word cider comes from the Latin *sicera*, but it is unlikely that the beverage was made in Britain in Roman times. It has, however, always had a connection with the Celts who fled from the various invaders to the West of England.

the time of the Norman Conquest cider orchards were flourishing and the British climate was not regularly suitable for growing vines. Both produced a fermented drink that in the minds of people unaccustomed to writing and precise expression, could reasonably be regarded as the same. The French may well have called the cider orchards by the same word that they used to describe their own land that produced fermented drinks.

By the 18th century, however, apple growing and cider-making began to decline, taxation adding another nail in the coffin. It was not until 1890 that the situation began to improve again in Hereford-

The first documentary evidence of cider-making in England comes from Norfolk and is dated 1205. Cider grew in popularity until its Golden Era in the 17th century when the Hereford orchards set a pattern for all England. In 1676 John Worlidge who invented the apple mill (or cider press, as we would call it), wrote a wonderful book entitled *Vinetum Britannicum*. The sub-title was *A treatise of Cider and other wines and drinks extracted from fruits growing in the United Kingdom. With the method of propagating all sorts of vinous fruit trees. And a description of the newly invented Ingenio or Mill for the more expeditious making of Cider. And the right way of making Methyglin and Birch wine.*

In the course of his treatise Worlidge states, 'The cider made in Herefordshire, Gloucestershire and Worcestershire being in great quantities carried to London and several other places of this Kingdom and sold at a very high rate, is valued over the wines of France, partly from its own excellency and partly from the deterioration of the French wines which suffer in exportation and adulteration that they receive from those who trade in them'.

Worlidge advanced the theory that the old word vineyard was really applied to apple orchards and not to vineyards as the word is now understood. About

shire and Somerset. Today cider-making is mainly in the hands of a few large firms with modern machinery and methods of distribution, working from factories rather than farms.

True cider apples are not easy to come by for most people, and so cider-making at home, rather like mead-making, is available only to those who have access to the base ingredient. But, like mead-making, cider-making is well worth the effort once in a while. Well made, it is a most enjoyable and satisfying drink, superior to the commercial variety, now so widely available.

The best known cider apples are 'Sweet Coppin' (sweet), 'Bulmer's Norman' (bitter sweet), 'Yarlington Mill' (bitter sweet), 'Crimson King' (sharp) and 'Kingston Black' (bitter sharp). They are customarily blended to ensure an adequate mixture of sweet, sharp and bitter varieties to make a cider of a specific style. Quite a palatable cider, however, can be made from a mixture of dessert and cooking apples, the more so if some true cider apples or even crab apples are included.

Apples are by nature hard and therefore difficult to crush and press in the home. They should be allowed to ripen and mellow as much as possible before crushing them. The food freezer is an excellent

Making cider 100 years ago. The apples were crushed, mixed with straw and made into a cheese-shaped pile for pressing. The principles have not changed. The straw filtered the juice as does a nylon bag today

tool at this stage, for once a frozen apple is thawed it becomes very soft and can be pressed without much difficulty. It follows that a good press is a necessity, especially since at least 7 kg (about 15 lb) of apples will be required to make six bottles of cider. A juice extractor may also be used.

As soon as the juice is extracted, 100 p.p.m. of sulphite should be added together with some pectin-destroying enzyme. Before doing so, however, it is desirable to check both the specific gravity and the acid content of the juice. The specific gravity registering the sugar content will be a guide to the alcohol content at the end of fermentation. An S.G.

of 1.046 is about average and will produce a dry cider with a final S.G. of about 1.004. In general a reading of between 1.042 and 1.050 is desirable. An acid content on titration should be in the region of 0.4% or 4 ppt, equivalent to a pH of 3.8. The tannin content or bitterness should be about 0.15% — not easily measurable in the home. If necessary the juice may be adjusted, but this is best done by varying the quantity of different apple varieties rather than by dilution with water or the addition of sugar, acid or tannin. This is why it is so important to have a good blend of sweet, sharp and bitter apples.

The addition of the sulphite not only kills off unwanted micro-organisms, but also prevents oxidation or browning and tainting of the cider. The pectin-destroying enzyme ensures a clear cider free from pectin haze. There are no specific yeasts for cider fermentation but the Unican 'Super yeast' or a Chablis yeast would produce a clean, dry cider, whilst a Vinotex All-Purpose, a Hock or a Mosel wine yeast would be suitable for a sweet cider. Fermentation is conducted in the same way as for wine or mead.

When fermentation has finished, the cider should be fined or filtered if necessary, sulphited at the rate of 50 p.p.m. and stored for three months to mature before bottling. Cider does not keep well and does not

improve with long storage because of the relatively low alcohol content. It is best consumed when it is about six months old.

If the initial gravity should be 1.060 or higher, a sweet cider can be made by terminating the fermentation with sulphite at the rate of 100 p.p.m. when the specific gravity has fallen to about 1.016. Then rack fine and filter. Alternatively a dry cider may be sweetened with saccharin or lactose. Sweet ciders need more acid and tannin to balance the sweetness.

A dry cider may be made into a sparkling cider in the same way as a sparkling wine. Alternatively, a beer pressure barrel may be used in conjunction with a CO_2 bulb. A home-made draught cider with a bit of a sparkle in it is a most attractive drink. The cider should have been allowed to clear naturally, so that a few yeast cells remain, or some yeast cells should be added to the barrel with the priming sugar in the same way as for priming beer.

Cooking pears may be added to apples when making cider. If the apples available are low in bitterness or tannin, the cider will be the better for a few pears which have a naturally high tannin content.

Perry is the name given to the fermented juice of certain pears. Only special varieties such as 'Barland', 'Blakeney Red', 'Moorcroft', 'Taynton Squash' or 'Thorn' are suitable. Do not peel the pears but use skin and core thoroughly squashed and pressed.

Perry is made in the same way as cider, but produces a lighter and more elegant beverage that is at its best when made into a sparkling drink.

The following recipe will make an acceptable dry cider from fruit available from most greengrocers:

Sweet apples ('Golden Delicious' or 'Worcester Pearmain' or 'Cox's Orange Pippin').	3.5 kg (8 lb)
Sour apples ('Bramley' or 'Derby' or 'Granny Smith').	2 kg (4 lb)
Bitter apples ('John Downie' crab apples or any hard pears)	1 kg (2 lb)
Sulphite	
Pectin-destroying enzyme	
Chablis yeast	

Method: Wash the fruit but do not peel or core them.

Place the fruit in a natural polythene bin a few at a time and crush them with the end of a rolling pin or something similar.

As soon as the first juice appears add 2 crushed Campden tablets and the pectic enzyme.

When all the fruit is well crushed, transfer it to a pressing bag inside a strong press.

After the free juice has run off, apply pressure on a go/stop basis.

When no more juice flows, open the pressing bag, stir up the pulp and re-apply the pressure — more juice will flow. Repeat until the 'cake' is dry.

Make the cider from the juice as already described.

Fruit Wine Vinegars

VINEGAR is probably older than wine itself, since it is unlikely that the first wine had not begun to acetify before it was tasted. The English word 'vinegar' comes from the French word *vinaigre*, meaning sour wine. One of the earliest references to vinegar is in the Bible, the *Book of Ruth, Chapter 2, Verse 14*: 'And Boaz said unto her, "At mealtime come thou hither and eat of the bread, and dip thy morsel in the vinegar"'. In Roman times a vinegar vessel was called an *acetabulum*. The distinctive ingredient in vinegar is acetic acid. The bacteria which changes wine into vinegar is *mycoderma aceti*, sometimes called *acetobacter*. It is clear that all these words stem from the ancient Latin and that vinegar has been well known for thousands of years.

Because vinegar is so old, mankind has flavoured it with countless fruits, vegetables, herbs, flowers and spices. There is wine vinegar, beer or malt vinegar, cider vinegar, distilled vinegar, mustard, onion, shallot, garlic, tarragon, raspberry, rose and indeed almost any other kind of vinegar you care to name.

Any low alcohol wine or beer or cider will turn to vinegar if left exposed to the air. Low alcohol is defined as about 4% and a good vinegar should consist of at least 4% acetic acid. All the alcohol should be converted to acetic acid by acetobacter. It is a somewhat risky business to allow an alcohol liquor to become vinegar without some control, and vinegars should therefore be made deliberately.

An orthodox wine or cider with an initial S.G. of 1.036 should first be made and fermented to dryness in the usual way. A grape juice concentrate, either red or white, would be excellent for this purpose. Other fruits may be used, but keep the fruit content low, otherwise the fruit flavour of the vinegar becomes too strong. Alternatively a few bottles of wine of a known alcohol content may be diluted with water. For example, 1 bottle of wine of 12% alcohol diluted with $1\frac{1}{2}$ bottles of water will produce $2\frac{1}{2}$ bottles of wine containing just under 5% alcohol. The important factor is to produce a liquor of between 4% and 5% alcohol.

The low alcohol wine should be poured into a standard fermentation jar, and then to 5 parts of liquor add 1 part wine vinegar. Lightly plug the neck of the jar with unmedicated cotton wool to keep out dust and insects. Note that the jar is only half full and there is plenty of air space above the wine. Place the jar in a warm position – 25°C (76°F) for two months by which time conversion should be complete.

If you use a colourless demijohn you will be able to see the conversion of the wine into vinegar. First a light veil or haze will appear in the wine. Later a thick, crumpled, sticky-looking skin, called 'the mother of vinegar' will develop on the surface. At the end of conversion the vinegar should fall bright.

Rack the vinegar into clean bottles, filtering if necessary, and filling each bottle to halfway up the neck. Cork each bottle lightly and stand all of them on a cloth or board in a deep pan. Fill the pan with water to the shoulders of the bottles – half bottles are obviously best for this – and place the pan on a stove. Steadily raise the temperature of the water to 60°C (140°F) and maintain this for at least 20 minutes to pasteurise the vinegar. Cork the bottles tightly and leave them in the water to cool, then remove, dry, label and store them for a few months to mature.

If any air space is left in the bottles, or if they are not thoroughly pasteurised and corked, the process of oxidation of the acetic acid into water and carbon dioxide will occur. The finished vinegar should be as bright as a good wine. If it is made from a white wine it will be practically colourless. If it is made from a red wine it will be but a pale pink. The vinegars may be coloured if you so wish with turmeric (yellow), caramel (brown), or cochineal (red). Cider vinegar has an attractive yellowish tint; so, too, has a vinegar made from a bitter beer.

Flavoured vinegars are made by placing the flavours in the wine whilst it is being converted into vinegar. If fresh fruit is used add $\frac{1}{10}$th of the weight of the liquor in the form of clean, prepared fruit, free from stalks and stones. So for the quantity already mentioned you would need 250 grams (9 oz) of fruit.

A basic recipe for a fruit vinegar could be as follows:

1 bottle of red or white wine and $1\frac{1}{2}$ bottles of cold boiled water or $2\frac{1}{2}$ bottles of cider or $2\frac{1}{2}$ bottles of pale ale
$\frac{1}{2}$ bottle wine vinegar
250 g (9 oz) of a fruit such as blackcurrant, blackberry, raspberry, loganberry, red currant.
or
90 g (3 oz) of fresh, prepared herbs such as borage, dill, mint, tarragon, etc. washed and trimmed from root and stalk.

Note: A bottle in this context is one of 75 cl equal to $26\frac{2}{3}$ fl oz. If cider or beer is used the Imperial quantity is 3 pints 7 fl oz. The USA quantity is 4 pints 3 fl oz.

This recipe will produce six half-bottles full of vinegar, flavoured to your own taste and enough to last most small families for some months.

A worthwhile variation is to make up your basic quantity of wine and vinegar and instead of pouring it into a demijohn, pour it instead into six full-size, 75 cl, bottles so that each is only half full. Into each half-bottle place 42 g ($1\frac{1}{2}$ oz) of a different fruit or 15 g ($\frac{1}{2}$ oz) of a different herb. In this way you can make six different bottles of vinegar. The fruit should, of course, be crushed before adding it to jar or bottle

An 'improved' barrel in which to make vinegar in the 19th century. Cotton wicks were suspended through the many holes so that the vinegar solution, poured on top, dripped down the wicks and were, therefore, exposed more fully to the air

Casks half full of vinegar solution were exposed to as much air as possible in a vinegar 'field'

so that the juices and flavours may be thoroughly mixed with the liquor.

Great care must be taken when making vinegar to ensure absolute cleanliness, not only before and during conversion, but also afterwards. Vessels and equipment should be washed in very hot water containing a detergent, rinsed several times in clean cold water and then sterilised in a sulphite solution. Failure to do this adequately, could cause a vinegar taint in any other wines, meads, beers or ciders that you may subsequently prepare. Vessels once used for vinegar should be kept for vinegar and not used for other liquors.

It is asking for trouble to attempt to make a wine or beer in the same room or at the same time as you make vinegar. Wine, mead, beer and cider will pick up the distinctive smell and even if the liquor does not turn to vinegar it will almost certainly taint the bouquet and flavour to the discerning palate. If you must make wine and vinegar at the same time, do make them in different places in the house. For example, you might make your wine in the kitchen and your vinegar in the bathroom, provided this is some distance away and not in an adjoining room.

Vinegars have many uses other than for sprinkling on fried fish and chips, or for pickling onions. Wine, fruit and herb vinegars are excellent for use in oil and vinegar dressings for salads, or as an ingredient in a mayonnaise. Vinegar is a beneficial addition to the liquor in which certain meats or fish are cooked.

Mulled Wines & Cold Cups

MULLED wines make party starters of incomparable speed. Faces light up just at their sight. And cold wine cups can accompany cold turkey with the merriment that makes the meal 'fly'. Great-grandma need not be left out; an egg nog or caudle will keep her well and happy.

Imagination rather than effort is called for. Costs are minimal and home winemakers are on to winners with their variety of wines available. The spices help them too!

Serving

Mulled wines look their absolute best when served from a silver bowl, but few of us have such a vessel ready to hand and there are many alternatives. Soup tureens of silver or stainless steel are next best. Pyrex glass bowls are very good too, and often can be bought with ladle and glasses. If the party is a large one, a stainless steel mixing bowl or aluminium preserving pan will do just as well. Tie a fancy cloth or flag around the sides.

Temperature

The great secret with a mulled wine is the temperature. Alcohols boil about 66°C (150°F) and just above, and if you boil your wine all the alcohols will come off in the steam and none will be left in the wine. *So never boil wine.* Always use a kitchen thermometer – never a medical thermometer (they break). Keep the thermometer in the warming wine and as soon as the temperature reaches 60°C (140°F) turn off the heat. At this temperature the wine tastes quite hot and still has all its alcohol. Temperature is absolutely critical when making a mull. The wrong temperature can ruin the drink.

Temperature is equally important with cold wine cups. It is usual to float small cubes or balls of ice in these but use your thermometer to ensure that the wine has cooled to 10°C (50°F). Above this temperature and the wine ceases to taste cool and crisp and begins to get 'flabby'.

Suitable wines

In either mulls or cups use second-rate rather than first-rate wines. In mulls use wines from red grape juice concentrates, elderberry, damson or plum. In a wine cup use wines from white grape juice concentrates, gooseberry, apple, orange, greengage and the like.

Fresh lemons, oranges, root ginger, whole cloves and fresh mint make suitable additives for mulled wines or wine cups. A small bottle of rum added to a mull just before it is served, gives a nice finish to it,

as does a bottle of cold sparkling wine – or cold ginger beer to a wine cup. When apples are mentioned in a recipe, small Cox's Orange Pippins have proved best, but a Russet will also do. When raisins are mentioned, large stoneless or pre-stoned raisins are essential.

Glasses

Since the wine is neither too hot nor too cold, an ordinary wine glass, such as a Paris goblet, may be used. This has a good-sized bowl, with a decent stem, so that you can keep your hands away from the heat or the cold. For preference ladle the wine, but if you haven't a suitable one use a small jug and dip it into the wine before serving.

A quarter of a slice of lemon looks good in each glass of a mull and a red maraschino cherry adds colour to a cold wine cup. A hot mince pie with short crust pastry is much better than anything else with a mull. If you are in doubt, try it and you will be convinced.

Here is the simplest mull of all; it has never been known to fail. The recipe is basic and you can make almost any addition to suit your palate. One bottle of wine is nearly enough for six, just enough for five and plenty for four.

PUNCH

Ingredients:
1 bottle red wine
6 whole fresh cloves
1 tbs brown honey
1 medium to large fresh lemon
1 large piece root ginger
3–4 tbs sugar to suit your palate

Method:
Pour the wine into a saucepan, add the sugar, honey and cloves. Well bruise the ginger root with a steak hammer or rolling pin and add to the wine, together with the thinly pared rind of the lemon. Warm the wine slowly, stirring it gently with a wooden spoon. Watch the temperature carefully and do not let it rise above 60°C. Strain it into a heated serving bowl and stir in the expressed juice of the lemon from which particles of pulp have been strained. Serve in pre-heated glasses.

Some simple additions are a small stick of cinnamon, a single grating of nutmeg, a small bottle of rum and a dozen large and pre-stoned raisins. These may be served in the glass together with a

This exquisite silver punch ladle was fashioned in the form of a shell in 1752

quarter of a thin slice of lemon including the peel.

This punch tastes magnificent in bed. Try it when you get the flu' or a cold, or when you are 'browned off' with the boss. Make it as described, pour it into a vacuum flask and take it to your bedroom with a mug (and one for your wife – or husband). When you are in bed, pour out the Punch and sip it slowly. Soon a wonderful sensation of satisfaction and contentment sweeps slowly over you. The realisation that you are already in bed enhances the drowsiness and sleep comes quickly.

He who goes to bed mellow, lives as he ought and dies an honest fellow
AMERICAN COLONIAL MAXIM

BISHOP

Five oranges
Well roasted, with sugar and wine in a cup
They'll make a sweet Bishop when gentlefolks sup.
SWIFT

Ingredients:
1 small sweet orange
1 small piece of cinnamon
1 small blade of mace
1 pinch all-spice
6 cloves
1½ cups water
1 tbs sugar
1 bottle port-type wine

A Monteith silver punch bowl made in 1705. Note the carrying handles on either side

149

Method:

Stick half a dozen cloves in a small orange and roast it very slowly. Take a small piece of cinnamon, six cloves, a piece of mace and a pinch of all-spice, put them in a saucepan with a cup and a half of water and boil gently until it is reduced by half.

Pour a bottle of port-type wine into a saucepan and gently heat it to 60°C (140°F) – no more – then mix in the spices. Rub the rind of a lemon with sugar lumps to extract the zest and place them in the wine. Squeeze out the juice from half a lemon and also add to the wine. A little grated nutmeg is now added, the wine sweetened to taste and the baked orange carefully placed in the hot spiced wine.

Keep it hot for another 10 minutes and serve it with the oranges and spices still floating in it.

There are many variations of this very old recipe. It is one of the earliest recorded. A red table wine may be substituted for the port but more sugar will be needed and a miniature bottle of brandy or rum.

Alternatively cider may be used but not only will even more sugar be required in this, but also twice the quantity of brandy or rum.

WHITE WINE WHEY OR POSSET

Ingredients:
1 bottle cream-sherry type wine
1 bottle full-cream milk
1 large fresh lemon
3 tbs white sugar
A little grated nutmeg

Method:

Pare the lemon very thinly or remove the zest with lumps of sugar. Pour the milk and wine into a saucepan and stir in the sugar and lemon zest or finely chopped parings. Warm gently to 60°C (140°F) and keep the temperature steady until the milk curdles and remains firm. Carefully strain the liquor from the curds, sprinkle on a little nutmeg and serve in heated glasses. The milk curd is very good too.

Other recipes are given in the Calendar – see June.

COLD WINE CUPS

These delicious drinks may be made with any white wine. Fresh, frozen or canned fruit is added instead of the herbs and spices, although some mint and cucumber are occasionally used. Crushed ice, small ice cubes or ice balls are added to make the drink really cool and refreshing. At the last moment you can add a bottle of sparkling wine or cider or ginger beer so that the bubbles enhance the appearance and give that little extra appeal to the drink.

Because wine cups must be served cold, they taste better if the drink is slightly sweet. Chilling emphasises dryness and makes it less acceptable. Always use sweet white wines or add a tablespoonful or two of sugar, preferably fine white caster sugar which dissolves quickly.

'SHERRY' COBBLER

Ingredients for each person:
1 large glass of sweet sherry-type wine
2 or 3 pieces of finely pared lemon skin
½ tumbler crushed ice
1½ tsp caster sugar
Some strawberries, pineapple or other fruit

Method:

Thoroughly crush some ice cubes by placing them in a clean cloth and hitting them frequently with a wooden mallet or the like. Half fill a large tumbler with the finely crushed ice. Add the sugar and lemon peel. Top up with sweet sherry-type wine and add some cut strawberries or other fruit in season. Stir the cobbler to dissolve the sugar and ice, then drink it whilst it is still cold.

MINT JULEP

Behold this cordial Julep here.
That flames and dances in his crystal bounds,
With spirits of balm and fragrant syrups mixt.

MILTON

Ingredients:
1 bottle of cold, cream sherry-type wine
4 tbs clear honey

12 small cubes or balls of ice
1 good sprig of fresh mint

Method:

Remove the leaves of mint from the stem, wash them, shake off the surplus water and chop them finely. Place the ice in a suitable bowl, pour on the honey then sprinkle the chopped mint leaves over the honey. Pour on the cold sherry and leave for six minutes. Stir gently and serve in cool glasses.

RASPBERRY CUP

Ingredients:

1 bottle chilled rosé wine
2 tbs white sugar
12 small ice cubes
12 large raspberries, fresh or frozen

Method:

Place the ice cubes in a bowl with the raspberries, sprinkle them with sugar and pour on the cold wine. Stir gently to dissolve the sugar and serve some raspberries in each glass of the wine.

This same basic recipe may be used with other white, rosé or light red wines and other fruits.

ORANGE CUP

Ingredients:

1 bottle of cold sweet white wine
2 tbs gin
1 small bottle fizzy orange
1 large sweet orange
4 cubes sugar
12 small ice cubes

Method:

Rub the orange thoroughly with the sugar cubes to extract all the zest and place them in a bowl with the ice. Peel the orange carefully, removing all the white pith remaining, cut into thin slices and mix these with the ice. Pour on the gin followed a minute or two later by the wine. Stir gently to dissolve the sugar, then add the fizzy orange and serve quickly in cool glasses.

BLACKCURRANT CUP

Ingredients:

1 bottle of ginger beer
2 tbs Bacardi white rum
1 tbs fresh or frozen blackcurrants
1–2 tbs white sugar to taste
12 small ice cubes

Method:

Wash, stalk and prick the blackcurrants with a needle. Place them in a glass or small jug, pour on the rum and leave for five minutes. Place the ice in a bowl, sprinkle on the sugar, add the rum and blackcurrants and finally the pre-cooled fizzy ginger beer. Stir gently and serve in large glasses.

PUSSYFOOT

Ingredients:

1 large bottle of sparkling wine
1 each small bottle of lemon and orange squash
Half each small orange, dessert apple, ripe peach
1 tsp grenadine syrup
12 small ice cubes

Method:

Peel the fruits, cut into small pieces and mix them with the ice cubes. Add the bottles of squash, the grenadine syrup and finally the wine. Serve at once with fruit and wine in each glass.

A WHITE WINE CUP *for a formal function*

Ingredients:

1 bottle sweet white wine
1 bottle tonic water or ginger ale
4 tbs vodka
1 thinly sliced lemon
12 small ice cubes
Some thinly sliced cucumber

Method:

Place the ice cubes in a bowl with the lemon. Pour on the Vodka and then the wine. Stir gently. Float some thin slices of cucumber on the Cup and finally pour in the fizzy drink. Serve at once.

Reference Tables

Contents

1 Comparative Weights

Metric	British/USA		Metric	British/USA	
28.35g	1	.035oz	.45kg	1	2.20lbs
56.70g	2	.07oz	.91kg	2	4.41lbs
85.05g	3	.115oz	1.36kg	3	6.61lbs
113.40g	4	.14oz	1.81kg	4	8.82lbs
141.75g	5	.175oz	2.27kg	5	11.02lbs
170.10g	6	.21oz	2.72kg	6	13.23lbs
198.45g	7	.245oz	3.18kg	7	15.43lbs
226.80g	8	.28oz	3.63kg	8	17.64lbs
255.15g	9	.315oz	4.08kg	9	19.84lbs
283.50g	10	.35oz	4.50kg	10	22.00lbs

Centre figures can be read as either metric or British/USA
eg 1kg = 2.20lbs or 1lb = 0.45kg

2 Comparative Liquid Measures

British	Metric	American
1 gallon (8 pints)	4.56 litres	10 pints
1 pint (20 fl oz)	0.57 litres	$1\frac{1}{4}$ pints
1 fl oz	28 mls	1 fl oz
1 tablespoon ($\frac{5}{8}$ fl oz)	15 mls	$\frac{1}{3}$ fl oz
1 dessertspoon ($\frac{1}{3}$ fl oz)	10 mls	1 tablespoon
1 teaspoon ($\frac{1}{6}$ fl oz)	5 mls	$\frac{1}{7}$ fl oz

American	Metric	British
1 gallon (8 pints)	3.8 litres	$6\frac{2}{3}$ pints
1 pint (16 fl oz)	.475 litre	$\frac{4}{5}$ pint
1 cup (8 fl oz)	.237 litre	$\frac{2}{5}$ pint
1 tablespoon ($\frac{1}{3}$ fl oz)	10 mls	$\frac{1}{3}$ fl oz (1 dessertspoon)
1 teaspoon ($\frac{1}{7}$ fl oz)	4 mls	$\frac{4}{5}$ teaspoon

Metric	British	American
5 mls	$\frac{1}{6}$ fl oz (teaspoon)	$\frac{1}{7}$ fl oz
10 mls	$\frac{1}{3}$ fl oz (dessertspoon)	$\frac{1}{3}$ fl oz (tablespoon)
$\frac{1}{4}$ litre	$8\frac{3}{4}$ fl oz	$8\frac{1}{2}$ fl oz
$\frac{1}{2}$ litre	$17\frac{1}{2}$ fl oz	1 pint + 4 tablespoons
$\frac{3}{4}$ litre	$1\frac{1}{3}$ pints	1 pint 10 fl oz
1 litre	$1\frac{3}{4}$ pints	2 pints + 8 tablespoons

3 Comparative Temperatures

Centigrade	Fahrenheit	Centigrade	Fahrenheit	Centigrade	Fahrenheit
0	32	35	95	70	158
5	41	40	104	75	167
10	**50**	45	113	80	176
15	59	50	122	85	185
20	**68**	55	131	90	194
25	77	**60**	**140**	95	203
30	86	65	149	100	212

10°C   Suitable temperature for serving cold cups, white and rosé table wines, sparkling wines. Also for fermenting lager type beer.

20°C   Suitable temperature for serving red table wines, dessert wines and liqueurs. Also for fermenting wines and beers.

60°C   Suitable temperature for serving mulled wines.

65–75°C   Suitable temperatures for mashing malted grains for beer.

4 Sugar Content

Specific Gravity	In 1 gal lb	In 1 gal oz	In 4.54 litres Kg	% Potential Alcohol
1.005		2	.050	0.69
1.010		4	.113	1.39
1.015		6	.170	2.04
1.020		8	.226	2.70
1.025		10	.283	3.40
1.030		12	.339	4.07
1.035		14	.396	4.75
1.040		16	.453	5.43
1.045	1	2	.510	6.10
1.050	1	4	.567	6.79
1.055	1	6	.624	7.47
1.060	1	8	.680	8.15
1.065	1	9½	.723	8.83
1.070	1	11½	.780	9.50
1.075	1	13	.822	10.19
1.080	1	15	.880	10.87
1.085	2	1	.937	11.55
1.090	2	3	.994	12.23
1.095	2	4½	1.035	12.90
1.100	2	6	1.078	13.57
1.105	2	8	1.134	14.27
1.110	2	10	1.190	14.95
1.115	2	11½	1.232	15.62
1.120	2	13	1.275	16.30
1.125	2	15	1.334	16.98

Note: Half the weight of a quantity of sugar is equal to the equivalent volume. For example, 2 lb sugar dissolved in a must occupies 1 pint in volume.

5 Comparative Hydrometer Tables

Specific Gravity	Potential % Alcohol	Balling & Brix	Baumé	Twadell
1.005	0.69	1.3	0.7	1
1.010	1.39	2.5	1.4	2
1.015	2.04	3.8	2.1	3
1.020	2.70	5.3	2.8	4
1.025	3.40	6.5	3.5	5
1.030	4.07	7.8	4.2	6
1.035	4.75	9.0	4.9	7
1.040	5.43	10.3	5.5	8
1.045	6.10	11.5	6.2	9
1.050	6.75	12.5	6.9	10
1.055	7.47	13.8	7.5	11
1.060	8.15	15.3	8.2	12
1.065	8.83	16.3	8.8	13
1.070	9.50	17.5	9.4	14
1.075	10.19	18.5	10.0	15
1.080	10.87	19.8	10.7	16
1.085	11.55	20.8	11.3	17
1.090	12.23	22.0	11.9	18
1.095	12.90	23.0	12.5	19
1.100	13.57	24.2	13.1	20
1.105	14.27	25.3	13.7	21
1.110	14.95	26.4	14.3	22
1.115	15.62	27.5	14.9	23
1.120	16.30	28.5	15.5	24
1.125	16.98	29.6	16.0	25

4a Specific Gravity

Variations in reading caused by different temperatures

Temperature in degrees C	F	Adjustment to last figure of S.G.	
10	50	Subtract	0.6
15	59		NIL
20	68	Add	1
25	77	Add	2
30	86	Add	3.4
35	95	Add	5
40	104	Add	6.8

6 Proof Spirit Conversion Table

British Proof	Canadian Proof	USA Proof	% Alcohol by volume
0	100 U.P.	0	0
25	75 U.P.	28	14
50	50 U.P.	58	29
70	30 U.P.	80	40
75	25 U.P.	86	43
87	13 U.P.	100	50
100	PROOF	114	57.1
125	25 O.P.	143	71.5
140	40 O.P.	160	80
175	75 O.P.	200	100

Convert British Proof to percentage alcohol by multiplying by 4/7.

Convert Percentage Alcohol to British Proof by multiplying by 7/4.

7 Sugar Content of Grape Juice Concentrates

Most cans of concentrate quote the strength of the concentration in degrees Baumé. The following tables convert various concentrations to units of measurement more familiar to the home winemaker.

Baumé	S.G.	Sugar in Imp gallon	Sugar in US gallon	Sugar in 5 litres
20	1.160	3lb 8oz	2lb 10oz	2.00kg
25	1.208	4lb 8oz	3lb 6oz	2.55kg
30	1.261	6lb 8oz	4lb 14oz	3.70kg
35	1.318	8lb 4oz	6lb 6oz	4.85kg
36	1.330	8lb 8oz	6lb 8oz	4.95kg
37	1.343	8lb 12oz	6lb 12oz	5.10kg
38	1.355	9lb 4oz	7lb 2oz	5.40kg
39	1.368	9lb 8oz	7lb 6oz	5.55kg
40	1.381	10lb	7lb 8oz	5.70kg
45	1.450	11lb 8oz	8lb 10oz	6.55kg
50	1.526	13lb 8oz	10lb 2oz	7.65kg
55	1.611	15lb 8oz	11lb 10oz	8.80kg

8 Myerhof's Path

Fermentation of sugar to alcohol

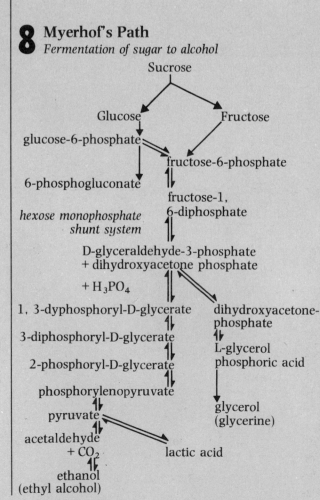

9 Yeast Strains

Current name	Wine type	Strain derivation	Alcohol tolerance
ALL-PURPOSE	Wine	Selection from strain testing	M
ALL-PURPOSE 'SUPER YEAST'	Wine	Winningen strain	H
BEAUJOLAIS	Red burgundy, very young	Beaujolais strain	M
BERNCASTELER DOKTOR	White Moselle, dry	Berncasteler Doktor strain	L
BORDEAUX	Red Bordeaux, dry	Margaux strain	M
BURGUNDY	Red Burgundy, dry	Chambertin strain	M
CABERNET	Red Bordeaux (claret)	Cabernet Sauvignon Isolate	M
CEREAL	Wines with starch material	*Saccharomyces distaticus nov. sp.*	M
CHABLIS	White burgundy, dry	Chablis strain	M
CHAMPAGNE	Sparkling white	Abbey of Hautvillers strain	M,L
CHIANTI RED	Red Italian, dry	Chianti Isolate	M
CHIANTI WHITE	White Italian, dry	Chianti Isolate	M
CLARET	Red Bordeaux (claret)	Château de la Tour de Mons strain	M
GRAVES	White Bordeaux dry/medium	Graves Superieurs strain	M
HOCK	White, Dry	Geisenheim strain	L
LIEBFRAUMILCH	White Hock type dry	Oppenheimer strain	L
MADEIRA	Oxidised white (fortified) dry to v. sweet	Maderia strain	H
MALAGA	Red wine, v. sweet	Malaga Pedro strain	M
MARSALA	Red fortified v. sweet	Marsala strain	H
MEAD	Honey Wine sweet or dry	English mead Isolate	M
POMMARD	Red Burgundy, dry	From commune of Pommard	M
PORT	Red fortified sweet	Douro Laurero strain	M
SAAR	White Mosel, dry	Zeltingen strain	L
SAUTERNES	White Bordeaux very sweet	Sauternes strain	M
SHERRY FLOR	Pale Sherry (fino) v. dry	Flor strain J.7	H
SHERRY	Sherry Rich, sweet	Oloroso strain	H
SCHLOSS JOHANNISBERG	White Hock-type dry	Schloss Johannisberg strain	L
TOKAY	White heavy & very sweet	Tokay Tallya strain	H

Average alcohol tolerance:
L = LOW (11–12% by volume), M = MEDIUM (12–15% by volume),
H = HIGH (15–18% by volume).

10 The Yeast to use

Main ingredient	Type of wine	Suitable yeast
Apple	Sparkling	Champagne
Apple	Sweet	Sauternes
Apricot	Dry	Bordeaux or Chablis
Apricot	Sweet	Sauternes
Banana	Sweet	Cereal
Blackberry	Dry	Burgundy
Blackberry	Sweet	Port
Blackcurrant	Dry	Burgundy
Blackcurrant	Sweet	Port
Currants	Dry	Hock or Sherry Flor
Currants	Sweet	Sauternes or Sherry
Damson	Dry	All-purpose
Damson	Sweet	Port
Elderberry	Dry	Burgundy
Elderberry	Sweet	Port
Flowers	Sweet	All-purpose
Gooseberry	Dry	Chablis or Champagne
Gooseberry	Sweet	All-purpose
Red grape concentrate	Dry	Bordeaux or Burgundy
Red grape concentrate	Sweet	Port
White grape concentrate	Dry	Chablis or Sherry Flor
White grape concentrate	Sweet	Sauternes or Sherry
Loganberry	Dry	Burgundy
Loganberry	Sweet	Port
Orange	Dry	Sherry Flor or Chablis
Orange	Sweet	Sauternes
Peach	Dry	All-purpose
Peach	Sweet	Sauternes
Pear	Sweet	All-purpose
Plum, Golden or Victoria	Dry	Bordeaux or Sherry Flor
Plum, Red	Sweet	Madeira or Port
Raisins	Dry	Hock or Sherry Flor
Raisins	Sweet	Sauternes or Sherry
Raspberry	Sweet	All-purpose
Redcurrant	Dry	Bordeaux
Rhubarb	Sweet	All-purpose
Flower leaf and sap wines	Sweet	All-purpose
Sultanas	Dry	Hock or Sherry Flor
Sultanas	Sweet	Sauternes or Sherry
Vegetables	Sweet	All-purpose or Cereal

11 Average alcohol content of some commercial table wines

Wine type	% Alcohol	equivalent to Initial S.G.
Dry White		
Alsace	8.0%	1.063
Mosel	9.2%	1.070
Rhine	10.0%	1.075
Hungary	11.2%	1.083
Bordeaux	11.8%	1.087
Burgundy	12.1%	1.089
Dry Red		
Bordeaux	11.5%	1.085
Burgundy	12.1%	1.089
Chianti	12.8%	1.094

12 Some bottle and cask sizes

Description	Metric		Imperial	
Miniature	2.8	cl	1	fl oz
Quarter	18.5	cl	6⅓	fl oz
Half bottle	34	cl	13⅓	fl oz
Hock bottle (slender shoulders)	72	cl	25½	fl oz
Sauternes bottle (square shoulders)	75	cl	26⅔	fl oz
Burgundy bottle (sloping shoulders)	80	cl	28½	fl oz
'Large' bottle	1	litre	35½	fl oz
Large Chianti bottle (spherical bowl in wicker basket)	1.75	litres	63	fl oz
Demijohn	4.8	litres	170	fl oz
Magnum	2	bottles		
Jeroboam	4	bottles		
Rehoboam	6	bottles	1	gallon
Methuselah	8	bottles		
Salmanazar	12	bottles	2	gallons
Balthazar	16	bottles		
Nebuchadnezzar	20	bottles		

Wine Casks			
Hogshead	52½	Imp gals	approx 315 bottles
Pipe	115	Imp gals	approx 690 bottles
Butt	108	Imp gals	approx 648 bottles
Tun	210	Imp gals	approx 1260 bottles

Beer Casks			
Pin	4½	Imp gals	36 pints
Firkin	9	Imp gals	72 pints
Kilderkin	18	Imp gals	144 pints
Barrel	36	Imp gals	288 pints

13 A guide to the acidity of popular ingredients

VERY HIGH	Black, red and white currants, rhubarb, lemons, grapefruit and morello cherry.
HIGH	Gooseberries, loganberries, raspberries, crab apples, quince, plum, oranges, strawberries, bilberries and blackberries.
MEDIUM	Apples, apricots, cherries, grapes, greengages, damsons and peaches.
LOW	All dried fruits, elderberries, pears, bananas, pineapples and pawpaw.
ALMOST NONE	Cereals, dates, figs, flowers, leaves, rosehips, vegetables, melon, mango and guava.

The degree of variation is very high between different varieties of the same fruit or between the same varieties grown in different locations or in different years. It is impossible to give more than a general guide and even then there can be overlapping between the gradations given.

Mostly Citric	*Mostly Malic*	*Mostly Tartaric*
Bananas	Apples	Grapes
Black/Red/White currants	Apricots	
Citrus fruits	Blackberries	
Elderberries	Cherries	
Pears	Damsons	
Pineapples	Gooseberries	
Raspberries	Greengages	
Strawberries	Loganberries	
	Peaches	
	Rhubarb*	

*(some oxalic acid also)

14 Acid comparison tables

A Comparative 'parts per thousand' of various acids

Sulphuric	Citric	Tartaric	Malic
0.5	0.72	0.77	0.68
1.0	1.43	1.53	1.37
1.5	2.14	2.29	2.05
2.0	2.86	3.06	2.73
2.5	3.57	3.83	3.42
3.0	4.29	4.59	4.10
3.5	4.99	5.36	4.78
4.0	5.71	6.12	5.47
4.5	6.43	6.89	6.15
5.0	7.14	7.65	6.84

B Additional acid required per demijohn of wine

oz per demijohn	gram per demijohn	Citric p.p.t.	Tartaric p.p.t.	Malic p.p.t.
$\frac{1}{8}$	3.5	0.55	0.51	0.57
$\frac{1}{4}$	7	1.09	1.02	1.14
$\frac{3}{8}$	10.5	1.64	1.53	1.71
$\frac{1}{2}$	14	2.18	2.04	2.28
$\frac{5}{8}$	17.5	2.73	2.55	2.85
$\frac{3}{4}$	21	3.27	3.05	3.42
$\frac{7}{8}$	24.5	3.82	3.56	3.99
1	28	4.36	4.07	4.56
$1\frac{1}{8}$	31.5	4.91	4.58	5.13
$1\frac{1}{4}$	35	5.45	5.09	5.69
$1\frac{3}{8}$	38.5	5.99	5.60	6.26
$1\frac{1}{2}$	42	6.54	6.11	6.83

Note It is sometimes easier to measure small quantities by dissolving a larger quantity of acid in water and then using the appropriate quantity of acid solution *eg* Dissolve $2\frac{1}{2}$ oz of acid in 19 fl oz water to make 20 fl oz of acid solution. 1 tablespoonful is equivalent to $\frac{1}{8}$ oz.

15 Dried fruit analysis

Fruit	Fresh fruit equivalent of dried fruit		Water content fresh fruit	Sugar content dried fruit	Acid content dried fruit	Tannin content dried fruit
Apples	6–9	measures	85%	54%	M	L
Apricots	5½	measures	85%	46%	M	L
Bananas	3	measures	75%	65%	L	L
Bilberries	4	measures	83%	18%	L	A
Currants	4	measures	80%	65%	M	A
Dates	2	measures	25%	60%	VL	L
Elderberries	4	measures	80%	15%	VL	H
Figs	3½	measures	78%	56%	VL	L
Muscatels	4	measures	80%	64%	M	A
Peaches	5½	measures	89%	43%	L	A
Pears	3	measures	83%	39%	L	L
Prunes	4	measures	82%	44%	L	L
Raisins	4	measures	81%	66%	M	A
Rosehips	3	measures	65%	20%	L	L
Sloes	3	measures	65%	16%	L	A
Sultanas	4	measures	82%	68%	M	A

VL = VERY LOW   M = MODERATE   H = HIGH
L = LOW   A = ADEQUATE

16 Poisonous Ingredients

The following list, by no means exhaustive, is of plants which all contain some harmful chemical. Not all of them will actually cause death but they will at least make you feel very unwell. For this reason they are best avoided.

A   Acacia, aconite, alder, anemone, aquilegia, azalea

B   Baneberry, belladonna, berberis, bitter almond, bay tree leaves, beech nuts, box tree leaves, black nightshade, bindweed, bluebell, bryony, broom, buckthorn, buddleia, buttercup

C   Campion, celandine, charlock, cineraria, clematis, clover, cotoneaster, columbine, cow-bane, crocus, crowfoot, chrysanthemum, cuckoo-pint, cyclamen

D   Daffodil, dahlia, deadly nightshade, delphinium, dwarf elder

F   Fool's parsley, figwort, foxglove, fungi of all kinds

G   Geranium, gladiolus, goosefoot, green potatoes

H   All members of the helebore family, hemlock, henbane, holly, honeysuckle (both flowers and berries), horse chestnut flowers and conkers, hydrangea, hyacinth

I   Iris, ivy,

J   Jasmine, jonquil

L   Laburnum, laurel, lilac, lilies of the valley, lilies of all kinds, lobelia, lucerne, lupins

M   Marsh marigolds, meadow rue, mezereon, mistletoe, monkshood

N   Narcissus

O   Orchids

P   Pheasant's eye, peony, poppy, privet

R   Ragwort, rhododendron, rhubarb leaves

S   Snowdrop, spearwort, spindleberries spurge, sweet pea

T   Thorn apple, tobacco plant, tomato stems and leaves, traveller's joy, tulip

W   Wood anemone, woody nightshade

Y   Yew

Index

Acknowledgements

The author and publishers would like to thank the following sources for providing photographic illustrations in *The Compleat Home Winemaker and Brewer*. Credits are given spread by spread.

Pages
10–11	Cooper Bridgeman Library/Kunsthistorisches Museum; Michael Holford
12–13	Mary Evans Picture Library; Michael Holford/British Museum; Mary Evans Picture Library
14–15	Mary Evans Picture Library; Michael Holford; Mary Evans Picture Library
18–19	Mary Evans Picture Library
22–23	Both photographs from Keith Hocking
26–27	Reproduced by the kind permission of the Boots Company from their publication *The Boots Book of Home Wine Making & Brewing*
32–33	Reproduced by the kind permission of the Boots Company from their publication *The Boots Book of Home Wine Making & Brewing*
34–35	W. R. Loftus Ltd.
42–43	Reproduced by the kind permission of the Boots Company from their publication *The Boots Book of Home Wine Making & Brewing*
44–45	Reproduced by the kind permission of the Boots Company from their publication *The Boots Book of Home Wine Making & Brewing*
46–47	Both photographs by Mike Sheil
48–49	Both photographs by Mike Sheil
54–55	Mike Sheil
56–57	Mike Sheil
64–65	Paul Forrester
68–69	Terence Woodfield Collection/Derek Balmer
70–71	Out of copyright; Harry Scotting
120–121	Radio Times Hulton Picture Library; Werner Forman Archive
122–123	Radio Times Hulton Picture Library
126–127	Mansell Collection
130–131	Out of copyright; Mike Sheil
132–133	Ken Hill
134–135	Mansell Collection
136–137	Mansell Collection
140–141	Terence Woodfield Collection/Derek Balmer
142–143	Angelo Hornak; Terence Woodfield Collection/Derek Balmer
144–145	All from Mansell Collection
146–147	Both from Mansell Collection
148–149	Both photographs from Sotheby Parke Bernet & Co.

Picture Research by Kate Parish and Phyllida Holbeach

Black and two colour illustrations throughout the book by Roger Bourne assisted by Allan Rees, Bob Brett, Lee Brooks, Peter Arnold, Max Ansell and Keven Diaper.

The author and publishers would also like to thank W. R. Loftus Limited of Charlotte Street, London, for the assistance and co-operation so generously given by Derek Pearman.

Thanks are also especially due to the following for information so generously and willingly supplied: K. V. J. Hockings, F.I.M.L.T. of Unican Foods Limited, Bristol; G. C. Leigh-Williams of Vinotex Yeasts, Tattenhall; and The National Dried Fruit Trade Association.